I0883675

SELMA

SELMA

A Bicentennial History

Alston Fitts III

The University of Alabama Press ~ Tuscaloosa

The University of Alabama Press
Tuscaloosa, Alabama 35487-0380
uapress.ua.edu

Hardcover edition published 2017.
Paperback edition published 2021.
eBook edition published 2017.

Typeface: Garamond

Cover images: (*top*) Perspective map of Selma, Alabama, county seat of Dallas County 1887, Milwaukee, Henry Welge & Co. (1887); (*bottom*) Florida B. Kencey Memorial in Selma's Live Oak Cemetery, courtesy of RuralSWAlabama, Billy Milstead

Cover design: Todd Lape/Lape Designs

Paperback ISBN: 978-0-8173-6021-4

A previous edition of this book has been cataloged by the Library of Congress.
ISBN: 978-0-8173-1932-8 (cloth)
E-ISBN: 978-0-8173-9065-5

For Anne, whose "yes" made it all possible,
and for Lida, Mary Alston, and Ruth,
who helped more than words can say

Contents

Illustrations

Preface

The Selma City Council commissioned the original version of *Selma, Queen City of the Black Belt* way back in 1988, in hopes that the city would have an up-to-date history in time for the 125th anniversary of the Battle of Selma and the 25th anniversary of Bloody Sunday and the Selma-to-Montgomery March. The council entrusted the job to Clairmont Press, a local publishing company. Clairmont in turn gave me six months to research and write the book in my spare time (I still had a full-time job with the Edmundite Missions).

I was not a trained historian; my degrees were in English literature. A Tuscaloosa native who had only moved to Selma in 1978 to work for the Edmundites, I was not kin to the old families who "built the river." But I had written articles on some positive but largely forgotten aspects of the city's history, like its election of Alabama's first black congressman (Ben Turner) in 1870 and of Alabama's first female legislator (Harriet Hooker Wilkins) in 1922. So Selma's five black and five white council members decided I was the man to tell Selma's story in a fashion that would be fair to all concerned.

Some of the city's history was controversial. The woman who found me doing research into slavery in the basement of the Dallas County Courthouse was dismayed. "You look like a decent human being," she told me. "Why are you doing this terrible thing?" Fortunately, my publisher, Claire Ralston, and I agreed that if we did not tell the truth about the bad things in Selma's history, people might not believe us about the good things. So I felt free to depict the Queen City "warts and all," and neither the mayor nor the city council asked to review my book before it appeared.

To some outsiders, Selma's history is all "warts." For generations, Selmians have had to struggle against the negative stereotypes that so many people have of the town. It was true after the Civil War, when ex-slave Ben Turner had to plead with his Radical Republican colleagues in the US House of Representatives for the people of Selma: "They may have sinned wonderfully, but they have suffered terribly. . . . I have no coals of fiery reproach to heap upon them now." And it was still more true after the civil rights movement, when Selma seemed to bear the blame not only for its own sins (which were bad enough!) but for the sins of the entire South as well. Some people still saw the city as frozen in time, never moving past the racial confrontations of the 1960s.

The Selma City Council has since created a new city seal featuring Sturdivant

Hall, the Edmund Pettus Bridge, and a butterfly along with the slogan "From Civil War to Civil Rights and Beyond." Sturdivant represents Selma's antebellum heritage and the Pettus Bridge its role in the civil rights movement. What about the butterfly? Well, Selma has been officially named "the butterfly capital of Alabama," but the butterfly represents more than the city's natural beauty. It has come to symbolize the city's emergence after the disasters of the past, its ability to move "beyond" the traumas generated by the Battle of Selma and by Bloody Sunday.

I did the best job I could in the limited time that I had, and when *Selma, Queen City of the Black Belt* appeared in print in 1989, my fellow Selmians seemed to appreciate the result in spite of its flaws. It is now out of print and increasingly out of date.

Since my retirement, I have had the time to do more research and to gain a more detailed knowledge and deeper understanding of the city's history prior to 1989. I have learned a good deal more. For example, I have learned about the founding of an integrated charity hospital in the 1880s, the town fathers' attempt to keep the Ku Klux Klan out of Selma during the 1920s, and their desperate struggle to keep its schools open during the Depression of the 1930s. And I can now offer a more detailed and accurate picture of the two events that loom largest in the city's history—the Battle of Selma and the Selma-to-Montgomery March.

In addition, events have taken place in the quarter century since 1989 that are of keen interest to anyone wanting to know "the rest of the story." The resegregation of Selma's public schools in 1990 and the election of its first black mayor in 2000 were both events that attracted national attention. These events force us to take a fresh look at earlier periods of Selma history, notably the era of integration—the twenty years from 1970 to 1990 when many of the institutions that had traditionally served the black community were struggling to survive and a majority of Selma's white students still attended public schools.

The past can never be completely forgotten, but we can learn from its sins and mistakes as well as from its successes. The mythical Selma that Macpherson wrote about in *The Songs of Ossian* was "a city of heroes"; the real Selma that I write about had its heroes and heroines as well, men and women who strove to make the Queen City a better place to live. It had its villains too, alas; some people still see the city as populated entirely by villains and victims. I hope that this edition will help readers see the city in its human complexity. And I hope and pray that it will help my fellow residents of the Queen City come to terms with our past and join together to create a positive future for our beloved Selma.

SELMA

I

Selma in Pioneer Days

"Moore's Bluff" Strives to Make the Big Time, 1819–1845

On March 16, 1819, two men appeared at the Federal Land Office in Cahawba to purchase some land in the Alabama Territory. Between them, William Rufus King and Dr. George Phillips bought 460 acres on the Alabama River.

The original land grant describes the purchase as "the fractional Section West of the Alabama River Number Thirty-Six in Township Number Seventeen of Range Ten." Travelers who knew the river well usually referred to the area as "Moore's Bluff," after Thomas Moore, a Tennessean who had built a cabin on the site in 1815.

King and Phillips had a vision of a town to be created at Moore's Bluff, a town they would call "Selma," after the royal fortress described in James Macpherson's *Songs of Ossian*, the international best seller of the day. They were part of a group calling itself the Selma Town Land Company. John Hardy's *Selma: Her Institutions and Her Me*n (1879) describes the group. "W. R. King, George Phillips, Gilbert Shearer, Caleb Tate, Jesse Beene, and George Mathews . . . organized, under articles of association, the 'Selma Town Land Company,' the objects and purposes of which were to buy and sell lands in the then territory of Alabama. The company organized by the election of George Mathews, president; and Gilbert Shearer, secretary and treasurer, and proceeded at once to issue $500,000 of certificates of stock in $100 shares." The sagacity of these men conceived the idea at once of the construction of a town on the beautiful level lands on the high bluff of the Alabama River, surrounded, too, as it was with such rich and productive soil—"a nice creek on the East, to which George Mathews gave the name of 'Beech Creek,' in consequence of the immense number of beech trees found along its banks, and on the West by another pretty little stream, which George Phillips gave the name of 'Valley Creek,' from the level lands through which it meandered; bounded on the South by the

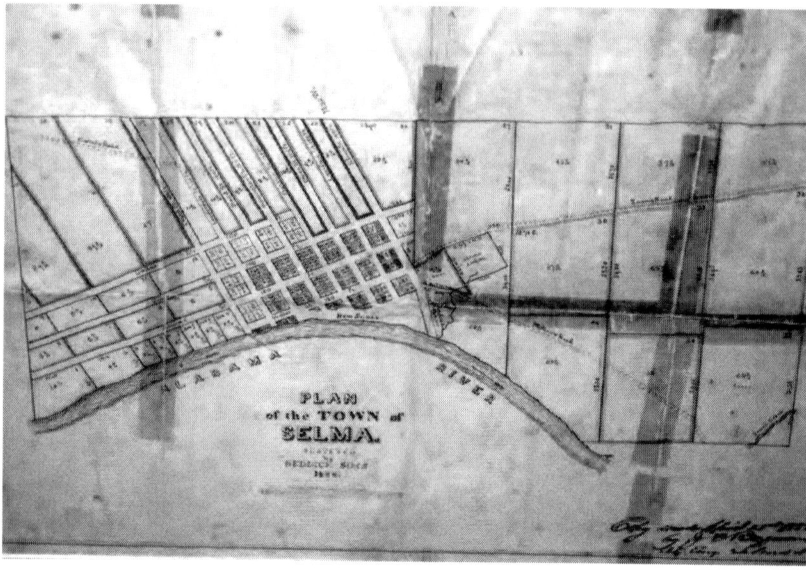

Figure 1.1 Plan of the town of Selma in 1828; courtesy of Selma–Dallas County Museum of History and Archives, Selma, Alabama.

noble River, Alabama, and on the East and West by these creeks, the present site of Selma was selected" (pp. 141–42). King, Phillips, and their associates seem to have been fairly successful in selling their vision of a city on the bluff. Thirty-three men bought 360 shares. The company then had a surveyor named Redick Sims plot out the town-to-be's major streets and intersections and lay out 125 choice downtown lots and 37 "out-lots." Not all of these lots were to be offered for sale: four particularly nice ones were set aside for churches. One lot, at the corner of Church and Alabama, would be for the Baptists, another for the Methodists, and two lots would be reserved for the Presbyterians—that is, one for the Cumberland Presbyterians and one for the "regular" variety. Other lots would be kept back for a public square, a school, and a cemetery. The 101 lots that were auctioned off went rather briskly. The highest price bid was $800 for lot twenty-nine on Water Avenue—the future site of the St. James Hotel. The total proceeds from the auction came to $37,930.

King and Phillips were called away from their town making to help write a constitution for Alabama. They were among the forty-five delegates chosen to assemble at Huntsville on July 5, 1819. King was representing Dallas County, and Phillips, Shelby County. A third member of the constitutional convention, Reuben Saffold of Clarke County, would later move his family to Dallas County and set up a mansion in Pleasant Hill and a "winter home" in the town of Selma.

FIGURE 1.2 Reuben Saffold helped write Alabama's 1819 Constitution and later became chief justice of the Alabama Supreme Court; courtesy of Selma–Dallas County Museum of History and Archives, Selma, Alabama.

Saffold (1788–1847), a native of Georgia's Broad River valley, had previously served in Mississippi's territorial legislature. He was appointed to the Alabama Supreme Court and served until 1836, becoming chief justice shortly before his resignation. His sons were to play significant roles in the politics of Dallas, Lowndes, and Montgomery Counties.

All three men were chosen as part of the Committee of Fifteen charged with writing the constitution, and King wound up as the one of the three who did most of the actual work. The document that resulted was among the most democratic for any southern state, providing, as it did, for universal white manhood suffrage. By contrast, Georgia voters were required to own property and Mississippi voters to serve in the militia.

The most difficult problem faced by the Committee of Fifteen was selecting the state capital. At that time, much of south Alabama was still Indian territory, and

FIGURE 1.3 Gov. William Wyatt Bibb addresses the Alabama legislature meeting in Cahawba; courtesy of Alabama Department of Archives and History, Montgomery, Alabama.

the majority of the settlers lived in north Alabama. Territorial governor William Wyatt Bibb had already chosen Cahawba, the seat of Dallas County, as the site for the new state capital. His decision was bitterly opposed by the Tennessee Valley delegates, who wanted a capital as far north as Tuscaloosa. The committee finally decided to postpone the decision until 1825 and allowed Cahawba to serve as the capital until that time.

After the convention was over, King started back to North Carolina to settle his affairs there. En route, he was pleased to learn that the Alabama legislature had elected him as one of the state's first US senators, giving him fifty-six out of sixty-nine votes on the first ballot. John W. Walker of Huntsville, who had served as president of the constitutional convention, came in second with eleven votes. Walker was then elected to Alabama's other seat in the US Senate, beating George Phillips by a wide margin. Because of this election, King's "business trip" was extended by quite a few months. In addition to his personal interests, it was necessary for King to go on to Washington and be sworn in on December 17, 1819, three days after Alabama's admission to the Union.

The business of building Selma went on without King's presence and, within a year, the Selma Town Land Company was ready to ask the legislature for a char-

FIGURE 1.4 Loading cotton on the Alabama River; courtesy of Alabama Department of Archives and History, Montgomery, Alabama.

ter. Dr. Phillips, who had recently been chosen one of Alabama's three presidential electors to cast the state's vote for James Monroe's reelection, presided at the historic meeting called by the land company to prepare their petition. In addition to that request, Gilbert Shearer expressed Selma's willingness to serve as the site for a public university.

On December 4, 1820, the legislature responded to the company's request by granting Selma a charter and fixing the date on which Selmians would elect their town councils. The elections were to be held on the first Monday in April between ten o'clock in the morning and three o'clock in the afternoon, and the five councilmen elected would, in turn, choose one of their number to serve as intendant, or presiding officer, roughly equivalent to a mayor. The council's term of office would last exactly one year, until the following April.

One of the exciting events during Selma's early years was the landing of the steamboats. The *Tensas* was one of the first of these to come up the Alabama River from Mobile. Hardy describes its arrival with relish.

> It landed at the Selma ferry, in the spring of 1822, and was considered a wonderful sight. Many persons stood upon the bluff and looked down at it with a strange commingling of fear and astonishment, and but few could be persuaded to go aboard and examine the works of the "belching craft." It had been twenty-three days from Mobile to Selma, and when it landed Captain Sonsby

> jumped up and cracked his heels together and offered to bet one hundred dollars that he would make the next trip in less than fourteen days. The Tensas was a sternwheel boat, and her pilot stood on deck and guided the boat with a long lever, instead of a wheel. It was covered like an open shed and could carry about two hundred bales of cotton. (168)

The coming of the steamboats meant that at least part of the Selma Town Company's dream was coming true: Selma would become a major inland port, shipping cotton from surrounding plantations down to Mobile for resale in England and Europe.

The Founding Fathers

What sort of men founded Selma? The six men who seem to have dominated the Selma Land Company—George Mathews, Major Caleb Tate, Dr. George Phillips, Gilbert Shearer, Judge Jesse Beene, and Senator William Rufus King—typify in many ways the settlers who poured into Alabama during its last years as a territory and its first few years as a state.

Most of these settlers were from the Piedmont areas of Georgia, the Carolinas, and Virginia: areas like the Broad River valley of northeast Georgia, the Abbeville district of South Carolina, and Mecklenburg County in North Carolina. They tended to be Presbyterians of Scotch Irish descent, rather than Episcopalians of strictly English heritage, though many of them had become Methodists through the efforts of that denomination's evangelists. By and large, they were farmers, ready to leave the exhausted soil of the Piedmont in search of new, rich lands in which to grow cotton. Four of the six founders—Mathews, Tate, Phillips, and Shearer—had ties with one specific area: Georgia's Broad River valley in Elbert, Oglethorpe, and Wilkes Counties.

George Mathews, president of the Selma Land Company, was the grandson and namesake of Gen. George Mathews, who had led the first group of Virginians to the Broad River area in 1784. The transplanted Virginians who made up the Broad River aristocracy were a powerful and cohesive group. General Mathews was twice elected governor of Georgia, and his success at politics and planting inspired several additional waves of immigration from Virginia to northeast Georgia. By 1817, the Broad River valley had placed one of her sons, William H. Crawford, in Pres. James Monroe's cabinet and two more, William Wyatt Bibb and Charles Tait, in the US Senate.

Sen. Charles Tait was from a different branch of the same family as Selma founder Caleb Tate, a branch that spelled its name differently. Charles and Bibb discovered that their political fortunes in Georgia had been severely damaged by their vote to raise their own salaries. Because of this, they started looking around for new states in which to run for office, and their eyes fell on the Alabama Territory. Since Secretary of the Treasury Crawford hoped to run for president and could use Alabama's electoral votes, he was happy to cooperate with his friends from Broad River. Thus, he arranged Senator Bibb's appointment as Alabama's territorial governor and worked with Senator Tait to secure Alabama's admission to the Union. (Tait later moved to Wilcox County and became the new state's first federal judge.)

Given the great power exercised by the Broad River allies, George Mathews was a perfect figurehead for the Selma Land Company. Once the stock had been sold, however, he took little further interest in Selma. Mathews's brothers and cousins settled in Dallas County, but Mathews himself became a prominent planter in Montgomery.

Maj. Caleb Tate (1783–1841) was part of the last wave of Virginians to move to the Broad River valley. There he married Mary Middleton, the daughter of another Virginia family that had emigrated to Georgia. After serving in the War of 1812 and earning the title of major, Tate found himself ready to move again. This time he settled his family in Valley Creek, ten miles north of Selma, and helped build up that community. When the Alabama legislature granted a charter to Valley Creek Academy in 1829, it was with the condition that the school be set up within two miles of Major Tate's house.

Dr. George Phillips (1786–1835) married into the Broad River group. Born in Delaware to Irish immigrants, young George grew up and studied medicine near Charlotte, North Carolina, before moving to Georgia in 1805. There he married Jemima Pope, daughter of the rich and influential Col. Leroy Pope, who later helped found both Huntsville and the largest bank in north Alabama. Phillips followed his in-laws to Huntsville. However, after serving in the War of 1812 as an army surgeon under Gen. Andrew Jackson, he decided to strike out on his own. His first move was to Shelby County, where he was elected a delegate to the constitutional convention. By 1820 Phillips had bought a large plantation near Valley Creek and moved to Selma. He, his sons, and his sons-in-law played a big role in helping to develop Selma as a commercial center. Dr. Phillips also became one of the fathers of Alabama's Whig Party, formed in opposition to the policies of his old comrade-in-arms, former general and now president, Andrew Jackson.

At first glance, Gilbert Shearer (1789–1840), a German American businessman from Newburgh, New York, seems like an outsider among these southern planters. But he, like Phillips, moved to Georgia as a young man and married into the Broad River aristocracy. His wife was Martha Ann Cowles. His in-laws bought stock in the Selma Land Company. Once established in Selma, Shearer threw himself into promoting his new home. He served on seven of the town's first eight councils, four times being chosen intendant. In later years, this enterprising man served as presi-

Figure 1.5 Dr. George Phillips, founder, Selma, Alabama; courtesy of Selma–Dallas County Museum of History and Archives, Selma, Alabama.

dent of Selma's first bank and its first railroad; he also organized the local militia and was given the rank of general.

"General" Shearer was only the first of a host of energetic northern immigrants who helped shape Selma's destiny. Journalists from Pennsylvania, educators from New England, and a host of German American businessmen were to follow in his footsteps.

The last two of Selma's six "founding fathers," Judge Jesse Beene and Sen. William R. King, were not tied to the Broad River group by either birth or marriage. Indeed, these two strongly opposed the "Georgia machine," as the Broad River group was called, in most political matters. In 1824, for example, Beene and King both supported General Jackson for president against the Georgia candidate, Secretary William H. Crawford. While King was carrying the banner of Jacksonian democracy in national affairs, Beene was fighting Jackson's battles at the local and state level. In 1835, when the Whigs, or anti-Jackson forces, were sweeping the Black Belt, Beene beat out the Whig candidate for Dallas County's senate seat by a single vote. And,

FIGURE 1.6 William Rufus King, founder, Selma, Alabama, later a US senator, and finally vice president of the United States; courtesy of Selma–Dallas County Library.

in 1837, the same year in which King was elected president pro tempore of the US Senate, Beene was chosen president of the Alabama senate.

Though King and Beene were closely allied in politics, in other respects they were almost opposites. Beene (1792–1845) grew up "in poverty and ignorance," to use Hardy's words, in east Tennessee. By fifteen, he was earning a living carrying the mail on horseback from Wytheville, Virginia, to the Cumberland Gap.

William Rufus DeVane King (1786–1853) was the son of a prominent family in Sampson County, North Carolina, who spent his fifteenth year at the University of North Carolina. By 1816, when Beene became a lawyer, King had already been elected to Congress twice and was about to leave the United States for diplomatic assignments in Naples and Saint Petersburg.

It was after the young Jesse Beene came to Dallas County in 1818 that he finally "made good." He served briefly as county judge and as clerk of the Alabama Supreme Court and also worked hard to build up Cahawba. Judge Beene became prosperous enough to marry Catherine Bird, a young woman from a South Caro-

FIGURE 1.7 Merchant prince Philip J. Weaver; courtesy of Alabama Department of Archives and History.

lina family, and invited her nephews to join him in his law practice. By 1839 he was prominent enough in Alabama to be talked about as a Democratic candidate for governor, but his tactless denunciations of the Whigs as subversive ruined his chances. Unlike King, Beene was no diplomat.

King was already both well known and well-to-do when he moved to Alabama with his brothers and brothers-in-law and bought a large plantation at King's Bend. King never married. His closest friend during his twenty-nine years in the US Senate was James Buchanan of Pennsylvania, another lifelong bachelor. The two dreamed of the day in which Buchanan would be elected president and King vice president of the United States. Their wishes came true, but not quite in the way either hoped. King was elected vice president in 1852, only to die in office, and Buchanan became president four years later, only to see the Union begin to dissolve during his administration.

King and Beene were the earliest of a series of Dallas County politicians who were to play an important role in state and national affairs. John Tyler Morgan's career in the US Senate (1877–1907) outlasted King's, though he never became, or wished to be, vice president. Since Jesse Beene served as presiding officer of the Alabama senate, five other senators from Dallas County have followed in his footsteps by winning that high honor.

Philip J. Weaver has some claim to be considered one of Selma's "founding fathers," though not a member of the Selma Town Land Company. Weaver (1797–1865), a native of Uniontown, Maryland, was the son of German immigrants. He grew up half-crippled from a snakebite and without much formal education. But his native intelligence and drive more than made up for these handicaps. Weaver first came to Dallas County in 1815 but did not settle in Selma until 1820, when he bought Thomas Moore's cabin and set up one of the first stores in "Moore's Bluff," trading with American Indians and white alike. In 1830 Weaver set up a similar store in Mississippi to trade with the Cherokees. In the same year he assisted Gen. John Coffee in his 1830 survey of south Alabama, acquiring the knowledge of land values that enabled him to make a fortune as a land speculator. By 1855 the merchant prince was making a fortune from his cotton plantations as well, producing thirteen thousand bales of cotton and selling them for $83,000. He cared enough about Selma to invest generously in various projects to build up the city.

The Black Population of the Black Belt

Most of the men and women pouring into Dallas County were not ex-congressmen from North Carolina or planters from Virginia by way of Georgia or businessmen from New York. Most of them were slaves. Hardy describes the yearly arrival of hordes of slaves from other southern states.

> Large droves, some hundreds daily, were brought to the town by men like James Hall, Watson, Willis and Jordan, whose business it was to trade in negroes. Several large buildings were erected in the town especially for the accommodation of negro traders and their property, the largest of which was erected on the present site of the Central City Hotel building [at the corner of Water Avenue and Green Street]. This was a large three story wooden building, sufficiently large to accommodate four or five hundred negroes. On the ground floor, a large sitting room was provided for the exhibition of negroes on the market, and from among them could be selected blacksmiths, carpenters, bright mulatto girls and women for seamstresses, field hands, women and children of all ages, sizes and qualities. To have seen the large droves of negroes arriving in the town every week, from about the first of September to the first of April, no one could be surprised that the black population increased in Dallas County, from 1830 to 1840, between twelve and thirteen thousand. The im-

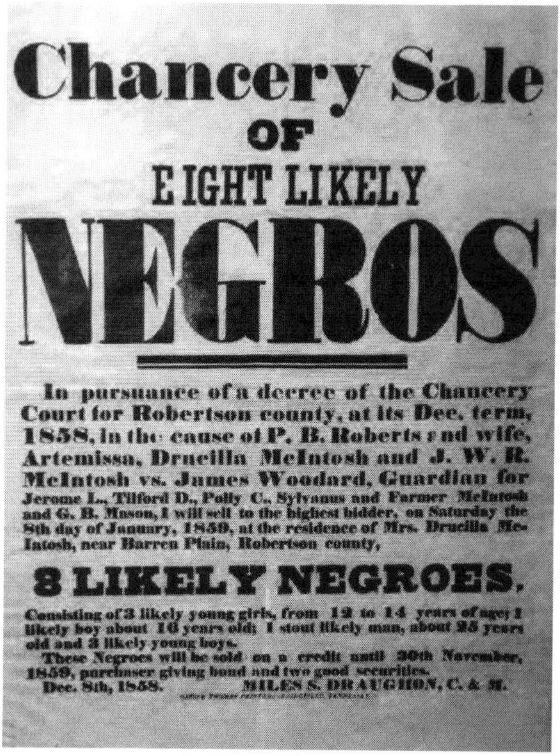

Figure 1.8. Poster advertising a slave auction; courtesy of a private collection.

mense wooden building thus used for twenty years, on Water Street, was taken away in 1854, . . . and some five or six buildings made out of it. (*Selma*, 16)

The reason for the large number of slaves included in the population was the extreme fertility of the black-colored soil, which, before the arrival of African slaves, caused the region to be given the geological name of "Black Belt." The soil, especially suited to the production of cotton, made plantation owners anxious to seek an adequate number of workers for the hand labor required in that endeavor. Slaves were, to them, the solution to their problem. Dallas County's rich soil and army of slaves made it the largest cotton-producing county in the state, sending 63,410 bales to market in 1860. The average slaveholder in Dallas County owned seventeen slaves, while the average owned by Montgomery Countians was only ten. Of course, even in Dallas County, only 1,280 out of 7,788 whites, about 16 percent, actually held slaves, and many of these owned just one family. But when you counted the slaveholder's wife and children, it can be asserted with some assurance that at least a third of Dallas County whites were attached to a slaveholding family. In any case, it was the slaveowners and their dependents who dominated society.

FIGURE 1.9. A slave auction in Montgomery, Alabama, during the 1850s; courtesy of Alabama Department of Archives and History, Montgomery, Alabama.

Very little is known about most of these slaves. However, the history of one woman who was brought from Africa to the Selma area in 1859 is known. Her name was Redoshi, and her father was chief of a small tribe in West Africa. She was twelve years old when the fierce Dahomey warriors raided her peaceful village, slew her father, and carried her and the other survivors off. After days of marching, Redoshi saw her first white man, Capt. Billy Foster of the *Clotilde*, who picked her and 115 other "Tarkars" to be chained up and taken aboard his ship. Two of the Dahomey warriors followed her on board to mock at her tears and were startled when Captain Foster told them smilingly that they, too, were going to America as slaves. The ship had slipped out to sea without their realizing it.

Most of the kidnapped Africans were still alive when the *Clotilde* sneaked into Mobile Bay and began unloading its cargo. (The African slave trade had been illegal in the United States since 1807.) A few escaped into the swamps, but the rest were sent with Redoshi up the Alabama River to a plantation near Mount Vernon. Then "those disposed to [buy] . . . were piloted to the place of concealment. . . . The Africans were placed in two long rows, the women on one side, the men on the other. Some with tears streaming down their faces and shouting, 'Ele, ele! Home,

home!' . . . were sold and sent to Selma." Zora Neale Hurston tells the story in the October 1927 issue of the *Journal of Negro History*. (Sylviane A. Diouf's *Dreams of Africa in America* fills in much of the African background, including the fact that there was no "Tarkar" tribe, that the slavers must have gotten the name wrong.) The chief's daughter was paired off with Yawith, an older man from another tribe, who did not speak her language, and the two of them were sold as man and wife. They were purchased by Col. Washington Smith, a Selma banker, who wanted them for his Bogue Chitto plantation. Once on the plantation, Redoshi was given a new name, "Sally," and beaten for not "speaking American." Redoshi and her husband, now "Billy," learned English, became Christians, and worked hard at the tasks given them. However, a Smith family legend says that although "Aunt Sally" lived to be 115, she never forgave the Dahomey warriors who labored beside her in the fields of Colonel Smith's plantation.

What was it like to be a slave in Dallas County? According to the Alabama Supreme Court, a slave was both a human being and a piece of property. Alabama chief justice A. J. Walker spelled out the legal theory of slavery in a famous decision rendered in 1857, which declared that in terms of civil law, slaves had no rights at all. They could not own property, inherit property, sign a contract, or sue for damages. They were not people but a piece of property. However, in terms of criminal law, slaves were recognized as human beings with an intellect, a conscience, and a will. Thus, they could be justly tried and punished for a wide variety of crimes. Some of these "crimes" sound strange to modern ears. One of the more serious offenses against Alabama's slave code of 1831, for example, was trying to learn how to read and write. A field hand caught struggling with his ABCs was liable to receive thirty-nine lashes on his bare back. It was feared that education might "spoil" farm workers, or even turn them into dangerous revolutionaries.

In practice, these laws were not always enforced. Most masters took them seriously, but a few did not. When Ben Turner—who will be discussed in more detail below—was a field hand in Bogue Chitto in the 1840s, the overseer caught him with a spelling book and reacted with threats: thirty-nine lashes if you are caught again! However, after Ben was sold to James McGee, a hotel keeper in Selma, his new mistress was pleased to learn he had picked up his ABCs on the sly: good, you can help run the hotel!

This suggests that it was better to be a slave in Selma than in rural Dallas County. As the abolitionist orator Frederick Douglass put it, "A City slave is almost a free citizen. He enjoys privileges almost unknown to the whip-driven slave on the plantation."

Many Selma slaves were skilled artisans—carpenters, blacksmiths, gardeners, and

FIGURE 1.10 Benjamin Sterling Turner, the slave who later became a congressman; courtesy of Selma–Dallas County Museum of History and Archives, Selma, Alabama.

seamstresses—whose masters allowed them to "hire their own time." Blacksmith Alex Goldsby (1820–91), a native of Charleston, attained remarkable status in the white community and was made a deacon at the First Baptist Church.

In those days, slaves attended their masters' churches. Indeed, some congregations had a black majority. In 1845, for example, Church Street Methodist Church had 140 members, all but 40 of them slaves. Of course, slaves were not usually voting members of the churches and had little influence over their policies. First Baptist was unusual, according to Wilson Fallin's *Uplifting the People*, in that it permitted its black members an unusual amount of autonomy. Goldsby and his fellow slaves were allowed to worship separately on the lower level and even got to bring in a preacher of their own color, Sam Phillips, who had been freed for his service in the Mexican-American War.

No Selma slave was more privileged than Benjamin Sterling Turner (1825–93), a native of Halifax County, North Carolina, who was brought to Alabama at the age

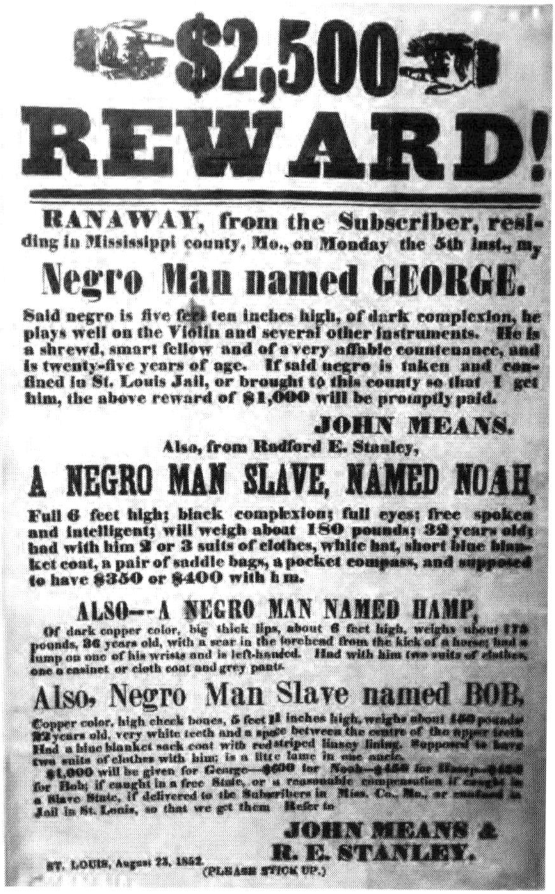

FIGURE 1.11 Poster offering a reward for the capture and return of runaway slaves; courtesy of a private collection.

of six. When his young master, Dr. James Gee, joined the Confederate Army, he took Ben with him as his body servant. After a few months, he sent him back to Selma to help his mother, Mrs. Susan B. Gee, run the hotel. Ben not only helped bring customers to the Gee House (now the St. James Hotel) but also set up a livery stable and wood yard on his own behalf. In 1862 he was wealthy enough to buy $200 worth of Confederate bonds. After Turner's wife, Independence, was bought by a white man to be his mistress, the humiliation was so bitter that it broke the marriage and left Turner vowing he would never again love a black woman with "the fatal gift of beauty." Thus, even privileged slaves had reason to long for freedom.

The US census for 1830 lists sixty-three free black people in Dallas County, including one farmer, Tom Smith, who himself owned four slaves. "Free Tom" was one of eight slaves belonging to Baxter ("Bat") Smith who were freed after Smith's death in 1826. The other seven included Tom's wife, Charity, and their two daughters, Malinda and Sarah, as well as Charity's three children by an unidentified white man. Each of the eight was given forty-five acres of land. "Free Tom" worked hard, bought more acres, and eventually purchased slaves to help work the land. By the time he died in 1850, he owned 450 acres and 11 slaves and his estate was valued at $11,000.

Unfortunately, "Free Tom" had failed either to draw up a will or to emancipate his second wife, also named Charity, or their three children. Selma representative Ben Woolsey persuaded the Alabama legislature to free Tom's widow and children and to divide the estate among them. Malinda and Sarah objected, saying they should not have to share the estate with their stepmother and their half-brothers and half-sister, who as slaves were actually part of the estate. The case went to the Alabama Supreme Court, which ruled in *Malinda and Sarah v. Gardner et al.* that since slaves could not contract marriage, none of the Smith children had any legal rights other than those conferred by the legislature. Malinda and Sarah, each of whom already owned a slave, had to be content with sharing in the proceeds from the sale of their father's estate. The legislature assigned them a "guardian" and ordered them to leave the state within two years, a step it took with all newly freed slaves. However, the Smiths quietly ignored the order.

In 1860, despite everything the state of Alabama could do to force freedmen to emigrate, there were almost fifty freedmen in Selma alone, most of them mulatto washerwomen or artisans. Even these free people had to be careful. In 1859 Selma passed a city ordinance forbidding all black citizens, whether slave or free, from playing cards, shooting dice, or enjoying any other game of chance. The penalty for slaves who were caught and convicted was thirty-nine lashes. The penalty for freedmen was hard labor on the city streets. Three years later, the city passed similar laws prohibiting "any negro [from being] found upon the streets of the city smoking a cigar or pipe, or carrying a walking cane."

Sometimes, when slaves were charged with serious crimes like assault and murder, they fared better than one would expect. In 1848 there was a famous case in which a Greene County slave, Emmanuel, was arrested for killing an overseer. Although Emmanuel confessed to the crime, there were some extenuating circumstances, so Selma lawyer William Mitchell Murphy was hired to defend him. Murphy, one of the most effective defense lawyers of the day, pleaded Emmanuel's case with such emotional force that the all-white jury was unable to agree on a conviction. By the time a second jury was sworn in, Murphy had found a loophole that won a complete acquittal for Emmanuel. Of course, it was a rare and lucky slave who had the good fortune to be defended by Murphy.

However, that sort of luck did not always work for slaves. When a Lowndes

County slave was accused of the rape and murder of a white girl in 1859, there was no talk of getting a lawyer for him. The victim's angry neighbors first took up a collection to reimburse the slave's owner for the loss of his property and then proceeded directly to lynch the accused.

In times of social tension, even white citizens could not always count on a trial. When two strangers were found bringing abolitionist literature into Selma during the 1830s, there was no bother about legal processes. The strangers were tarred, feathered, and chased out of town. This incident set off one of the periodic panics that afflicted the Black Belt throughout the antebellum period. During these times, owners who normally bragged about the fidelity of their slaves would become terrified that a slave rebellion was about to take place.

When Major Benjamin Grumbles of Old Town in south Dallas County heard about the presence of the two abolitionist strangers, he became convinced that the slaves of Selma were about to revolt. He called together the local militia and led them on an eleven-mile march to the city's rescue. Reaching the Alabama River at nightfall, the men camped for the night. At two in the morning the sound of thunder convinced Grumbles that the fight had already begun. Hardy describes Grumbles' response: "The Major whipped his troops into line, and made them a flaming speech, winding up by saying, 'Boys, the niggers are now killing the white people of Selma, you must go and kill the niggers. The most of you are young men; I am an old man; I have a wife and ten children at home; I must go protect them; good bye, boys.' The Major, wheeling his mare, put spurs to her, and off he went at a gallop" (*Selma*, 15). The leaderless militia pressed bravely on through the storm that broke out, leaving them knee-deep in mud. It was noon before the exhausted would-be rescuers reached Selma, only to find everybody going about business as usual. General Shearer gave them a good dinner and thanked them for their trouble, but it was a long, long time before they forgave the excitable major.

In the Shadow of Cahawba

In its early years, the bustling river town growing up on Moore's Bluff was overshadowed by a town ten miles away at the confluence of the Alabama and Cahaba Rivers. It was Cahawba, which Governor Bibb had selected as the state's "permanent" capital, that drew all the attention. Since James Monroe had run unopposed for president in 1820, Alabamians were preparing for their first contested presidential election in 1824. It was at Cahawba that the partisans of Andrew Jackson, John Quincy Adams, and William H. Crawford gathered to choose their electoral slates. Justice Reuben Saffold of Pleasant Hill was chosen a Jackson elector, and Andrew Pickens of Carlowville, head of the Alabama State Bank, an Adams elector. There was no Dallas County man on the Crawford slate, but George Phillips and other members of the "Georgia Machine" were active on behalf of their former patron. Selmians had to read about the goings-on in the *Cahawba Press*, since they had no newspaper of their own.

In 1825, General Lafayette visited the United States, and Senator King managed to arrange for the Revolutionary War hero to pass through Alabama. Steaming down the Alabama River on the *Charles Carroll of Carrollton*, Lafayette paused only briefly at Selma before going on to the state capital, where he was lavishly entertained by state officials.

Cahawba's hour of glory was shortly followed by one of defeat. The heavy floods of late 1825 gave north Alabama forces in the legislature the excuse they needed to urge the capital's removal to higher and drier ground. Legislators from the Tennessee River valley and the Tombigbee–Black Warrior Counties joined in proposing Tuscaloosa for the new capital, while the legislators from the Alabama River valley stayed loyal to Cahawba. On December 6, 1825, the Alabama senate finally voted 11 to 10 to move the capital to Tuscaloosa.

The glory had departed from Cahawba, along with the state house, the state bank, the Supreme Court, and the legislature. Dallas County residents, such as George Phillips, Jesse Beene, and others who had served as directors of the state bank, were swiftly replaced by residents of Tuscaloosa County who, so the story goes, would find it easier to attend meetings. Many erstwhile residents of Cahawba followed the state capital to its new setting on the Black Warrior.

Cahawba was still the county seat and was still surrounded by rich plantations, so in a few years it was prospering once again. However, it no longer overshadowed Selma as it once had. Indeed, the two were becoming rivals for the domination of Dallas County.

In 1827 Selma got its own newspaper when Selma millionaire Philip J. Weaver sent off to Pennsylvania for Thomas Jefferson Frow, a young journalist. The *Selma Courier*, which Frow founded, later became the *Selma Free Press*, one of the leading Whig newspapers in Alabama. Frow himself quit journalism in 1848 and left for Texas. His paper continued under a new name, the *Selma Reporter*. Indeed, Frow's paper, now known as the *Selma Times-Journal*, currently ranks as the twenty-seventh oldest newspaper still publishing in the United States.

During those days, Selma's city government showed a lot less staying power than its newspaper. After Intendant Edward Gantt resigned in 1827, nobody bothered to replace him. Not until 1830 was a new city council elected. With Gilbert Shearer as its intendant, the council set busily to work repairing the streets, digging wells, and trying to repress vice and immorality. The council had a difficult row to hoe, since the Selma of 1830 smacked more of the Wild West than of the Old South. As Anson West's *History of Methodism in Alabama* puts it, "Jockey Clubs were better supported than churches, and more appreciated than religion" (534). Selmians were making fortunes on cotton and losing them betting on the horse races in east Selma, where Elmwood Cemetery now stands. They also played such games of chance as "bucking the tiger," also called faro, at the Alhambra Saloon on Broad Street. One famous brawl at the Alhambra ended in the death of Selma postmaster Patrick McMullen, but "the tiger" continued to be a very popular game.

On May 8, 1832, Shearer and his fellow reformers on the town council went too far. They passed a law that said anyone caught drinking liquor on Sunday would be arrested and fined. At that time, according to Hardy, there were only two adult males in Selma who did not visit McKeagg's saloon every Sunday. The council lost support and went out of existence for a number of years.

In 1835, however, a dramatic change began in this river town. It started in January when the Methodists erected a wooden building on the lot set aside for them by the Selma Land Company. Within a year, the Cumberland Presbyterians were also building on their lot, and their young pastor, Samuel M. Nelson, set up the town's first "Sabbath School." The school was at first an interfaith project, with staunch Episcopalian William Waddill Jr. serving as superintendent and Methodist Sarah Maples and Presbyterian A. H. Lloyd as two of the teachers.

Nelson also launched a public crusade against gambling. As Hardy describes it, Nelson "opened his batteries of eloquence against gambling: in his pulpit, on the streets, around the family fireside, did this able man let no opportunity pass, without inflicting a wound against gambling; and, finally the public sentiment commenced changing" (*Selma*, 14).

The outbreak of war may also have had a sobering effect. A troop of militia left Selma on February 26, 1836, under the leadership of Capt. William T. Minter, to take part in the Seminole Wars.

Minter (1805–65), a native of Georgia, came to Selma in 1830 and was elected sheriff of Dallas County in 1834. His father and grandfather had both served in the Revolutionary War, and it was only natural for him to assume a leadership role. His company landed at Tampa Bay and was soon embroiled in a battle in which several of his men were severely wounded.

Shortly after Minter's company returned safely from Florida, war broke out with the Creek Indians in east Alabama. Another troop of volunteers, "the Selma Rangers," this one captained by John F. Conoley, set out in May. This company returned to Selma without having lost a man, something that would not often be true in future wars.

FIGURE 1.12 William T. Minter, the militia leader who later founded a railroad, and his wife, Susan Bell; courtesy of Selma–Dallas County Museum of History and Archives, Selma, Alabama.

Other signs of civic progress were soon to follow. Jesse Beene attended a railroad convention in Memphis, Tennessee, and came back convinced that Selma could not rely just on steamboats and stagecoaches for its commerce. The town must have a railroad. Beene met with Selma lawyer John W. Lapsley and a few other "go-getters" to launch a campaign for public support.

Lapsley (1806–89), a native of Tennessee, had first come to Selma in 1826 to work as a clerk. Success in business did not satisfy him, however, and he left for Kentucky to study law under Henry Clay at Transylvania University. When he returned to Selma in 1835, it was as a lawyer convinced that railroads were the wave of the future and that Selma needed to ride that wave.

On December 22, 1836, the Alabama legislature granted a charter to the Selma and Tennessee Rivers Railroad. Senator Beene and Rep. James M. Calhoun had forced the bill through, over bitter opposition from north Alabama legislators. Before the company could become a reality, its supporters were required to raise $500,000 in pledges. This proved easy enough, with Selma merchants P. J. Weaver and William Johnson pledging almost $100,000 between them. By March 1837, the Selma and Tennessee River Railroad Company organized with the election of Gilbert Shearer

FIGURE 1.13 Railroad promoter John W. Lapsley; courtesy of Alabama Department of Archives and History, Montgomery, Alabama.

as president and hired Col. A. A. Dexter of Montgomery to prepare the line as far north as Montevallo.

Selma was not only undergoing religious and economic changes but also a political one. In 1832 the city had cast every single vote in support of Andrew Jackson. Now, however, Jackson's clash with the National Bank of the United States disturbed Selma capitalists like J. W. Lapsley, while his harsh treatment of South Carolina during the nullification crisis alarmed such states' right devotees as J. M. Calhoun. A strong Whig, or anti-Jackson, party now emerged, with the *Selma Free Press* as its spokesman. In 1836 the "Whigs and nullifiers" (as the Democrats called their foes) carried Dallas County by a 2 to 1 margin. Calhoun and most of his fellow nullifiers returned to the Democratic fold by 1838, but the Whigs continued to be a dominant force in the Black Belt for years to come.

Of course, Senator King and Judge Beene were not about to let the area go Whig without a fight. They imported a young journalist from South Carolina, William Lowndes Yancey (1814–63), and helped him set up the *Cahawba Democrat* in oppo-

FIGURE 1.14 William Lowndes Yancey, the Cahawba journalist who became the great orator of succession from the Union; courtesy of Selma–Dallas County Museum of History and Archives, Selma, Alabama.

sition to the *Selma Free Press*. In South Carolina Yancey had been a Union Democrat who denounced nullifiers like John C. Calhoun. After moving to Alabama, however, he gradually became more and more devoted to states' rights. A few years later, Yancey left Dallas County for Wetumpka and ultimately for Montgomery, emerging as a major spokesman for the "fire-eater" or secessionist wing of the Democratic Party in opposition to the moderate wing led by King.

By 1838 Selma was bustling with civic activity. The city's first bank, the Real Estate Bank of South Alabama, was being organized with Gilbert Shearer as its first president. A medical society was organized, a fire engine was ordered, and a library was about to open its doors.

While Selma's menfolk were talking about banks and railroads, its women were talking about the city's need for quality schools. Soon the Ladies' Education Society of Selma was prodding the men into action. Selma intendant Dr. Uriah Grigsby chaired a public meeting on March 24, 1838, to discuss raising money to build a female academy in connection with the Episcopal Church. A committee of six men (including Mayor Grigsby and Reverend Nelson, as well as future intendants William Waddill Jr. and Philip J. Weaver) was set up to raise money. Then, after a motion from the floor, six women, including Mrs. Grigsby, Mrs. Waddill, and Mrs. Weaver, were added to the committee. The ladies wanted to make sure that their husbands did the right thing.

The Alabama legislature granted the Ladies' Education Society a charter on January 30, 1839, and Episcopal pastor Lucien B. Wright set up a "Male and Female School" in the church basement. The ladies were pleased but not satisfied. By 1841 they joined with the Masons in establishing a combination school and lodge at Alabama and Mabry on land donated by William Johnson. The two-story brick building they erected was soon full to overflowing with students from Selma and surrounding areas. In the years that followed, the ladies helped to build another in 1845 at Church and Selma (site of the present Dallas Academy). Some sources suggest that they were also involved in the 1847 erection of the Central Masonic Institute (the present Vaughan-Smitherman Building). The ladies' contribution proved so significant that their organization in 1838 has traditionally been taken to mark the birth of public education in Selma.

Meanwhile, the town's "boom" had been brought to a grinding halt by the national depression following the Panic of 1837. The Real Estate Bank had to suspend its payments, leading the *Cahawba Democrat* to chortle on March 16, 1839, that "the Selma bubble has burst at last." The Selma and Tennessee River Railroad also had to cease its operations temporarily.

Tuscaloosa's *Independent Monitor* poked savage fun at Selma's ambitions. In a June 25, 1845, editorial prompted by fears that the Black Belt might reclaim the state capital, the paper sneered:

> [Selma] pompously refers to ten miles of old graded rail track, which points to the Tennessee Valley, forgetting that for years it has been a cow-path, and is likely to be nothing more. The present generation will never see a steam locomotive, or even mule power, breaking the solitude of this tremendous folly. The Selma and Tennessee railroad began with a flourish of trumpets, and ended with a retreat on tin pans. So ends the mighty thorough-fare that at one time threatened to draw North Alabama, East Tennessee, and North-western Georgia in contact with Mobile Bay, with Selma as the grand Southwestern depot.

One of the town's leading citizens, Dr. Grigsby, died; others left town for good. According to Sam Will John's essay in *Northern Alabama* (1888), the early 1840s were years of deep discouragement, "Selma's darkest hour."

However clouded Selma's prospects may have seemed, its womenfolk and churches kept expanding. In 1842 the Baptists started building on their lot. Within a year, their membership jumped from eleven to sixty-six. The Ladies' Education Society also kept right on going. In 1845 they got a new charter from the legislature and another plot of land from the ever-generous Mr. Johnson and began erecting a school on the corner of Selma and Church. The brick building on Alabama Avenue would be for the boys and the new wooden building (the present Dallas Academy) for the girls. Two outstanding teachers, Dr. Lucius B. Johnson (1805–53) and Mrs. Harriet Benham Johnson (1805–85), were lured from Summerfield, north of Selma, to take charge of the Dallas Male and Female Academy. Dr. Johnson was a native of Vermont, his wife of Connecticut, and under their direction the school flourished.

2

The Queen City Grows As Storm Clouds Gather, 1844–1861

DURING THE SIXTEEN YEARS PRIOR to the Civil War, Selma went through a period of dramatic growth. The amount of cotton received at Selma for shipment down the Alabama River doubled between 1840 and 1850 and doubled again by 1860. In that year Dallas County produced 63,410 bales of cotton, more than any other county in the state (Marengo was second, Montgomery third).

The town's population grew threefold, from 1,053 citizens in 1840 to 3,073 just ten years later, and the Alabama legislature renamed this booming river town "the City of Selma." To its boosters, Selma was "the Queen City of the Black Belt," dominating west central Alabama with its expanding network of railroads and growing financial institutions. In addition, Selma took great pride in the accomplishments of William Rufus King, who, in 1853, became the first Alabamian elected to national office when he became vice president of the United States.

All this progress came at a time of growing strife between North and South, as northern abolitionists became more and more agitated against slavery and southern "fire-eaters" became increasingly anxious to set up a separate southern republic. During the first great political crisis of this period, which ended in 1851, King and other moderates were able to persuade Alabama to stick with the Union. However, during the crisis that ended in 1861, Selma's unionists were no match for the tide of popular feeling, encouraged by William Lowndes Yancey, which swept Alabama into secession and war.

KING AND THE SECTIONAL CRISIS, 1844–1853

Bad feelings between the North and South developed dramatically between 1844 and 1846, while William R. King was serving as US ambassador to France. Pres.

FIGURE 2.1 Bishop James O. Andrew, whose ownership of slaves split the Methodist church; courtesy of Selma–Dallas County Museum of History and Archives, Selma, Alabama.

John Tyler had asked King to use his diplomatic skills to keep France from interfering with US efforts to annex Texas. King accepted this challenge as a patriotic duty and stayed on as minister plenipotentiary to France after James K. Polk succeeded Tyler as president in 1845.

While King was in Paris, Alabama's two largest denominations severed ties with their fellow believers in the North. The Methodist Episcopal Church split along sectional lines in 1844, and Alabama Baptists broke away from their national organization in the following year. The Methodist split has long had particular interest to Selmians because it developed over the second marriage of Bishop James Osgood Andrew (1794–1871). Bishop Andrew was a son of the Broad River valley who, like so many other natives of that region, ended his days in Dallas County. His father had been the first native Georgian to become a Methodist "circuit rider," and James himself had been an outstanding bishop for twelve years when the trouble started. When he married Mrs. Leonora Greenwood in 1844, her slaves became his property, and northern Methodists were horrified that a bishop would defile himself by owning slaves.

Bishop Andrew offered to resign his position, but his fellow southerners would not hear of it. Within a year, a separate Methodist Episcopal Church of the South had been set up, with Andrew as its presiding bishop. When his wife died, Andrew married Emily Sims Woolsey Childers and moved to Summerfield in Dallas County. His new spouse's son by a previous marriage, Benjamin M. Woolsey, was already an up-and-coming lawyer and a leading figure in Dallas County politics.

In 1846, the Democratic Party, following the pattern set by Methodists and Baptists, began to split along sectional lines. This split grew out of the Mexican-American War, which was wildly popular in the South but bitterly resented in New England. Pres. James K. Polk's call for volunteers to repel a Mexican "invasion" of American soil woke an eager response in Selma. Sixty sons of Dallas County enlisted in the company organized by Capt. Thomas Evans Irby of Wilcox County and Lt. Andrew Bogle of Selma. This group became Company B of Maj. J. J. Seibels' Alabama Volunteers, who arrived in Vera Cruz barely too late to join the triumphant march on Mexico City. However, the company did good service and was given a hero's welcome when it returned home in 1847.

Irby (1824–63), a native of South Carolina, attended three different colleges (Spring Hill, the University of Alabama, and Mount St. Mary's in Maryland) and read law. However, he preferred planting cotton to practicing law. According to Brewer's *Alabama*, Irby was "six feet high, handsome, and of commanding presence." Thus it is no surprise that after his return to Wilcox, he was promptly elected to the Alabama House as a Democrat on the strength of his war record. Irby later moved to Dallas County and was elected to the House twice more from his new home.

When Pennsylvania Democrat David Wilmot urged that none of the territory acquired from Mexico be open to slavery, Alabamians like Irby understandably responded with indignation. It seemed to them the height of injustice that southern men should be forbidden to take slaves into territories that southern men had fought and died to acquire. It was discrimination! The controversy over the "Wilmot Proviso" grew more and more bitter. The new territories could not even be organized until Congress resolved the issue, and Congress seemed hopelessly split.

When Ambassador King returned from France and sought to resume his old place in the US Senate, he found out how divided feelings had grown. The Democrats of Alabama had split into two factions, the "Hunkers," loyal to the national party, and the "Chivalry," devoted to southern rights at all costs. The Chivalry insisted on keeping Sen. Dixon H. Lewis of Lowndes County in King's seat and, after days of bitter balloting, won the day.

FIGURE 2.2 Capt. Thomas E. Irby led the Selmians who served in the Mexican-American War; courtesy of Irby Pope.

Mobile judge John A. Campbell explained to Sen. John C. Calhoun in a December 20, 1847, letter that "Col. King was bound up with the Northern Democrats, and . . . [so] this was a work very well done." Actually, King's closest northern friends were strong defenders of the South. But at this point, almost all northerners were under suspicion.

This was the one great defeat of King's career. Within a year, Alabama's senator A. P. resigned to become minister to Russia, and King was appointed in his place. However, he now knew how dangerous it could be for an Alabama politician to be too "friendly" with northerners or too devoted to the Union.

"I am again in the Senate," King wrote his Montgomery friend M. P. Blue on April 11, 1850, "and am engaged in making efforts . . . to protect the rights of the South, and save the Union—whether these efforts will prove successful is I fear exceedingly doubtful."

FIGURE 2.3 Senator King is second from the left in the back row of this 1852 lithograph, Tompkins Matteson's *Union*, honoring the senators responsible for working out the Compromise of 1850. The front row was reserved for Gen. Winfield Scott (who was not actually in the Senate), Henry Clay, John C. Calhoun (who actually opposed the compromise), and Daniel Webster; courtesy of the Library of Congress, Prints and Photographs Division.

A ray of hope broke through the storm clouds when Sen. Henry Clay of Kentucky presented a series of bills designed to compromise the territorial controversy. California would be admitted as a free state, but the territories of New Mexico and Utah would remain open to slaves. Slave trade would be abolished in Washington, DC, to appease the North, but a stronger fugitive slave act would be passed to please the South.

King and Clay had been adversaries for many years, but the chance of saving the Union now made them allies. King urged all senators to join in working out a compromise. He even went so far as to confess that he himself found the slave trade in the District of Columbia a disgusting spectacle—a shocking admission from a southerner! (The *Cahawba Gazette* was not pleased by King's admission.)

Back home in Dallas County, however, the Compromise of 1850 was less popular. Cahawba was now the home of the most rabid group of "fire-eaters" in all Alabama, and the *Cahawba Gazette* responded to Clay's proposals with fury. If these bills pass, said the *Gazette*, "let us have disunion—a secession of the slave states—a

FIGURE 2.4 Fire-eater George Washington Gayle; courtesy of the Selma Chapter 53 of the United Daughters of the Confederacy.

Southern republic—a division of the public property [i.e., the territories] upon equitable terms—or the blood of our enemies!"

Cahawba lawyer George W. Gayle (1807–75), a native of South Carolina who had formerly served as King's campaign manager, had become an extreme secessionist. "If secession brings on a conflict of arms," he said, "let it come!"

King found such attitudes alarming. "In the present excited state of mind in Alabama, I find myself in great danger of being denounced by my old friends," he wrote his nephew by marriage, Cahawba planter Dr. Alanson Saltmarsh, on August 25, 1850. "The day is not far distant when the [*Gazette*] will brand me a subservient—one thing is certain, I am no disunionist."

Representatives from every slave-holding state were urged to attend a May 1850 convention in Nashville to decide on a common response to "Yankee aggression." King was appalled by the keynote address by South Carolina's Barnwell Rhett, which he felt was "intended by exaggerated statement to inflame the public mind" and break up the Union. It was his old adversaries, the Whigs of the Black Belt, who

FIGURE 2.5 Judge John Starke Hunter of Cahawba; courtesy of Gaylord C. Lyon Jr.

stood up against Rhett's overheated rhetoric and helped the convention calm down. John Starke Hunter of Cahawba, William M. Byrd of Marengo, and William Mitchell Murphy of Greene were among the leading moderates who drew up resolutions that King considered "temperate and dignified." (Byrd and Murphy both later moved to Selma.)

Judge Hunter (1796–1865) played a particularly important role because of his position on the resolutions committee. He was a native of South Carolina and had served both in the Alabama senate and on the circuit bench. As the largest slaveholder at the convention, with 201 slaves and plantations in two states, the judge used his influence to urge moderation. In the end, the convention adjourned until the fall to see what would happen to Clay's compromise bills.

It was a long, agonizing summer for Congress, as the compromise came under savage attack from both the North and the South. Pres. Zachary Taylor, who opposed Clay's proposals, died, and was succeeded by his vice president, Millard Fillmore, who supported them. King took over as president pro tempore of the Sen-

FIGURE 2.6 James M. Calhoun of Carlowville, longtime champion of southern rights; courtesy of Alabama Department of Archives and History, Montgomery, Alabama.

ate and saw the last bills making up the historic Compromise of 1850 enacted in late September.

When the Nashville convention met again in November, only a few delegates showed up, most of them southern rights zealots like James M. Calhoun of Carlowville in Dallas County. But the rhetoric was as feverish as always. "It is already done," proclaimed the delegate from South Carolina, "the Rubicon is crossed, even now the Union is divided!"

James Martin Calhoun (1805–77) was a native of South Carolina and a nephew of Sen. John C. Calhoun. He had supported his uncle during the nullification crisis of the 1830s and only returned to the Democratic Party after Andrew Jackson left office. The regular Democrats welcomed him and his fellow nullifiers back into the party and even chose him to serve as president of the Alabama Senate in 1840. While less extreme than Gayle and Yancey, he was clearly opposed to accepting the compromise.

When King returned to Alabama, he discovered, to his horror, that the Chivalry still planned to campaign against the compromise. Such a course, he wrote Democratic leader Bolling Hall, would only deliver the state to the Whigs. Whig leaders had already established a "Unionist Party" and were recruiting union Democrats to serve as candidates for the Alabama legislature in 1851. Ignoring King's advice, the Chivalry formed a "Southern Rights Party" and asked anticompromise Whigs to join them. A few Whigs did so, including a young Talladega lawyer named John Tyler Morgan, but not many. Thousands and thousands of Democrats, among them King's nephew, Franklin K. Beck of Wilcox County, rallied around the banner of the Unionists.

In Dallas County, the Unionist ticket consisted of two Whigs (Francis A. Saunders and Benjamin M. Woolsey) and one Democrat (Elijah Wilson). The Southern Rights Party responded with a ticket of two Democrats (James M. Calhoun and R. L. Scott) and one Whig (Hezekiah Bussey). During the heated campaign that followed, the *Cahawba Gazette* beat the drum for secession, while the *Selma Reporter* rallied around the Union. Both sides were a little taken aback by the results when Dallas County voters elected all three Whigs, even though two were Unionists and one a secessionist! The secessionist Whig won by a single vote, Woolsey by almost a hundred.

Across the state, Unionists won an overwhelming victory, electing five out of Alabama's seven congressmen and two-thirds of the Alabama legislature. At this point, Senator King set about trying to pull the Democratic Party back together. With help from Gov. Henry Collier, he persuaded Hunkers and Chivalry alike to join forces once more on the basis of accepting the Compromise of 1850. By December 1851, the wily old diplomat had accomplished both his major objectives: keeping Alabama in the Union and restoring Democratic Party unity.

Alabama's senior senator was now at the height of his power and influence. As chairman of the Foreign Relations Committee in 1850, he had been largely responsible for passing the Clayton-Bulwer Treaty, which resolved a conflict between the United States and Great Britain over Nicaragua. As president pro tempore of the Senate, he had commanded the respect of such giants as Calhoun, Webster, and Clay.

In 1852 King finally achieved the prize he had long sought. When the Democratic National Convention met in Baltimore, it took the delegates forty-nine ballots to finally decide on "dark horse" Gen. Franklin Pierce as their candidate for president, but it took them only two ballots to choose William Rufus King over Jefferson Davis and other potential nominees as their candidate for the vice presidency.

Washington's *Daily National Intelligencer*, a Whig newspaper, reported the nomination on June 7. The *Intelligencer* expressed puzzlement that the Democrats had not chosen King for the first place on their ticket, since his qualifications were clearly superior to those of Pierce. A few southern rights newspapers did denounce King

FIGURE 2.7 Pres. Franklin Pierce and Vice Pres. William Rufus King, the winners of the 1852 election, portrayed in *Gleason's Pictorial*; courtesy of Selma–Dallas County Museum of History and Archives, Selma, Alabama.

as a "wishy-washy ninny-nanny," but their complaints were drowned out in a national chorus of praise.

George W. Gayle and a few other fire-eaters organized a third party in opposition to the Pierce-King ticket but to no avail. The Democrats carried Dallas County for the first time in twenty years, as well as Alabama and all but four of the other states in the Union.

King's hour of triumph was brief and bittersweet. An advanced case of tuberculosis drove him to Cuba in search of a healthier climate, where a special act of Congress allowed him to take his oath of office. Realizing that death was near, the vice president asked to be taken "home." He reached his plantation at King's Bend on April 17, 1853, and died the following day.

President Pierce and other national leaders joined in praising King for "a career of public service and devotion to this Union which for duration and usefulness is almost without a parallel in the history of the Republic."

Selma Strives to Become "The Queen City"

In 1845 Alabama voters approved a constitutional amendment allowing the state capital to be moved from Tuscaloosa, provided two-thirds of the legislature agreed. While thirty-nine legislators wanted to keep the capital in Tuscaloosa, a majority of the legislature wanted to move it back to the Black Belt. Selma, Marion, Mobile,

FIGURE 2.8 Dr. Albert G. Mabry, founder of the Alabama Medical Association; courtesy of the Bryce Hospital Archives.

Wetumpka, and Montgomery all hoped to be chosen. Dallas County had sent a strong bipartisan delegation, consisting of Democrat George W. Gayle and Whigs E. W. Saunders and William H. Norris, to argue Selma's case. Even though Gayle and Norris were both from Cahawba, they realized that Selma offered the county's best chance to recapture the capital. Voting began on January 28, 1846, and continued for sixteen ballots. In the end, it was Montgomery's forces that triumphed, winning sixty-eight votes to Selma's eleven.

Selma was not to make its mark through politics, at least not in the antebellum years. Starting in 1847, however, the enterprise of a group of outstanding Selmians, including Dr. Albert G. Mabry, William Waddill Jr., John W. Lapsley, Philip J. Weaver, and W. J. Norris, was to launch a series of projects that were to benefit the state and reflect credit on the town. These were men who served the city in a variety of ways. Waddill and Weaver both served as intendents, Mabry as a state representative.

The first project was in the medical area. Dr. Albert G. Mabry (1810–74), a na-

FIGURE 2.9 The Central Masonic Institute, now the Vaughan-Smitherman Historic and Civic Building; courtesy of the Vaughan-Smitherman Historic and Civic Building, Selma, Alabama.

tive of Southampton County, Virginia, and a graduate of the University of Pennsylvania's medical department, came to Selma in 1843. Mabry was a man of medium height and delicate health, but with great force of personality. He and his partner, Dr. Drury Fair, became convinced of the state's need for a mental hospital. In 1847 they issued a call for all Alabama physicians to meet in Mobile to discuss important medical issues. The immediate result of the meeting was the organization of the Alabama Medical Association, which Mabry served twice as president during the following decade. The establishment of the Alabama Insane Hospital took longer, but in 1861 this, too, became a reality, with Dr. Mabry (now a member of the Alabama legislature) as one of the first trustees.

A second project was to make Selma an educational center. Dallas County already had a Methodist college (Centenary) at Summerfield; why couldn't the Masons establish one in Selma? The Selma Fraternal Lodge No. 27 of the Free and Accepted Masons (John M. Strong, "worshipful master;" William Waddill Jr., "senior warden") had already established the Dallas Masonic Academy in cooperation with the Ladies Education Society. Now the lodge spent $15,000 erecting a three-story brick building at Alabama and Union and in October 1848 the Central Masonic Institute opened its doors.

The institute added a military department in 1849 and in January 1850 was authorized to receive from the secretary of war a supply of arms (151 muskets) suitable for the military training of the pupils. By 1852 it was enrolling students from as far away as Florida and Louisiana and had changed its name to the Masonic University of Alabama, as a mark of its ambitions. But the school was also having financial problems; on April 13, 1852, the trustees had to borrow $5,000 from a local landowner, with the school itself as security.

But the yellow fever epidemic of 1853 hit Selma's schools hard, forcing the Masonic University to postpone its opening till November and claiming the life of Dallas Academy's principal Lucius Johnson. When November came, the Masonic University's president, Dr. Alexander Mitchell, had received the offer of a better job and left for Michigan. The widow Johnson kept the Dallas Female Academy going by herself for another decade, but within a few years the Masonic University had closed its doors for good.

In spite of this setback, the city maintained its reputation as an educational center; on July 24, 1856, forty-seven teachers from around the state gathered at the Dallas Female Academy to establish the Alabama Educational Association (AEA) and elect Dr. L. C. Garland, president of the University of Alabama, as its first president.

The third major project was the revival of the Selma and Tennessee Rivers Railroad. In March 1848 John W. Lapsley and Col. Thornton B. Goldsby got a new charter from the legislature for the enterprise, under the new name of the Alabama and Tennessee Rivers Railroad. In the following year Selma's enthusiastic promoters were able to outwit their competitors from Montgomery, which also aspired to be a railroad center.

During the summer of 1849, a railroad convention was held at Shelby Springs for all counties interested in building a railroad to connect the hill counties of north Alabama with the Alabama River. Dallas County's delegation arrived to find representatives from eight other counties—but none from Montgomery! Several counties, and particularly Talladega, that had previously been leaning toward Montgomery as the southern terminus of the proposed railroad were easily persuaded to swing their support to Selma. Two days of warm debate ended with Selma as the victor.

A second convention was held at Talladega on September 23, 1849, to complete the plans. This time there were twelve counties represented, and a very strong delegation from Montgomery planned to take the terminus away from Selma. The balloting ended in a tie. The convention's presiding officer, Philip Phillips of Mobile, was a good friend of William Rufus King, and cast his deciding vote for King's beloved Selma.

The Alabama legislature, believing that the proposed railroad would bind north and south Alabama more closely together, agreed to turn over $190,000 in federal funds to the Alabama and Tennessee Rivers Railroad. The legislators also authorized Selma to invest $50,000 of its own money in the project.

In early 1851 the company began laying track. Soon Selma's first locomotive arrived from Philadelphia, a thirty-ton engine called the *Alabama*. On May 10, a day almost as exciting in Selma history as the arrival of the first steamboat, the *Alabama* made its first run down the track, carrying a bevy of excited ladies. Some of the gentlemen present recalled the *Independent Monitor*'s mockery of the project as "a stupendous folly" and rejoiced all the more as the *Alabama* steamed back and forth on its four-mile track.

It was on February 9, 1852, that the legislature granted Selma a charter as a city. Selmians now had the privilege of electing a mayor directly, rather than having the council choose an intendant. John M. Strong (1794–1885), a native of North Carolina who had previously served several terms as intendant, became the city's first mayor.

During the same year, Lapsley stepped down as first president of the Alabama and Tennessee and was replaced by William S. Phillips. Phillips (1806–72), the son of Dr. George Phillips, had followed in his father's footsteps as a planter and a Whig politician, serving in both houses of the Alabama legislature. He was one of several second-generation Selmians, sons of the city's founders, who began to play a major role in the city's expansion and growth. Under its new president, the Alabama and Tennessee acquired a second locomotive and laid tracks all the way to Montevallo, sixty-three miles from Selma. There building stopped for some fifteen months because the line had run out of ready cash.

The epidemic that hit Selma in late 1853 did not help things. The city had been plagued by a series of mysterious deaths for weeks. Then, on October 13, Selma's physicians announced their diagnosis of yellow fever. "A terrible panic at once ensued," according to Hardy, "and in one day the place was almost deserted. . . . A few young men, the ministers, house servants, and occasionally a female in charge of a house, were the only citizens found in the city." The epidemic lasted until November 3. However, unlike the "sickly season" of 1840, which left Selma in a stupor for years afterward, the epidemic of 1853 proved to be only a temporary setback for the city.

In 1854 Thornton B. Goldsby became president of the Alabama and Tennessee, and work got underway once more. Goldsby (1810–58) was yet another son of the Broad River valley who had settled in Dallas County. In 1855 the tracks reached the Coosa River, and cotton from piedmont counties began moving down the railroad to Selma on its way to the Port of Mobile. The Alabama legislature voted to give more money to the struggling railroad, but Gov. John A. Winston, who suspected all banks and railroads of being conspiracies against the common man, refused to let the Alabama and Tennessee have a penny. Once he left office, the funds were re-

FIGURE 2.10 William S. Phillips, Whig leader and railroad builder; courtesy of Alabama Department of Archives and History, Montgomery, Alabama.

leased. In 1859 the railroad reached Talladega and, by 1861, had gotten as far as Blue Mountain, 135 miles from Selma.

In the meantime, Selma's enterprise had snatched a railroad from its old rival Cahawba. The Alabama and Mississippi River Railroad, first chartered in 1850, was supposed to run from Uniontown to Cahawba. The planters of the Canebrake, as that section of the state was known, soon discovered that Cahawba was not very interested in the project. As Sam Will John tells the story in *Northern Alabama: Historical and Biographical*,

> The wealthy men of Cahaba refused to subscribe a dollar to its building, and greeted the public statement of its first advocate "that if they would build thirty miles of railroad and put a train on it, it would never stop till it reached the banks of the Mississippi," with shouts of derisive laughter, and with the bold statement that a rail-road could never be built through the canebrake, "the cars would sink out of sight in the mud."
>
> This conduct on the part of the people of Cahaba opened the way for Selma to step in and give the desired aid, which she did, following the lead of Philip J.

FIGURE 2.11 Five-dollar bill with a railroad (and Philip Weaver's picture), issued by the Commercial Bank of Selma; courtesy of the Vaughan-Smitherman Historic and Civic Building, Selma, Alabama.

> Weaver and Thornton B. Goldsby, and at the next session of the Legislature the charter was so amended as to allow the road to be built from Selma, west. (653)

By 1855, building on the Alabama and Mississippi River Railroad was underway, and by 1860 the line had reached Uniontown. James L. Price, Gilbert Shearer's son-in-law, served as president of the railroad, which helped fulfill Shearer's old dreams of Selma as a rail center.

J. W. Lapsley and Selma's other railroad enthusiasts were not content to have the city involved in building just two railroads. They looked south and dreamed of a railway connecting the city with the Gulf of Mexico. In January of 1858, the Alabama legislature granted a charter to the Selma and Gulf Railroad Company. Col. William T. Minter was elected president, and Judge W. S. Burr secretary treasurer. The Selma City Council pledged to purchase $60,000 worth of stock and the company began preparing the route. However, the coming of war put a temporary end to the activities of the Selma and Gulf.

Clearly, a city so full of enterprise needed its own bank. In 1856 the legislature overrode Governor Winston's veto and granted a charter to the Commercial Bank of Selma. It was necessary for the bank's stockholders to raise $100,000 in subscriptions, half of it in gold or silver, before the Commercial Bank could begin operation, which they did in short order. William J. Norris (1808–85), a native of Georgia's Broad River valley, served as president and built the bank up into one of the state's top three financial institutions.

It quickly proved that one bank was not enough for the growing city. A second one was founded the following year by Washington M. Smith (1814–69), a native of Kentucky who had served as a state legislator from both Mobile and Marengo Counties before moving to Dallas County. He began the Bank of Selma with a cash

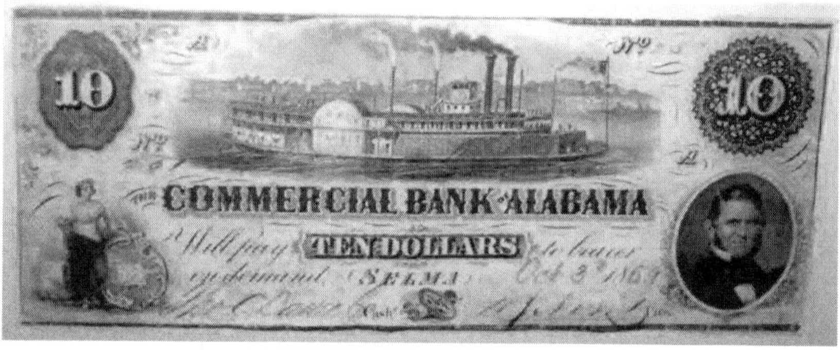

FIGURE 2.12 Ten-dollar bill with a steamboat issued by the Commercial Bank of Selma; courtesy of the Vaughan-Smitherman Historic and Civic Building, Selma, Alabama.

capital of $300,000; Col. Charles Lewis, Dr. George Phillips' son-in-law, served as cashier. Both banks survived the Panic of 1857 and were in good shape in 1861, when they constituted a fourth of all the banks operating in the state of Alabama.

Selma's future was looking brighter from year to year. However, storm clouds continued to gather, and sectional conflict distracted men from the challenge of building a metropolis on the bluff over the Alabama River.

Selma's Path to Secession: 1854–1860

Dallas County was a beehive of political activity during the late 1850s. Each major political group in Alabama had its own newspaper. Madison J. Williams's *Selma Reporter*, a descendant of the city's first paper, spoke for the remnants of the old Whig Party, which was still powerful in central Alabama. The *Cahawba Gazette* continued to beat the drums for southern rights. The *Selma State Sentinel*, founded by John Hardy in 1853, followed an erratic course in state politics.

Hardy (1823–83) had run away from home at the age of fifteen to become a journalist. He worked for Yancey's paper in Wetumpka for several years but later became a bitter foe of his former employer. When he returned to Dallas County, Hardy supported the American Party for a time before becoming a major voice for the national, or Unionist, Democrats.

In 1854 a new organization sprang into being that for a time seemed to be sweeping the state. The Order of the Star Spangled Banner had been founded in New York in 1849 to save Protestant Americans from being overrun by Catholic immigrants (i.e., the Irish). The order gradually spread throughout the country and for a brief time was all the rage in Alabama. Unionist Whigs like Ben Woolsey, national Democrats like John Hardy, and states' rights Democrats like John Tyler Morgan

FIGURE 2.13 Editor John Hardy, later mayor of Selma; courtesy of Selma City Hall, Selma, Alabama.

all joined the order and swore to keep its secrets from outsiders by claiming they "knew nothing" about it. The order ventured into politics by setting up the American Party, but its foes sneered at it as the Know Nothing Party. Dallas County elected an American delegation to the legislature in the 1855 state election. The *Gazette* suggested that the county had been moved not by anti-Catholic prejudice but by the popular appeal of the American candidates for the legislature, including Robert Hatcher and Ben Woolsey. But the American Party started running out of steam in 1856, when most Alabamians decided that the pope of Rome was less of a threat than the other new party taking shape in the North. White Alabamians viewed the Republican Party, organized in 1854, as a group of radical abolitionists and referred to them as "Black Republicans." Dallas County voted Democrat for president in 1856 and elected Democratic state legislators (Sen. James M. Calhoun, Reps. Thomas Irby and Dr. A. G. Mabry) for the rest of the decade.

In Alabama, Yancey's forces were not preparing just for an election but for the creation of an independent southern republic. Yancey saw himself as a revolutionary. Political parties cannot save us, he wrote his ally, James S. Slaughter, in 1858, "but if we could do as our fathers did . . . at the proper moment, by one organized, concerted action, we can precipitate the cotton states into a revolution." Thus, his followers organized companies of "minute men," ready to take action at a moment's notice. They also sought to "fire the Southern heart" with constant warnings of Black Republican plots against the safety of every southern home.

Yancey was prepared for the presidential election of 1860 to prove the "proper moment" for his revolution, since the Republicans might well carry enough northern states to win the presidency. The Alabama legislature had already authorized Gov. A. B. Moore to call a state convention should such a fearful event happen. The convention would then decide whether Alabama should secede.

The *Selma Reporter* did not care for Yancey's plans to "precipitate . . . revolution" and expressed the moderates' determination to defeat secession in 1860 as they had in 1851. But growing fears of a possible slave uprising in Dallas County undermined the moderates' position. On October 9, 1859, Mayor M. J. A. Keith appointed a "secret Vigilance Committee . . . to arrest any suspicious person who might be found in the city tampering with negroes" (Hardy 75). George W. Gayle convinced himself that the founder of Judson College in nearby Marion, Milo Jewett, was a "vile Abolition scoundrel" who should be hung for "secret manoeuvering with our slaves." In the following year, "A number of negroes were arrested, belonging to planters in the country, upon the charge of being engaged in a contemplated conspiracy against the whites. W. H. Fellows, John Robbins, W. S. Knox, W. B. Haralson, J. R. John, Alfred Berry and W. Y. Lundie were appointed a committee to investigate the matter, and $500 were appropriated to pay the expenses of said investigation" (Hardy 76–77).

When Alabama Democrats met in January 1860 to choose their delegates to the Democratic National Convention in Charleston, Yancey's forces took control. They instructed the delegates that unless the national party accepted the "Alabama Platform"—that is, a federal slave code protecting slavery in all US territories—they were honor bound to withdraw from the convention.

Selma lawyer N. H. R. Dawson was one of the delegates who went to Charleston in April 1860. Dawson was a native Charlestonian whose parents had emigrated to Carlowville in 1842. He was chosen as one of the secretaries of the convention and listened proudly to Yancey's thundering denunciations of the North. When the convention rejected the "Alabama Platform," Dawson joined Yancey and the delegates from seven southern states in marching out of the hall. The convention then took fifty-seven ballots without being able to select a nominee and adjourned in despair. Its last act was to appeal to all the states to send delegations to a new convention to be held in Baltimore in June.

When the Baltimore convention met, it was confronted with two delegations from Alabama. The state's unionist Democrats, convinced that Yancey was deliberately trying to break up the party in order to pave the way for secession, had sent their own delegation, led by Robert A. Baker of Summerfield. Cahawba planter Thomas M. Mathews was also a member of the delegation. Baker (1802–65), a native of Tennessee, had served as speaker of the Alabama House of Representatives in 1840 while representing Franklin County. A wealthy commission merchant, he

FIGURE 2.14 N. H. R. Dawson, leader of Selma's "Minute Men"; courtesy of Alabama Department of Archives and History, Montgomery, Alabama.

was widely known for his activities on behalf of the Methodist church and the temperance movement.

According to party rules, Yancey's delegation should have been seated instead of Baker's. But the supporters of Sen. Stephen A. Douglas, who made up a majority of the convention, voted to seat Baker's group of loyalists. This prompted another massive walkout by southern delegates, along with a few sympathetic northerners.

The result was two separate conventions, each nominating a different candidate for the presidency. The national Democrats endorsed Sen. Stephen A. Douglas of Illinois; the southern Democrats, Vice Pres. John C. Breckenridge of Kentucky.

During the same time, the *Selma Reporter* was sounding the alarm: "Your country is in danger, and if the people do not take an interest NOW, and come to the aid of the weak against the mighty, they may soon be precipitated into a revolution of the Cotton States and then you will have to leave your home and take up the line of march for the battle field. If you desire to avoid this issue and live in peace elect BELL and EVERETT." Alabama's old Whigs, now calling themselves the Constitutional Union Party, gathered in Selma on June 27 to endorse John Bell of Tennessee for

Figure 2.15 Robert A. Baker of Summerfield led the loyalist delegation from Alabama at the Baltimore Convention; courtesy of Alabama Department of Archives and History, Montgomery, Alabama.

the presidency. Col. William S. Phillips presided over the convention, which selected Selma banker Washington M. Smith to be on its slate of electors. Another of the leading spirits of the convention was Selma lawyer William McKendree Byrd.

Byrd (1819–74), a native of Mississippi, had fought to preserve the Union during the territorial crisis of 1850–51, both at the Nashville convention and in the Alabama legislature. A devout Methodist, he had founded Selma's YMCA, one of the first in the state, in 1858. His keen intelligence and stern integrity made him one of the most respected lawyers in Alabama.

The Alabama national Democrats also chose Selmian and ex-congressman Alexander White (1816–91) to serve on their electoral slate. White, the son of an Alabama Supreme Court judge, had served from 1851 to 1853 in the US House of Representatives as a Union Whig. A tall, gaunt man with chiseled features and a guttural pronunciation, he was a brilliant orator and an erratic politician. Even though he still owned a plantation in Talladega, White had been practicing law in Selma for several years. Another Selma lawyer, ex-sheriff John F. Conoley, was selected as an alternate. Conoley (1811–83), a native of North Carolina, was the son of Scots immigrants. He first moved to Selma as a merchant but became an attorney after serving as sheriff from 1843 to 1847.

The southern rights Democrats did not neglect Dallas County either. They chose Cahawba lawyer John Tyler Morgan as their elector and Mexican-American War

Figure 2.16 Unionist leader William M. Byrd, later named to the Alabama Supreme Court; courtesy of Alabama Department of Archives and History, Montgomery, Alabama.

veteran Thomas K. Irby as his alternate. Morgan, like White, was an ex-Whig who had practiced law in Talladega. Unlike White, he had been born to poor parents in Athens, Tennessee, and was an ardent advocate of southern rights.

The campaign was a heated one. In early November Stephen A. Douglas became the first presidential candidate ever to visit Selma during his campaign. A large delegation of Selmians met Douglas in Montgomery and escorted him down the river on the steamer *Duke*. Arriving at the Selma wharf at eight o'clock Friday morning, November 3, Douglas rested briefly at a Selma hotel before making a two-and-a-half hour speech denouncing both abolitionists and fire-eaters as twin enemies of the Union. He then left on the *Duke* for his final campaign stop in Mobile.

Selmians cast their ballots overwhelmingly for Unionist candidates. Bell got 40 percent of their votes, Douglas 33 percent, and Breckinridge only 27 percent. The rural voters of Dallas County, however, cast most of their votes for the southern rights candidate. Breckenridge carried Dallas County with 833 votes, to 606 for Bell, and 344 for Douglas. He also carried the state at large by a good majority.

Once all the returns had come in from the North and West, Selmians realized

Figure 2.17 John Tyler Morgan as a young lawyer; courtesy of Selma–Dallas County Museum of History and Archives, Selma, Alabama.

with dismay that Abraham Lincoln had carried every northern state but one, and the Black Republicans would soon be in power. A mass meeting was held to discuss the results, at which John W. Lapsley urged a consultation between all the southern states to decide on a course of action. The leader of Selma's Minute Men, N. H. R. Dawson, replied with a resolution that stated, "That we, the citizens of Selma, are opposed to living under a government with a black Republican president." The resolution passed overwhelmingly.

Governor Moore announced an election for December 24, 1860, to choose delegates to a state convention that would decide Alabama's course of action. He also made it clear he agreed with Dawson: it was time for Alabama to leave the Union, regardless of what other states did. The opponents of this view responded by adopting J. W. Lapsley's position: Alabama should consult with other southern states before doing anything rash. Calling themselves "cooperationists," they set out to win a majority of the delegates to the convention.

However, the cooperationists suffered a stunning blow when Selma's Minute Men announced that William S. Phillips had agreed to serve as one of their delegates. The man who had presided over the Constitutional Union Party convention in June, a wealthy planter and former railroad president, was now supporting Yancey's views! Selmians may have been struck that while Dr. George Phillips had helped draw up Alabama's original constitution as one of the United States back in 1819, now his son Will would be voting Alabama out of the Union. The Minute Men's other candidate was John Tyler Morgan, whom J. Mills Thornton has described as "the self-educated son of a hill-county squatter" (*Politics and Power in a Slave Society*, 420). The conversion of Phillips, and that of a few other Whig leaders, had a devastating effect on the Unionists of central Alabama. The *Selma Reporter* endorsed secession and, throughout much of the Black Belt, resistance to secession collapsed completely. Even in Montgomery, the cooperationists offered only token opposition to the tidal wave of support for Yancey's revolution.

Selma's Unionists, however, were made of sterner stuff. "Union Men, to Your Posts!" trumpeted the *Selma State Sentinel* on November 21, calling on all Whigs and Douglas Democrats to unite in opposing secession. On December 4, 1860, William M. Byrd, Robert A. Baker, and Alexander White called together a small group of cooperationists to choose their candidates for the convention. Both their choices, Cahawba planter Thomas M. Mathews and Selma lawyer Ben F. Saffold, were sons of prominent Dallas County families. Mathews's father, Charles, had been one of the original members of the Selma Land Company, and Saffold's had been chief justice of the Alabama Supreme Court. Mathews had little political experience but was one of the county's richest men, with 142 slaves and $350,000 worth of real estate. Saffold, a lawyer with a degree from the University of Alabama, had supported Breckinridge but was now having second thoughts about the wisdom of immediate secession. The cooperationists issued an eloquent "Address to the People of Alabama," outlining the perils facing the state. "The immediate secession of Alabama is a leap in the dark, we have made no preparation for it, we do not know where we go, who is to accompany us, what government we are to have, what is to be our destiny. We make the plunge into the whirlpool of revolution." The voices of caution, however eloquent, are hard to hear in revolutionary times. It was in vain that the *Daily State Sentinel* insisted that as long as the Democrats still controlled Congress, the South had nothing to fear from such "an unfit, incompetent, imbecile (as) Lincoln." It was futile for Saffold to warn, as he did at Summerfield on December 8, that "the course which the separate state secessionist(s) propose will cause the abolition of slavery, and that it will be attended with scenes of carnage and conflagration which will shock mankind." (December 19, 1860).

When the voters of Dallas County trooped to the polls on Christmas Eve, most of them probably saw the election in the terms used by Sheriff Michael Kenan in writing up the official returns. To Kenan, Phillips and Morgan were "For Freedom," Mathews and Saffold "For Submission." The Minute Men's ticket won by 1,015 votes to 358.

When the Secession Convention met in Montgomery on January 7, 1861, its members unanimously chose William S. Phillips as temporary chairman. The Yanceyites then elected Judge William T. Brooks of Perry County permanent chairman, by a vote of 53 to 45, over the cooperationist candidate, Robert Jemison of Tuscaloosa. The convention sent two Dallas Countians as ambassadors to other states—Edmund W. Pettus to Mississippi, where his brother was governor, and James M. Calhoun to Texas, where Gov. Sam Houston refused to have anything to do with secession.

Pettus was present when Mississippi voted to secede on January 9, describing it as "a scene of moral grandeur—the doing of a brave deed by gallant people, trusting in God" (*Official Records of the War of the Rebellion*, hereafter *OR*, series 4, 77).

Morgan played a leading role at Alabama's convention, where he ranked second only to Yancey among the orators for secession. After listening to cooperationist protests for a few days, Morgan and Yancey forced through the Ordinance of Secession on January 11. By a vote of 61 to 39, the convention declared "the State of Alabama now withdraws, and is hereby withdrawn from the Union . . . and is, and ought to be, a Sovereign and Independent State."

Once the issue had been settled, the ladies of Montgomery were allowed to present the newly created flag of the Republic of Alabama. Yancey explained the symbolism of the flag, which showed the Goddess of Liberty holding a flag with a single star on one side, and on the other side a poisonous snake coiled beneath a cotton plant. Yancey said that the snake represented the people of Alabama, who are "peaceable and harmless until disturbed; but death to the individual who assaults [them]!" Tumultuous applause followed his statement.

The convention continued for two months longer, working on a new constitution for Alabama. John Tyler Morgan served on the three-man committee that sought to revise the 1819 constitution, just as William Rufus King had served on the three-man committee that wrote the original document. One of the things Morgan wanted was to have county judges appointed by the governor rather than elected by the people, but the convention rejected this proposal as too "undemocratic."

When the convention adjourned on March 21, Phillips and Morgan went back to Dallas County to prepare for the war that was to have such a dramatic effect on both Selma and Cahawba.

3

Secession and Civil War

Selma, Arsenal of the Confederacy

"We are not fighting for slavery," Jefferson Davis told a Yankee reporter in July of 1864. "We are fighting for Independence, and that, or extermination, we *will* have." White southerners have been making the same argument ever since. They point out that most Confederate soldiers were not slaveholders, that Gen. Robert E. Lee freed his slaves before Lincoln ever got around to issuing his Emancipation Proclamation, and that there were other issues dividing the country. There were even a few slaves, such as James Jefferson of Dallas County, who went into battle for the Confederacy.

And it is true that at one time the president of the United States, Abraham Lincoln, agreed with the president of the Confederacy that slavery was not the issue. Throughout 1861 and early 1862, Lincoln kept insisting that US troops were fighting to restore the Union, not to free the slaves. However, there were people on both sides who did think slavery was the issue. The vice president of the Confederacy, Alexander Stephens, in his celebrated "Cornerstone Speech" delivered March 31, 1861, told the citizens of Savannah that the agitation over slavery was in fact "the immediate cause of the late rupture and present revolution." The United States had failed because it was founded on the mistaken notion that "all men were created equal." "Our new government is founded upon exactly the opposite idea; its foundations are laid, its cornerstone rests, upon the great truth that the negro is not equal to the white man; that slavery subordination to the superior race is his natural and normal condition. This, our new government, is the first, in the history of the world, based upon this great physical, philosophical, and moral truth" (Henry Cleveland, *Alexander H. Stephens in Public and Private*, Philadelphia, 1866). John Tyler Morgan had similar things to say at Alabama's Secession Convention: "The Ordinance of Se-

FIGURE 3.1 Pres. Jefferson Davis; courtesy of William S. Hoole, Special Collections Library, University of Alabama.

cession rests, in a great measure, upon our assertion of a right to enslave the African race, or, what amounts to the same thing, to hold them in slavery." Since the chains of slavery were "Christian bonds, I shall not hesitate to keep them where they were placed by the ALL-WISE" (William R. Smith, *History and Debates of the Convention of the People of Alabama*, Montgomery, 1861, 196–97).

If there were slaveholders in the Deep South who thought of the war entirely as a means of protecting their human property, there were also abolitionists in New England and New York who saw the war as a heaven-sent chance to destroy the institution of slavery. Some had little regard for the Union and regarded Lincoln as no better than Jeff Davis.

Lincoln also hated slavery but was too shrewd a politician to argue for emancipation on moral grounds. When he issued the Emancipation Proclamation on January 1, 1863, he assured the North he was doing so simply as a "war measure." Davis responded on January 5, 1863, with an "Address to the People of the Free States" announcing his intent to reduce all free blacks in the Confederacy to slavery as of February 22, Washington's birthday. He then went on to proclaim his belief that "the day is not far distant when the old Union will be restored, with slavery nationally declared to be the proper condition for all of African descent" (*Black Confederates and Afro-Yankees in Civil War Virginia*, 320). By then, if not before, the war to save the Union had become also a war to free the slaves.

When the crunch came in 1865, Davis was willing to compromise or even sacrifice slavery in order to win independence for the South. But when he asked the Confederate Congress to free slaves who were willing to fight for the South, he ran into bitter opposition. Gen. Howell Cobb responded indignantly, "The day you make soldiers of [black people] is the beginning of the end of the revolution. If slaves will make good soldiers our whole theory of slavery is wrong—but they won't make good soldiers" (OR, series 4, vol. 3, 1009).

In contrast, the *Selma Morning Reporte*r had shown some interest in the idea as early as August 19, 1863, when it printed a letter outlining "Reasons Why the Negro Shall Be Made a Soldier." "The negro, if paid, fed, clothed and cared for when sick, as is the white soldier, will fight more earnestly for the South than for the North." Perhaps the Selma paper remembered that Dr. Samuel Watkins Vaughan's slave "Jim Jeff" had fought beside his master at the Battle of Manassas. (The story is told in Alice V. D. Pierrepont's *Reuben Vaughan Kidd: Soldier of the Confederacy*, 294.) Vaughan and his body servant James Jefferson went up to Virginia to check on his soldier son and were visiting with his unit on July 21 when the Union Army attacked. Most of the servants fled to the woods once the bullets started flying, but not Jim Jeff: "At the roar of the guns, Jim started to run but saw [Dr. Vaughan] firing as fast as he could. 'My place is there,' thought the negro; he seized a gun, and by his master, fired steadily at the attacking army."

After Robert E. Lee had joined Davis in appealing for black troops, the Richmond *Examiner* expressed doubts that Lee was truly "a good Southerner" (February 25, 1865). The *Charleston Mercury* made it plain it was unwilling to sacrifice slavery even to save the South from being conquered by the Yankees: "It was on account of encroachments upon the institution of slavery by the sectional majority of the old Union, that South Carolina seceded from the old Union. . . . We want no Confederate Government without our institutions" (January 13, 1865). By the war's end John Tyler Morgan himself was recruiting slaves to fight for the Confederacy; but by then, of course, it was too late.

The Boys Go Marching off to War

In almost every generation, young people take up arms and go into battle to protect their homes, families, and way of life. Their elected leaders tell them it is their

FIGURE 3.2 James Jefferson, better known as "Jim Jeff," a slave who fought for the South at Manassas (Bull Run) and at Selma; courtesy of Alabama Department of Archives and History, Montgomery.

duty, and their preachers tell them it is God's will. It was like that in Selma in the spring of 1861. Indeed, many of Selma's political leaders and a few of her ministers were going to war themselves.

Rep. Thomas E. Irby left the Alabama legislature, N. H. R. Dawson resigned from the Selma City Council, and James Dedman quit his post as Selma's city marshal to join the troops leaving for Virginia. One of the city's most popular young ministers, Noble Leslie DeVotie of the First Baptist Church, who became the chaplain for volunteers from Selma who were going to Fort Morgan, will be described in more detail below.

By and large, the men who campaigned for secession were ready and eager to fight for it. John Tyler Morgan enlisted in the Cahawba Rifles, even though he said his only military talent was playing the fife. He must have developed other aptitudes as well since, within a few months, he became a major of the Fifth Alabama.

By 1862 he was a colonel recruiting a regiment of mounted infantry, and in 1863 he was promoted to brigadier general.

Most of Selma's former Unionists now fell in line behind their secessionist friends and neighbors. Alexander White became as fervent an orator for the Confederacy as he had once been for the Union. His fellow Douglas Democrat, forty-nine-year-old John F. Conoley, enlisted and became lieutenant colonel and commanding officer of the Twenty-Ninth Alabama.

Former Unionists William Byrd, John W. Lapsley, and Washington Smith actually helped launch a campaign to make Selma the capital of the new Confederate States of America. A public meeting at the city council on April 16, 1861, presided over by Mayor M. J. A. Keith, adopted the following resolution:

> WHEREAS, It will soon become necessary for the Confederate States of America to locate permanently the Seat of Government, and in the opinion of this meeting the City of Selma possesses advantages not equalled by any other point in the Confederate States for that purpose, being central, accessible at all times by river navigation and network of Railroads to all parts of the Confederacy, located near the great coal fields, and iron and marble quarries, with healthful climate and surrounded by a rich Cotton growing region. Therefore, Resolved, That it is the earnest desire of the citizens of Selma that the Congress of the Confederate States shall locate the seat of Government in this city; and for the accomplishment of that purpose, hereby offer our most cordial aid and support.

Selma did not succeed; when the Confederate Congress left Montgomery, it was for Richmond, Virginia. But the advantages cited by the appeal did help the city become one of the new nation's major arsenals.

Cahawba planter Joel Early Mathews (1809–74), a long-time fire-eater, was too old to be a soldier, so he sent his money to war instead. On January 20, 1861, Mathews gave the newly formed Republic of Alabama $15,000 in gold to use in maintaining its independence. Governor Moore graciously responded by saying that the example of patriotism set by Mathews was worth even more than the money he had so generously given.

According to William G. Stevenson's *Thirteen Months in the Rebel Army*, Selma's ladies were as fervent as their menfolk in support of the Confederacy. Stevenson spent part of 1862 at the Confederate hospital here and discovered that: "The unmarried ladies were so patriotic, that every able-bodied young man was constrained to enlist. Some months previous to this, a gentleman was known to be engaged for an early marriage, and hence declined to volunteer. When his betrothed, a charming girl and a devoted lover, heard of his refusal, she sent by the hand of a slave, a

FIGURE 3.3 Joel Early Mathews put his money where the South was; courtesy of Emily Furniss Maxwell.

package enclosing a note. The package contained a ladies' skirt and crinoline, and the note these terse words, 'Wear these or volunteer.' He volunteered." Unfortunately, Stevenson's account does not tell us whether the young man survived the war, or if the marriage ever took place.

One young Selmian who did not survive was Rev. N. L. DeVotie, who became the first casualty of the Civil War two months before the firing on Fort Sumter. On February 12, as he was preparing to board a ship in Mobile Bay, his foot slipped off the gangplank and he fell into the water. His fellow Selmians tried to rescue him, but the undercurrent carried him off. His dead body washed ashore three days later. DeVotie, a graduate of Princeton Theological Seminary and the founder of Sigma Alpha Epsilon, seemed almost too appropriate a symbol of the youthful talent that was to be lost to death in the years to come. According to Alabama historian Dr. Thomas Owen, the Confederate flag that draped DeVotie's casket was the first one ever made.

That was how the War between the States began for Selma: with a tragic, accidental death by water. It was to end in much the same way. On April 30, 1865, after all the fighting was over, a steamboat taking Northern prisoners of war home exploded on the Mississippi River. These men, who had survived both the perils of

FIGURE 3.4 Rev. Noble Leslie DeVotie, the Baptist minister who became the first casualty of the War between the States; courtesy of Selma–Dallas County Museum of History and Archives, Selma, Alabama.

the battlefield and the horrors of Castle Morgan, the infamous Confederate prison at Cahawba, died much as DeVotie did: tragically, accidentally, by water.

Hardy calls the roll of companies that were formed here during the first year of the war:

> Selma did not stand still; her manhood was aroused, and in a few short months, five companies of gallant young men of the city were organized, ready to rally to the defense of the Southern movement. Capt. N. H. R. Dawson, with the "Magnolia Cadets," composed of the first young men of the place, took the lead; followed by the "Governor's Guards," led by Capt. Thomas J. Goldsby, one of the most gallant young men of the State; then came the more sober, settled men of the city, composing the "Selma Blues," led by Capt. Thomas C. Daniel, a most worthy citizen, who gave up his Cashiership in the Commercial Bank to lead the Company, and who fell, leading his men, at the Second Battle of Manassas; the fourth was the brave and hardy men of the "Phenix Reds," composed almost entirely of the working men of the city, led by Capt. James M. Dedman, who was severely wounded at Vicksburg, and who after-

> wards was promoted for his bravery and gallantry; the fifth was Dr. James Kent, with a company formed at Selma. Thus did our little city, in less than twelve months, furnish to the Confederate forces in the field, over six hundred men, rank and file. (*Selma*, 46)

In his catalog of companies, Hardy makes it clear that the whole range of Selma white society, from aristocrats like Dawson to working men like Dedman, were involved in the war effort. The crusade for Southern independence was not "a rich man's war and a poor man's fight," at least not in Dallas County.

Hardy's catalog leaves out some of the other companies organized by men from Dallas County, including the Cahaba Rifles led by Christopher C. Pegues. He also omits the Jeff Davis Artillery, which was organized by Rev. Joseph T. Montgomery of Summerfield in Selma itself on April 16, 1861. He also ignores the companies organized in the following year, after Davis had appealed for twelve thousand additional soldiers. Dr. Kent, who had been forced to resign from the Independent Blues because of poor health, promptly organized an entire regiment—the Forty-Fourth Alabama—at Selma on May 16, 1862. Unfortunately, his health gave way again once he was back in Virginia, and he was never able to lead his men into combat. In August 1862 John Tyler Morgan also returned to Alabama to organize a new regiment, the Fifty-First (Mounted) Infantry, consisting mostly of recruits from north Alabama.

What follows is a more inclusive list of the Selma and Dallas County companies that served in the Confederate Army, and the men who led them. The information is based on Dr. Thomas Owen's *Alabama*, and Willis Brewer's book of the same name.

Confederate Commands from Dallas County

INFANTRY

Fourth Alabama Regiment of Volunteers, Company A, the Governor's Guard
Capt. Thomas J. Goldsby, promoted
Capt. Reuben V. Kidd, killed
Capt. Jason M. West, captured

Fourth Alabama, Company C, the Magnolia Cadets
Capt. N. H. R. Dawson, resigned
Capt. Alfred C. Price, killed
Capt. F. C. Robbins, wounded and captured

Fifth Alabama, Company G, the Cahawba Rifles
Capt. C. C. Pegues, promoted and killed
Capt. E. B. Mosely

Eighth Alabama, Company D, the Independent Blues
Capt. James Kent, resigned
Capt. Robert T. McCrary, killed
Capt. W. R. Knox

Twentieth Alabama, Company K, the Phenix Reds
Capt. James M. Dedman, promoted
Capt. Thomas J. Ferguson

Twenty-Eighth Alabama, Company I, the Dallas Warriors
Capt. F. M. Hopkins, captured
Capt. P. G. Wood

Forty-Fourth Alabama, Company A
Capt. D. B. Edwards

Forty-Fourth Alabama, Company G, the Wash Smith Guards
Capt. Thomas C. Daniel, killed
Capt. William T. Dunklin, killed
Capt. W. P. Becker

Fifty-Eighth Alabama, Company H, the Ben Edwards Greys
Capt. Elias Fort, resigned
Capt. Calvin Harrell, wounded

Sixty-Second Alabama, Company H
Capt. J. J. Alston, captured

Sixty-Second Alabama, Company I, Rosser's Reserves
Capt. George D. Shortridge Jr., captured

CAVALRY

Third Alabama Regiment of Company 5, the Curry Dragoons
Capt. William Cathy, killed
Capt. R. W. Cole, resigned
Capt. Thomas Norris, killed

Third Alabama, Company I, the Mathews Rangers
Capt. James Boykin, transferred
Capt. Augustus Tomlinson, died
Capt. Thomas Lenoir, killed

Third Alabama, Company K, the Crocheron Light Dragoons
Capt. E. M. Holloway

Eighth Alabama, Company F
Capt. M. M. Burke

Fifty-First Alabama (Mounted Infantry), Company I, the Partisan Rangers
Capt. John Robbins

Fifty-Third Alabama (Mounted Infantry), Company E
Capt. W. R. Davis, captured

ARTILLERY

First Alabama Battalion of Company C, Gee's Battery
Capt. James T. Gee, promoted to lieutenant colonel and then captured

Jeff Davis Artillery
Capt. Joseph T. Montgomery, resigned
Lt. C. W. Lovelace, resigned
Lt. William Fitts, resigned
Lt. Robert Walker, resigned
Lt. John Mitchell

Selden-Lovelace's Battery
Capt. C. W. Lovelace, captured

Human nature being what it is, the aristocrats got more attention than their fellow soldiers of humble origin. Two Selma companies, Goldsby's Governor's Guards and Dr. Kent's Selma Blues, left town for Fort Morgan on January 12, 1861, without getting half the attention Dawson's Magnolia Cadets received when they departed for Virginia on April 26 of the same year. Of course, the shooting had actually begun by then.

Many years later, Georgia author Mary Gay recalled the departure of the Magnolia Cadets in her *Life in Dixie during the War*, which exults in the spectacle of "wealthy, cultured, young gentlemen voluntarily turning their backs upon the luxuries and endearments of affluent homes, and accepting in lieu the privations and hardships of warfare." She watched with interest as Captain Dawson accepted the company flag made for him by Elodie Breck Todd and Martha Todd White, sisters-in-law of Abraham Lincoln!

FIGURE 3.5 Elodie Breck Todd Dawson; courtesy of the Vaughan–Smitherman Historic and Civic Building, Selma, Alabama.

Both ladies were as fervent in their support of the Confederacy as their older sister, Mary Todd Lincoln, was in her devotion to the Union. It gives a romantic flourish to the story to know that Captain Dawson proposed to Elodie before leaving for Virginia and that she defied both her mother and her older sister Mary by accepting his proposal. When he returned triumphant from a year of battles, Dawson married Elodie and was then elected to the Alabama legislature as a war hero.

Not all members of the Magnolia Cadets or the Governor's Guards were as fortunate. Both companies became part of the Fourth Alabama Infantry, which suffered heavily at the first battle of Manassas, known also as the first battle of Bull Run. "We had one of the most dreadful conflicts that has ever been known on the American continent, in which the 4th Alabama was cut to pieces," wrote Sgt. Reuben V. Kidd on July 28, 1861. "You who have never witnessed the horrors of a battlefield have no idea what its horrors are" (Pierrepont, *Reuben Vaughan Kidd*, 297). Most of the Fourth Alabama's commanders were slain on the field or later died of wounds.

T. J. Goldsby, a planter's son who had attended Princeton and Yale, now became

Figure 3.6 Sgt. Reuben Vaughan Kidd of the Magnolia Cadets; courtesy of Alabama Department of Archives and History, Montgomery, Alabama.

lieutenant colonel of the "Fighting Fourth." Kidd, formerly a clerk in a dry goods store, succeeded him as captain of the Governor's Guards, now Company A. Goldsby left the army after being wounded at Cold Harbor, Kidd was killed at Chickamauga, and his successor, Selma clerk Jason M. West, was wounded at Hanover Junction. Dawson's successors as captain of the Magnolia Cadets, now Company C, fared the same. Lawyer Alfred C. Price died at Cold Harbor, and merchant F. C. Robbins was wounded and then captured at Nashville. The war took a frightening toll on the brave young men who marched off from Selma in 1861 and 1862.

Elodie Todd, confessing that she had no idea that war would prove so dreadful, wrote her fiancé on October 13, 1861, "I think my patriotism has cooled too much to allow a thought of your serving again [in the army]."

Many of the soldiers who had been lucky enough to survive needed serious medical care. The former Central Masonic Institute was converted into a Confederate hospital under the direction of Dr. William P. Reese, and the ladies of Selma stayed busy making bandages and providing care for the wounded soldiers brought in from battlefields in Mississippi, Tennessee, and other Southern states. By 1863 it was apparent that a second hospital was needed; the *Selma Morning Reporter's* September 30 issue included a plea from "some kind hearted ladies to suggest to the citizens of Selma the propriety of establishing a wayside hospital, for the benefit of unfortunate female refugees and other deserving exiles, who in sickness and distress are sometimes obliged to sojourn for a time in our city." Selma responded by setting up a hundred-bed Wayside Hospital at the corner of Water Avenue and Broad Street.

In early 1862, the paper money issued by the Confederacy was beginning to lose its value, and the Selma press expressed indignation because a few local merchants refused to accept it. Since the South had previously imported most of its goods from the North, including such necessities as table salt, serious shortages quickly developed. In south Alabama, a cow that would have sold for $15 before the war cost $127 in 1864. Because a pair of boots cost almost as much as a cow, many Confederate soldiers were going barefoot.

On September 4, 1863, a group of artisans and mechanics associated with the government works held a mass meeting at City Hall to protest that they were being charged "enormous prices for the necessaries of life." Four days later, the "residents and property owners of Selma" responded by holding their own mass meeting with Dr. A. G. Mabry as president. The meeting set up a Relief Association headed by William Byrd and included Gen. Andrew Bogle, Judge Jonathan Haralson, Capt. C. E. Thames, and Mabry himself "to supply the families of soldiers and the poor of Selma and Dallas County, with provision and fuel at prices existing prior to the war" (*Selma Morning Reporter*, hereafter *SMR*, September 5–9, 1863).

Conditions continued to worsen, both on the battlefield and on the home front. The *Reporter* began to print lists of deserters. Even the "Fighting Fourth," flower of Alabama's chivalry, suffered seventy-two desertions, most of them from north Alabama companies. Dallas County was producing enough crops to feed most of central Alabama, but some hill counties were seriously short of food. Some ragged soldiers, hearing that their families were near starvation, gave up on a war that looked increasingly hopeless after Vicksburg and Gettysburg.

"There are times when the heart is sick, sick of this life in the wilderness, this absence of pleasures, comforts, friends . . . this weary pilgrimage of freedom," wrote Lt. Paul Turner Vaughan of the Magnolia Cadets in late 1864. "I am nearly overcome by its depressing weight, and would . . . almost welcome the bullet which terminated so much trouble" ("Civil War Diary and Letters to Pa," manuscript, Old Depot Museum). Vaughan's brother Henry had been taken captive, his cousin Reuben had died at Chickamauga, and his "boy" John had fled into Union lines. He later left the Magnolia Cadets to serve in the Alabama militia, which would both bring him closer to home and give him a better chance of surviving the war.

Selma Becomes a Center of Confederate War Production

Selma's status as a transportation center and its budding industries gave the city new importance as the pressures of war forced the agrarian South to develop both its industries and its transportation systems.

The foresight of Selma's capitalists in launching the Alabama and Mississippi Rivers Railroad was vindicated when Davis asked the Confederate Congress to provide funds needed to complete the Alabama and Mississippi from Demopolis to Meridian. The South badly needed rail connections between its Atlantic Coast states and those further inland. Once the rails had been laid from Demopolis to Meridian (which was connected to Natchez by rail), it would be possible for trains to run from Selma to the Mississippi River.

On February 15, 1862, the Confederate Congress appropriated $150,000 to complete the Alabama and Mississippi. Unfortunately, the thousand tons of iron purchased for the railroad was captured by Union forces when New Orleans fell in May. The Alabama and Mississippi then purchased iron belonging to the Cahawba, Marion and Greensboro Railroad, which had gone bankrupt. Further problems developed in the fall when planters temporarily withdrew their slaves from work on the railroad. This additional crisis was overcome and, on December 15, 1862, the *Daily Morning Reporter* announced that trains were running regularly over the completed track.

The Alabama and Tennessee Rivers Railroad, running from Selma to Blue Mountain in Calhoun County, also proved an invaluable asset to the Confederacy. It made possible the transportation of coal and iron ore mined in Bibb and Shelby Counties to Selma for use at the armory and for shipment to other parts of the South. The Confederate Congress allocated a large sum of money to extend the Alabama and Tennessee to Rome, Georgia, where it would link with the extensive railroad system of the Atlantic Coast states. However, this road, which was to be renamed the Selma, Rome, and Dalton (and was soon nicknamed "the Slow, Rough, and Dangerous"), was not completed in time to help the war effort because of a shortage of iron.

Two dramatic consequences for Selma came about because the Union had a navy and the Confederacy did not. First, it forced the moving of Southern armories in-

FIGURE 3.7 Warship built at Selma's Confederate Naval Ordnance Works; courtesy of Selma–Dallas County Museum of History and Archives, Selma, Alabama.

land, where they would be safe from the US Navy. Second, it led to an attempt to build a navy. One of the sites selected for this effort was Selma.

After New Orleans fell in April 1862, the Confederate arsenal at Mount Vernon, Alabama, was moved upriver to Selma. This was the first of three major government installations—the arsenal, naval yard, and Naval Ordnance Works—to be established here. The arsenal produced ammunition, the naval yard built ships, and the ordnance works created artillery, both for shore defenses and for the Confederate navy. Capt., later Lt. Col., James L. White directed the arsenal, which grew to include twenty-four buildings manufacturing ammunition of all sorts. By the war's end, the Tredegar Iron Works in Richmond and the Selma Arsenal were the only sources of badly needed ammunition and arms for the Confederacy.

In April 1862, Confederate congressman Colin J. McRae suggested to the Department of the Navy that Selma would be an ideal spot to build ironclad ships for the defense of Mobile Bay. By September 1862, work was underway in the new na-

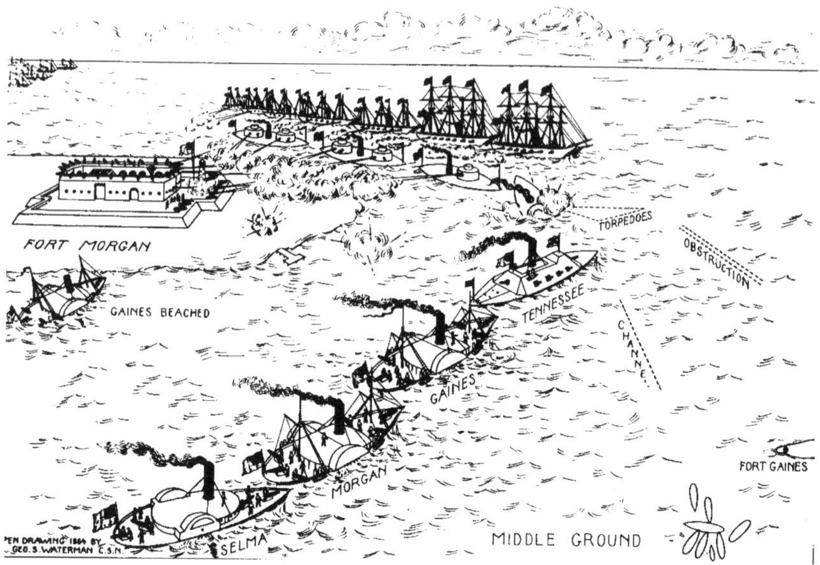

FIGURE 3.8 The Battle of Mobile Bay as depicted by George S. Waterman, CSN; courtesy of the US Naval Historical Center.

val yard in Selma. Joseph Pierce, CSN, had been working on the *Tennessee* in Memphis when federal forces captured that city. He began work on a new *Tennessee* and, this time, was able to complete the job without interruption.

On February 8, 1863, all of Selma turned out to watch the launching of the CSS *Tennessee.* The ship had cost roughly $595,800 to build and boasted two 7-inch Brooke cannons. There was a minor mishap when the ship struck and demolished the corner of a brick warehouse. However, a year and a half later, on August 5, 1864, this ship was the very heart of the Confederate forces in the Battle of Mobile Bay.

The battle pitted the *Tennessee* and three wooden gunboats (the *Gaines*, the *Morgan*, and the *Selma*) commanded by Adm. Franklin Buchanan against the Union's fourteen ships (including four ironclad "monitors") under Adm. David Farragut. One of the Union ships hit a mine and sank within two minutes even before the battle began. Two of Buchanan's gunboats, the *Gaines* and the *Morgan*, took refuge under Fort Morgan; the *Selma* fought valiantly but was forced to surrender. The *Tennessee* fought on alone against Farragut's thirteen surviving federal ships. Its guns took a terrible toll; the Union lost 222 men in the battle, the Confederacy only 8. Finally one of the monitors succeeded in disabling the *Tennessee.* Buchanan, who had been seriously wounded in the battle, had to surrender.

Two other ships, the *Tuscaloosa* and the *Huntsville*, were substantially finished

FIGURE 3.9 Capt. Catesby ap Roger Jones, one of the outstanding figures at the Selma Arsenal; courtesy of Selma–Dallas County Museum of History and Archives, Selma, Alabama.

by the Selma navy yard, but lack of iron plating prevented their being of any use in the battle.

A submarine, or "torpedo boat," was completed at Selma in 1864 and sent down the river to Mobile. However, its one attack on the US fleet, on January 27, 1865, was a failure, and no second attempt was made.

The third government installation established in Selma during the war, the Naval Ordnance Works, was created in February of 1863, when the Confederate government bought Colin J. McRae's Selma Foundry and began looking for men to create first-class artillery for the South. It found two men: Comm. Catesby ap Roger Jones (1821–77), a native Virginian and an Annapolis graduate, to serve as commander of the naval works; and George Peacock (1823–94), an Englishman and master iron worker, to be superintendent of the foundry.

Catesby Jones was already famous when he came to Selma. He had been second-in-command to Adm. Franklin Buchanan when the Confederacy's first ironclad, the CSS *Virginia*, almost destroyed the Union navy in Norfolk Harbor. When

FIGURE 3.10 George Peacock, one of the outstanding figures at the Selma Arsenal; courtesy of Selma–Dallas County Museum of History and Archives, Selma, Alabama.

Buchanan was wounded, Jones took command of the Confederate ship for its climactic struggle with the Union ironclad, the *Monitor*. The battle ended in a draw. Later, when Norfolk fell to Union forces, the *Virginia* was scuttled to prevent her capture. Jones was then sent, much against his will, to make cannon for others to fire.

However, Jones soon learned that making cannon could be almost as dangerous as a battle at sea. He always supervised the casting of large pieces of artillery such as the Brooke cannon and, thus, was present on the day a pit exploded just as molten iron was being poured into it. Two workers were killed, another lost an ear, and several others suffered painful burns. Jones was fortunate: he lost only his hat, his coat, and his trousers!

Afterward, Jones wrote Buchanan, "I consider my life in greater danger here than if I were in command of the *Tennessee*, though I should expect some hot work in her occasionally."

Jones and Peacock faced major problems in securing enough raw materials, recruiting enough skilled workers, and mastering the complicated techniques involved in producing what was then the finest cannon in the world. However, by January 8, 1864, the Selma Naval Ordnance Works had begun to produce impressive artillery. From then on, it turned out a cannon every five days—an impressive achieve-

FIGURE 3.11 The Brooke cannon outside Selma City Hall; courtesy of the author.

ment, since some of the larger pieces took six days to harden, and then required at least a hundred seventy-five hours of machining!

Jones's Naval Ordnance Works and Lt. Col. White's Selma Arsenal were supposed to work together, but the two men got along so badly that the Confederate government finally had to intervene. White was "kicked upstairs," and afterward the foundry and arsenal cooperated a great deal better.

All these war plants were handicapped by the South's shortage of raw materials such as iron, coal, and saltpeter. Jonathan Haralson, the Selma lawyer serving as agent for the Confederate Nitre Works, hit upon a novel method of collecting animal wastes from which nitre could be extracted. In the October 1, 1863 issue of the *Selma Sentinel*, he took out an ad which read:

> The ladies of Selma are respectfully requested to preserve all their chamber lye collected about their premises for the purpose of making Nitre. Wagons with barrels will be sent around for it by the subscriber.
>
> Signed, Jno Haralson
> Agent Nitre and Mining Bureau

In other words, the ladies were to save the contents of their chamber pots, since urine is a rich source of nitrogen and can be used in making gunpowder!

Selma's women served the Confederacy in many ways, most of them more dignified than the one specified by Mr. Haralson. They provided food and bandages for both local Confederate hospitals, the general hospital at the foot of Alabama Avenue and the "Wayside" hospital on Water Avenue. They also made up a major part of White's work force at the arsenal. The rolling of cartridges, unlike the casting of cannon, required more delicacy of touch than it did brute strength. Indeed, a number of children, some as young as nine or ten, worked at the arsenal day after day, preparing cartridges for their fathers and older brothers to use against the hated Yankees.

Of course, the largest part of the workforce in Selma, as in Richmond, was made up of slaves. It was also the slaves who, in 1863, began erecting the impressive fortifications around Selma, hoping to protect it from Union attack.

As the city became an increasingly important center of Confederate war production, Selma's population grew swiftly and in large numbers. By 1865, there were probably ten thousand men, women, and children living in and around the city, most of them serving the war effort in some way. In addition to the government plants, there was a host of private firms producing rifles, shovels, oil, whiskey, cotton cards, canteens, and a variety of other goods. Selma, where most of the people preferred an agrarian way of life, was rapidly being transformed into an industrial center, one that reminded some visitors of northern cities such as Pittsburgh.

Word of Selma's new prominence in the war effort was not slow in reaching the Union army. On January 25, 1864, former Selmian James Q. Smith wrote Gen. U. S. Grant from Nashville, identifying himself as "a refugee from Alabama, having escaped out of the Confederate lines, after some imprisonment in the military prison at Mobile for my uncompromising attachment to the Union cause and opposition to the rebel government." Smith informed Grant that "the city of Selma . . . has lately become the focus from which the rebel Government receives its war supplies. There is now located there a large and extensive arsenal, which supplies small-arms of every description; a naval foundry, machine-shops, and rolling-mills, which supplies the Army of Georgia and Mississippi with cannon of all sizes, and Charleston now is defended by shot and shell from this place; a powder-mill, wagon manufactory, and harness establishments."

He then suggested that Grant could "inflict an irreparable injury to the rebellion" by sending troops to destroy "Selma itself, and all the Government works there" (OR, series 1, vol. 44, 214–16). Smith felt sure that Union troops would face little resistance from the city's workers, many of whom were foreigners or Northerners.

A year later, the Union Army decided to take Smith's advice. Wilson's Raid-

FIGURE 3.12 Gen. Edmund Winston Pettus; courtesy of Alabama Department of Archives and History, Montgomery, Alabama.

ers, the cavalry commanded by Union general James H. Wilson, headed South in early 1865 to destroy the Confederacy's remaining transportation network and industrial capacity. This meant, of course, that a major target was Selma, the arsenal of the Confederacy.

Selma's "Stout-Hearted Soldier" Edmund Pettus

Selma's fighting men were mostly far from home, serving in the Army of Northern Virginia or the Army of Tennessee, when the attack came. Few of them saw more combat during the War between the States than Edmund Winston Pettus.

Pettus (1821–1907) had already seen combat during the Mexican-American War, having resigned his post as solicitor (district attorney) for the Seventh Judicial Circuit when the war broke out. Tall, broad-shouldered, and handsome, he proved a natural leader of men. After the war he visited California before returning to Sumter County, where he was elected circuit judge in 1855. In 1858 he resigned to move his legal practice to Cahawba, Dallas County.

Once the war had begun, he helped to organize the Twentieth Alabama Infantry and was elected its major. The Twentieth took part in the Confederate invasion of Kentucky in 1862, when the South's fortunes were at high tide. The tide began to ebb quickly; by December 21, Pettus was writing his wife that "the Kentuckians don't deserve to be free. They are not willing to risk position, prosperity or blood." In the following year, Pettus and many of his men were captured by Union soldiers after the battle of Port Gibson, Mississippi. He later gave an account of his escape in a May 9, 1863, letter to his friend N. H. R. Dawson: "I was marched that night fifteen miles with about 300 other prisoners to the Mississippi River. Then when we stopped to rest and get water I laid down to rest behind a plank fence and when the order was given to fall in I never moved. The guard and other prisoners moved off and left me there. So soon as they were gone, I passed across a field into the back water. It was about day, Saturday morning. After terrible suffering from hunger and exhaustion, wading ten miles through back water and living two days and a half without food, I joined my regiment here Tuesday morning." His regiment was trapped inside Vicksburg during Grant's siege of the city. It was during the siege that Pettus "won the admiration of every one by his daring on May 22d," when he personally led forty Texas soldiers in what looked like a suicidal attack on a Yankee position (Jackson, *The Story of Selma*, 392). (A previous attempt had resulted in the death of every Confederate soldier involved.) Pettus succeeded not only in taking the position but also in capturing fifty Union soldiers in the process. When told later that Gen. Stephen D. Lee had called his exploit "the bravest single deed he saw during the War," Pettus responded curtly that there had been no bravery on his part; his men had volunteered, but he was under orders (OR, series 2, vol. 24, 351–52).

Pettus's exploit delayed the loss of Vicksburg by only six weeks: on July 4, 1863, the same day that Lee met defeat at Gettysburg, the starving garrison surrendered to Grant.

After Pettus was exchanged, he was promoted to brigadier general and led "Pettus' Brigade" in the thick of the fighting in Tennessee and Georgia, taking part in the battles of Missionary Ridge (November 25, 1863), Kennesaw Mountain (June 27, 1864), Atlanta (July 22), and Jonesborough (August 31–September 1). His brigade was involved in Gen. John Bell Hood's disastrous invasion of Tennessee in late 1864. A January 9, 1865, letter to Dawson reveals his bitterness over the incredible blunder made by his commanding officer:

> We knew that General Hood with most of the army had succeeded in reaching Spring Hill before [Union General] Thomas' advances had arrived at that place. But none of us could guess that Hood's Army would sleep in one mile

FIGURE 3.13 The Battle of Nashville, as sketched by George H. Ellsbury for the January 14, 1865, issue of *Harper's Weekly*; courtesy of the National Archives, Washington, DC.

> of the only road over which Thomas could retreat with his artillery and wagons, and make no attempt to stop his march. Yet such is the truth.
>
> Thomas with his army passed Spring Hill that night, with his entire train, in sight of our pickets and in the hearing of the whole army, yet no attack was made—no effort to stop him. Here we lost the Campaign. (Jackson, *The Story of Selma*, 395)

Having failed to attack the Union forces when they were most vulnerable, Hood now threw all his forces into a desperate attack on their strongly fortified positions at Franklin. In so doing, he largely destroyed his own army. After a second, even more disastrous battle near Nashville, it took all of Pettus's skill and courage to hold his troops together during the nightmarish retreat that followed. "The extent of the labor and suffering on this campaign cannot be surely exaggerated. Through snow and mud, over frozen ground, and through deep creeks the men have marched and waded; most of them only half clad and very many barefooted." At the close of his letter, Pettus confessed that he had no idea what the Confederate army could do now. Soon he and his men, now under the command of Gen. Joseph Johnston, were futilely pursuing General Sherman into North Carolina. Johnston's forces "caught up" with Sherman near Bentonville, North Carolina, where one of the last battles of the war was fought on March 19–21. "The Yankees attempted an advance upon General Pettus," his commanding general later reported, "but that stout-hearted soldier and his noble brigade drove them back without difficulty. In this attack [Pettus] himself received a painful flesh wound, and his nephew and aide-de-camp, Lieutenant Pettus, was killed" (OR, series 1, vol. 47, 1096.)

On the day after the battle, March 22, 1865, when Pettus was recovering from his wound and many of Dallas County's other brave soldiers were also far from home, Wilson's Raiders crossed the Tennessee River and headed for Selma.

The Battle of Selma: April 2, 1865

The battlefields had been edging closer and closer to Selma for some time, and on April 2 they reached the city itself. The skirmishes leading up to the fall of Selma consisted largely of a series of clashes between two mighty opposites: Confederate general Nathan Bedford Forrest and Union general James Harrison Wilson.

Forrest (1822–79), Selma's defender, was one of the most spectacular and controversial of all the South's generals. A poor boy with little or no formal education, he had risen to be a wealthy Memphis businessman before the war. Forrest raised a battalion of cavalry and quickly developed a genius for guerilla tactics and psychological warfare that earned him a nickname, "the Wizard of the Saddle." He defeated large federal forces on several occasions, especially during Streight's raid into northern Alabama in 1863. Forrest's admirers, including Selma historian Sol H. Tepper, consider him one of the greatest military men who ever lived. The Confederate monument in Selma's Live Oak Cemetery ranks Forrest's name with those of Robert E. Lee and Jefferson Davis.

Black Selmians, remembering that Forrest was a slave trader before the war and grand wizard of the Ku Klux Klan for a time afterward, regard him with different eyes. They find it easy to believe the Union charges that Forrest's men massacred black prisoners at Fort Pillow—charges that some historians still dispute.

James Harrison Wilson (1838–1925) was a "boy general" from Shawneetown, Illinois. A West Point graduate, he served on Grant's staff for two years before being named chief of the war department's cavalry bureau. His greatest accomplishment in the job, according to James P. Jones's *Yankee Blitzkrieg*, was to secure large numbers of Spencer repeating rifles for Union forces.

In the spring of 1864, Wilson, at that time the youngest general in the US Army, got his first experience as a raider when he was sent to destroy the Confederate railroads south of Petersburg, Virginia. He succeeded in the mission but with heavy cost in men and materials. Later, however, Wilson and his men performed very well at the battle of Nashville. Brilliant, ambitious, and decisive, Wilson was also humor-

FIGURE 3.14 Gen. Nathan B. Forrest, "the Wizard of the Saddle," was charged with the defense of Selma; courtesy of Selma–Dallas County Museum of History and Archives, Selma, Alabama.

less and conceited. To some white Selmians, he ranks as a war criminal because he encouraged his men to terrorize private citizens.

It reveals something about both men to know that Wilson sent Forrest a formal challenge to battle during early 1865. Capt. Lewis M. Hosea was sent to Forrest's headquarters near Tupelo, Mississippi, under a flag of truce to deliver the challenge. Hosea was impressed with the charm and simplicity of the Confederate general, who replied: "Jist tell General Wilson that I know the nicest little place down here . . . and whenever he is ready, I will fight with him with any number from one to ten thousand cavalry and abide the issue. . . . I ain't no graduate of West Point; never rubbed my back up agin any college, but Wilson may take his sabers and I'll use my six shooters and agree to whup the fight with any cavalry he can bring." Heavy rains and flooding delayed Wilson's crossing of the Tennessee River until March 22, 1865, but then his fourteen thousand men headed south on their mission to destroy Ala-

FIGURE 3.15 Union general James H. Wilson; courtesy of Selma–Dallas County Museum of History and Archives, Selma, Alabama.

bama's railroads, iron works, and war supplies. Forrest had been distracted by news of a projected Union invasion from the south, and Wilson's men were several days on their way before Forrest learned of their rapid move through north Alabama.

The head start gave Wilson a crucial advantage. To have a fighting chance against the Union forces, Forrest had to pull together Gen. James R. Chalmers's Mississippi troops, Gen. W. H. Jackson's Tennesseans, and all the Alabama troops and militia he could find and concentrate them at Selma. While his couriers were racing to contact Chalmers and Jackson, Forrest and his men did all they could to delay Wilson's troops in their southward march.

The first real clash came at Montevallo, where the Union forces had been ordered to destroy the Bibb Naval Furnace and other facilities supplying Selma's war industry. Forrest's small force engaged in a fourteen-mile running fight with the advancing raiders for most of March 31. The Confederates camped near Randolph that night, and Forrest sent out urgent messages to other Confederate units scattered across west Alabama, thinking, no doubt, that if he could concentrate his forces in time, the wizard of the saddle might yet outfox the boy general.

Luck was against him, however. Wilson's men captured Forrest's messenger and, thus, discovered how few and scattered their opponents were. "If I could force the marching and the fighting with sufficient rapidity and vigor," the Union general wrote, "I should have the game entirely in my hands." He sent troops to destroy the Centerville bridge Jackson's forces would have to cross to reinforce Forrest, then pressed his advantage for all it was worth. In the battle of Stanton that followed, Forrest displayed his personal courage once more, killing a Union captain in hand-to-hand combat. However, his outnumbered forces could only delay, and not halt, the federal advance.

A council of war was held in Selma that same day, April 1, to decide whether or not to defend the city. Forrest's messages made it clear that without Jackson's and Chalmers's troops, there was little hope of holding the city. Chalmers's forces were moving toward Selma but too slowly to be of much help. Under the circumstances, Mayor John H. Henry suggested that the city be surrendered. Gen. Richard Taylor, commander of all Confederate forces in Alabama and Mississippi, responded by saying that everything of value to the Confederacy would be shipped out of the city but that Selma itself should be defended at all costs.

When Forrest arrived in Selma at noon on Sunday, April 2, all bloody from battle, he found that Taylor's men had been working furiously to make sure that nothing was left in the town that might benefit the Union forces. George Peacock and his crew had been busy pushing their newly made cannon into the Alabama River. Most of the city's cotton had been stacked into railroad cars and sent west to Demopolis, and every railroad engine but one had been sent away on the Alabama and Mississippi. The one remaining engine had been reserved for Taylor's personal escape and, after speaking briefly with Forrest, he "left the city as fast as a steam engine could carry him" (Hardy, *Selma*, 51). Before leaving, however, he confirmed his earlier decision that Selma must be defended at all costs.

Selma had an impressive line of fortifications about a mile and a half north of the city with parapets six to eight feet high and eight feet thick at the bottom, stretching from Summerfield Road to Range Line Road. Ditches five feet deep and five feet wide had been dug in front of the parapets to make things just a bit more difficult for attackers. The eastern and western approaches to the city were defended by stockaded rifle pits along Valley and Beech Creeks.

The city's defenses would have been formidable indeed, if there had been enough soldiers to man the parapets with riflemen two feet apart. However, the city had

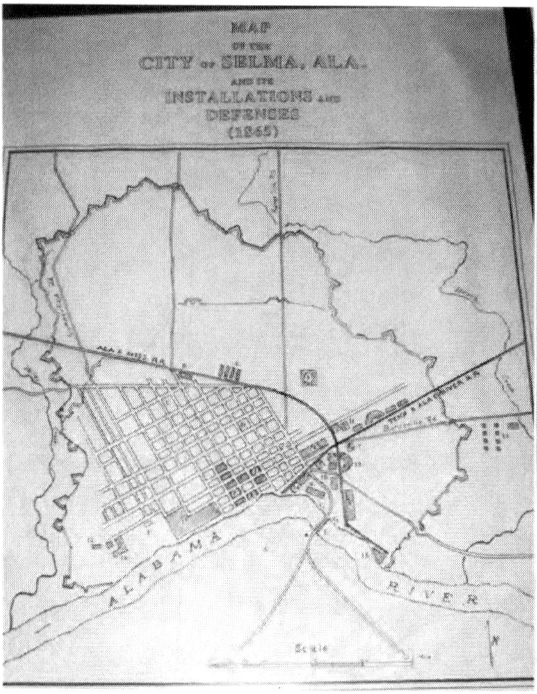

FIGURE 3.16 Map of Selma in 1865 showing breastworks.

only enough men, counting civilians, boys, and old men, to position a man every fifteen feet. By Forrest's judgement, this was not good enough. A second, shorter line of defenses closer to the city had been started but not completed.

Under Forrest's command were Gen. Frank C. Armstrong's Mississippi troops, Col. Edward Crossland's three Kentucky regiments, General Philip D. Roddey's five Alabama regiments, and about 2,700 civilians. According to Forrest's biographer, he issued the order that all male Selmians, regardless of their age or calling, must either go "into the works or into the river." Hardy describes the scene: "Everybody who could walk was called upon to go to the breastworks, with whatever arms could be procured. Squads of armed men were traversing the streets, and examining various buildings for soldiers to go to the breastworks, sparing nothing that wore pantaloons, and by Sunday, 12 o'clock, there were collected in the [parapets], around the city, about four thousand persons, not more than two thousand of them reliable, to meet a force of nine thousand of the flower of the Federal armies, and equipped in a manner unexampled in the history of ancient or modern armies" (Hardy, *Selma*, 51). Hardy's last phrase refers to the fact that Wilson's men were equipped with Spencer repeating rifles, while Selma's defenders had a wide variety of inferior arms.

It was three o'clock on Sunday, April 2, when Wilson's forces arrived just north of the city. The Union general had been favored with an extraordinary piece of good fortune: one of the engineers who helped build the breastworks, an Englishman named Millington, arrived at Plantersville that morning, and supplied Wilson with a sketch of the city's defenses. Now the attacking forces knew more about the situation than Forrest did!

The attack began shortly before five, with Gen. Eli Long's regiment attacking down the Summerfield road. Confederate sharpshooters took a heavy toll on the Northern troops charging five hundred feet across open ground, some of it swampy, to try and scale the eight-foot parapets. The *Cincinnati Commercial* later described the charge as witnessed by "an ex-rebel officer": "He said it was the grandest sight of the whole war, to see that Yankee cavalry come up the road under such a fire. Every now and then one of the batteries would sweep an avenue through their ranks, but the gap was no sooner made than filled. Wilson's men, said he, 'came at us with astonishing coolness; they neither yelled nor shouted, and the only thing you could hear, as they approached, was the order to "close up" after a cannon ball had cut down a few of them. They kept right on, and never stopped until they rode right into our fortifications. The charge of the six hundred at Balaklava wasn't equal to that'" (as reprinted in the May 20, 1867, *Selma Daily Messenger*). General Long was one of the hundred or so shot down in the charge. He survived but with a head wound that left him half paralyzed and unable to think clearly. Some men did reach the top of the parapet, however, and suddenly the Stars and Stripes was flying from within the breastworks. Gen. Emory Upton's men attacked from the Range Line road at almost the same moment, and once the Confederate line had been broken in two places, the breastworks were lost.

The battle was not over, however. Some of Forrest's soldiers made a brief stand in a heavily wooded area south of the breastworks, giving their comrades time to regroup at the second and incomplete line of defense. The Confederates were able to repulse a cavalry charge led by General Wilson himself, shooting the general's horse out from under him. A fresh regiment was called up and sent charging against the second line. This time, the men in blue were able to break through Selma's last line of defense.

At this point, rebel forces scattered in all directions. Forrest and the other generals were able to cut their way out of the city, escaping up the Burnsville road. Some fleeing Confederates remembered Taylor's last orders and set fire to the Central Cotton Warehouse. A building located on Water Avenue and Broad Street that had been used to house Union prisoners and Confederate deserters was also set on

FIGURE 3.17 Frances John Hobbs, who hid her husband's wealth in her petticoat; courtesy of Selma–Dallas County Museum of History and Archives, Selma, Alabama.

fire, supposedly by a former prisoner. The fires spread rapidly, until much of downtown Selma was in flames. Fire destroyed a full five blocks of the city, including St. Paul's Episcopal Church and several private homes.

It did not help matters that Selma merchants took their barrels of whiskey into the streets to be destroyed but were surprised by the enemy before they could empty them. The hot, battle-weary soldiers who found whiskey waiting for them must have thought it a gift from the gods, but it helped transform them into what Selma legend recalls as "devils from hell."

Some Selmians had planned ahead. Banker Washington Smith had hollowed out one of the columns of his home and hidden the Bank of Selma's funds there. Mrs. Frances John Hobbs, whose jeweler husband was off in the army, had sewed all the more valuable pieces into her petticoat. When Union officers demanded her jewels, she made a great show of reluctance about opening the family safe and distributing its contents, which were, of course, mere costume jewelry, the least precious things she had.

White Selmians were not the only ones who were robbed. Slave Charles Marven lost his watch at gunpoint that night and must have been startled Tuesday when General Wilson called him in and asked that he take a message to Mobile. Perhaps Marven thought gaining his freedom was worth losing a watch, since he agreed to do as Wilson asked. After getting permission from his master to "look for work," Marven set out on a raft down the Alabama River to carry the news of Selma's fall to General Canby.

According to Hardy, order was restored by Monday morning, and Wilson provided guards to protect the homes of any family who requested them. However, stories of that terror-stricken day and night have continued long in Selma legend. "Words cannot express what we underwent that memorable week of April," twenty-one-year-old Julia Kenan wrote her aunt in North Carolina on October 17, 1865. She went on to relate some of the atrocities that took place:

> At Mr. Crawford Phillips they hung a poor silver-haired man (Mr. Hyde from New Orleans, who with his family was boarding at Mrs. P's) to the bed post. Afterwards drove Mrs. Phillips & [Mr. Hyde's] wife from the house and burned it consuming his body in the flames. That horrible murder liked to have killed Mrs. Hyde and the daughters, tis feared the former will never recover, has declined quite rapidly since their return to New Orleans. Poor Mrs. Dr. Phillips was driven from her home in almost a dying condition & her house burned. She has since died. Four houses were burned in that immediate neighborhood. Mr. Small & Mr. Philpot who were in the trenches were both killed. . . . Mr. S. was shot after surrendering. His poor wife & his sister were so distressed or rather uneasy that he did not come home, learned he was not in the stockade as a prisoner, they obtained a permit from the Yankee Gen'l to look for him. They soon found his body near the fortifications. While sitting beside him weeping, a Yankee came up and asked why they were weeping over that "Johnny Reb," he knew they were glad to have him out of the way.

Rev. Alexander Small (1832–65), a native of Charleston, South Carolina, had served as pastor at First Presbyterian since 1858. After the battle of Gettysburg, he had gone up to minister to the troops and participated in the religious revival that swept through the Army of Northern Virginia. In a sense, Selma's Baptist minister had been its first casualty of the war; now its Presbyterian minister became one of the last.

The week that followed was given over to planned destruction. Gen. E. F. Winslow, who was in charge of destruction, compiled a list:

> First, Selma Arsenal, consisting of twenty-four buildings . . . among other articles destroyed were 15 siege guns and 10 heavy carriages, 10 field pieces with

FIGURE 3.18 Rev. Alexander Small, the Presbyterian minister killed in the Battle of Selma; courtesy of the Presbyterian Church of Selma.

60 field carriages, 10 caissons, 60,000 rounds of artillery ammunition, 1,000,000 rounds of small-arms ammunition, 3,000,000 feet of lumber, 10,000 bushels coal, 300 barrels resin, and 3 large engines and boilers. Second, Government Naval Foundry, consisting of 5 large buildings, containing 5 fire engines, 13 boilers, 29 siege guns unfinished, and all the machinery necessary to manufacture on a large scale naval and siege guns. Third, Selma Iron-Works, consisting of 5 buildings . . . Fourth. Pierce's Foundries, Nos. 1 and 2 . . . Fifth, Niter Works: these works consisted of 18 buildings, 5 furnaces, 16 leaches, and 90 banks. Sixth, Powder mill and magazine, consisting of 7 buildings . . . Seventh Washington Works; small iron-works with 1 engine. Eighth. Tennessee Iron Works, containing 2 engines. Ninth. Phelan & McBride's machine-shop, with 2 engines. Tenth. Horseshoe manufactury, containing 1 engine. About 8,000 pounds of horseshoes from this establishment were used by our army. Eleventh. Selma Shovel Factory; . . . Twelfth. On the Alabama and Mississippi Railroad, 1 round-house, 1 stationary engine, and much standing machinery, together with 20 box and 1 passenger cars. Thirteenth. On the Tennessee Railroad, 1 round-house, with machinery, 5 locomotives, 1 machine, 19 box and 50 platform cars.

FIGURE 3.19 The ruins of the Naval Arsenal; courtesy of Selma–Dallas County Museum of History and Archives, Selma, Alabama.

Slaves who had worked hard to make cannon and ammunition were set to work pushing it into the Alabama River. All the horses and mules not needed by the Union cavalry were shot. Hundreds of them were left for the people of Selma to bury.

Over two thousand Confederate prisoners, including most of the white men of Selma, were herded into a stockade north of the railroad, an area formerly occupied by Union prisoners. According to Hardy, there was not a dry spot to lie down on in the entire area. One Mississippi soldier was bothered less by the damp than he was by the Union band's bad habit of playing "Dixie" when he was trying to sleep.

During the week Wilson occupied Selma, he attended services at First Baptist with his men. There were no services at St. Paul's, which had been burned to the ground, or at First Presbyterian, whose pastor (Rev. Alexander Small) had died in the battle. Wilson also sent Captain Hosea out once more to meet with Forrest under a flag of truce. Hosea arranged for a meeting between the two mighty opposites, to be held near Cahawba at the home of staunch Unionist T. M. Mathews. Colonel Mathews treated the two generals to a sumptuous meal, after which they retired for a private discussion.

Jones, in *Yankee Blitzkrieg* (99), gives this account of the meeting:

> "Well, General," Forrest told Wilson, "you have beaten me badly, and for the first time I am compelled to make such an acknowledgment."

"Our victory was not without cost," Wilson truthfully replied. "You put up a stout fight." The Union had lost close to four hundred men and Forrest only twenty.

"If I had captured your force twice over it would not compensate us for the blow you've inflicted on us," Forrest said—and that was true too.

Three days later, Wilson's Raiders completed a pontoon bridge across the Alabama River and headed east toward Montgomery. Scores of slaves had joined the Union camp and been organized into a regiment—the 137th Regiment of Colored Infantry—on April 8 to assist Wilson in what might be called the first Selma–to-Montgomery March. Ben Turner went with them, in part to keep track of the horses, mules, and carriages of his that the army had taken.

The citizens of Selma learned a few days later that the Confederate capital, Richmond, had fallen the same day their city fell, and that Lee had surrendered his forces at Appomattox Court House on April 9, the day Wilson's troops began leaving Selma.

General Johnston's forces surrendered in Salisbury, North Carolina, on April 28. By that time, there were only 165 members left of the Twentieth Alabama (which had numbered 1,100 men only four years earlier) to surrender to Sherman. Pettus's farewell address to his brigade showed him "stout-hearted" to the last:

> The fortune of war has made you prisoners. You are to be marched in a body to your State, and there disbanded on parole. Your valor and good conduct has [been] my greatest joy and pride; and it is confidently expected that the reputation of this command will be still preserved in this new trial.
>
> Though others may desert and disgrace themselves & their kindred, let us stand together and obey orders! In this way we best contribute to our safety, and comfort; and preserve our characters untarnished. (Pettus Family Papers)

Pettus himself set out for home by ambulance, able to travel only twenty-five miles a day due to his wounded leg. To his wife he wrote, "I have heard nothing from home since the Yankees were in Cahaba. I am tortured by every Conceivable conjecture. As a Soldier and as a patriot I have lost all, save honor—I believe I have done my duty. But our dear country is a conquered province. It may be that our little property has all been destroyed, I feel it is so. . . . God bless you, my dear wife, and our dear children—and give you all courage to meet whatever trials which may be in our future" (Pettus Family Papers).

Pettus was not the only one worried about what the future might hold. Thousands of former slaves gathered in Selma on May 9 to hear Union general C. C. Andrews offer them some advice:

> You are free. I expect and certainly hope you will never again be slaves. I do

> not believe you hazard your liberty by remaining where you are and working for such compensation as your employers are able to give. . . . My advice to you, then, is to remain. . . . People used to say that you did not know how to use freedom; that if freed you would be indolent, violent, and cruel. It will greatly rejoice the hearts of your friends all over the world if you show you are worthy of freedom. Be industrious, be charitable and kind in your feelings; be peaceable, forbearing, sober; cherish no spite. . . . There is nothing makes people so beautiful, whether they are white or black, as virtue. Adorn yourself with that and you will have the affection of the nation. You may then feel sure of having all the rights you are entitled to. . . . In due time, no doubt, your interests, which now seem to you unsettled, will be arranged in a wise and humane manner. (OR, series1, vol. 49, 728–29)

How the former slaves of Selma felt about the general's advice is not known.

On the following day, May 10, a large group of white citizens of Dallas County assembled in Selma to appeal to Governor Watts to call the Alabama legislature into session and take the state back into the Union. Judge Byrd announced that the war had settled two questions for good: slavery was dead and the right of secession had ceased to exist. It was time for Alabama to face facts. According to General Andrews, "He counseled conciliation and moderation, and said it greatly depended on the generosity and magnanimity of the victors whether conciliation and harmony would be permanent and substantial" (OR, series 1, vol. 49, 727).

On the same day, May 10, 1865, Pres. Jefferson Davis was captured by Wilson's men near Irwinville, Georgia, leaving no further resistance possible on the part of the South.

The war was over at last.

4

Rebuilding and Reconstruction

Selma Rises from the Ashes, 1865–1880

SELMIANS SLOWLY BEGAN BUILDING new lives for themselves and their city after the war's destruction ceased. Institutions as well as buildings had been lost in the conflict. Both Selma banks went out of business after the war because their holdings consisted largely of Confederate money, which was now worthless. The city itself was penniless and had taken on a substantial debt in order to aid the railroads. War damage to the railroads had been heavy, and they needed extensive repairs.

On top of everything else, people were hungry. The Freedmen's Bureau set up a soup kitchen behind the Vaughan-Smitherman Building (which had been converted from a Confederate hospital into a freedmen's hospital) to feed the hundreds left destitute by the war. The citizens of Lexington, Kentucky, responded to Dallas County's distress by shipping 300 sacks of corn and 1,500 pounds of bacon to Selma; and Lexington was not the only town to do so. As late as May 1868, the bureau's soup kitchen was feeding 1,065 Selmians, mostly women and children; 769 of those being fed were white.

Selma's entrepreneurs and "go-getters" set out to revive or replace the banks, railroads, and professional associations that had been suspended or destroyed by the war. The indomitable Dr. A. G. Mabry resolved that the Alabama Medical Association, which he had founded and which had ceased to exist during the war, should be revived. By 1868 the AMA was up and running again, with Mabry serving as its president for the third time. In 1869 Selma dentist James C. McAuley followed Mabry's example by organizing the Alabama Dental Association, and in the following year Selma druggist Ed Galt joined forces with Mobile's E. P. Candidus to establish the Alabama Pharmaceutical Association.

Selma's railroad men were also busy. In addition to reviving the three lines already radiating out of Selma, the city launched a fourth line in 1867, optimistically named the New Orleans and Selma. A fifth line, the Cahawba, Marion, and Greensboro, was transferred from Cahawba and ambitiously renamed the Selma, Marion, and Memphis. A sixth line, the Western Railway of Alabama, was launched by Montgomery entrepreneurs to connect Selma to the capital city.

The abolition of slavery meant that both the freedmen and their former masters had to adjust to a new world. Under the old order, educating slaves had been a crime; now black people were hungry for schools and the white citizens were uncertain how to respond. Slaves had worshipped at their masters' churches before the war; now many of them wanted churches of their own.

The task of rebuilding Selma was complicated by the changing directions from the federal government. At first it was Pres. Andrew Johnson who was in charge of what later came to be known as "Presidential Reconstruction." At his instructions white Alabamians held a convention in 1865, drew up a new state constitution, ratified the Thirteenth Amendment abolishing slavery, and elected new leaders. The new government did not please the Radical Republicans in Congress, who refused to accept Alabama back into the Union until the state had approved the Fourteenth Amendment conferring citizenship on black people and barring former Confederate officials from holding office. Johnson urged white southerners to reject the amendment, and Alabama followed his advice.

Once the Radicals had achieved an overwhelming majority in the Congressional elections of 1866, Johnson could no longer dictate the terms of what was now "Congressional Reconstruction." In 1867 white Alabamians found themselves having to write another new constitution and elect new leaders—this time with the assistance of their former slaves. Selma's black residents found themselves playing a significant role in the politics of the state as the city produced Alabama's first African American congressman in 1870 as well as its first African American judge in 1874.

Congressional Reconstruction did not last forever; by 1875 the Republicans had lost control of Congress and the federal government was both less willing and less able to interfere. Once again the state drew up a new constitution, this time with minimal input from its black citizens.

Selma Rebuilds and Becomes a Railroad Town

Selma's city government also showed a good deal of energy, despite its financial difficulties. Madison J. Williams (1837–72), former editor of the *Selma Times*, became mayor shortly after the Battle of Selma.

Williams and the city council had $25,000 worth of city-backed currency, or "shinplasters," printed in New York and set to work on an extensive and expensive

FIGURE 4.1 Mayor Madison J. Williams led the city in rebuilding after the war; courtesy of Selma City Hall, Selma, Alabama.

rebuilding program. The mayor scored a major success in one area. When, in December 1865, the Alabama legislature authorized a local election to determine whether the county seat should stay at Cahawba or be moved to Selma, Williams tipped the scales in favor of Selma. He had the council buy the old Confederate hospital for $15,000 and offer it to the county, free of charge, as the new courthouse. When the election was held in May 1866, Selma won overwhelmingly.

The *Selma Daily Messenger* responded to the election by urging the citizens of Cahawba not to mourn the loss of the county records but to follow them to their new home and become residents of Selma. Many Cahawbans took the paper's advice, and, within a few years, the former state capital was little more than a ghost town.

Despite this triumph, Williams and a majority of the city council were swept out of office in elections held the following week. "This administration accomplished a great deal," observes Hardy, "but it was a costly one to the city." The council's biggest mistake, perhaps, was in raising the mayor's salary from $200 to $1,000 at the same time it was imposing new fees on the citizenry.

The new mayor, Dr. James T. Reese, did not have to face the danger of being

FIGURE 4.2 Sturdivant Hall, the antebellum mansion supposedly haunted by the Parkman family; courtesy of the Center for Commerce, Selma, Alabama.

defeated at the polls. By the time his term ended in May 1867, the Radical Republicans had taken control of Congress and President Johnson was no longer in a position to direct the reconstruction of the South. No election was held to choose Reese's successor since the US Army was going to appoint a new mayor and council.

During the Civil War, Europe had to find other sources of cotton. As a result, southern cotton faced more competition than it had before and no longer commanded the high prices it once had. The cotton problem caused the collapse of Selma's first postwar bank. John W. Parkman founded the First National Bank of Selma in 1866, with a capital of $100,000. He invested bank funds heavily in cotton futures and wound up with hundreds of bales selling for less than half of what he had paid for them. On April 10, 1867, Parkman announced that $160,000 had mysteriously disappeared from the bank and offered a reward for its recovery. When the military authorities sent officers to investigate (an action that Hardy considers "unwarranted intermeddling" [153]), Parkman fled town. He was caught in Wilcox County, brought back to Selma, and locked up in the jail at Cahawba. Before he could be brought to trial, Parkman tried once more to escape. On May 23, with the police hot on his heels and a bullet in his side, he tried to swim across the Cahaba River and perished in the attempt. The Parkman children's "ghosts" are still said to haunt Sturdivant Hall, where they had lived happily before their father's disgrace and death.

Selma was not without a bank for long. The Selma Fire and Insurance Company provided some banking services during the years that followed, and, under Maj. Joseph Isbell's leadership, it "took the plunge" in 1870 and converted itself into the City National Bank. Isbell died a year later, and his son-in-law, William P. Armstrong, administered the bank for thirty years until his own death in 1901. This bank, now a branch of PNC, stands on Broad Street to this day and ranks as Selma's oldest continually operating financial institution.

A second bank was organized in 1870 under the presidency of cotton broker A. G. Stollenwerck. The Selma Savings Bank had a capital of $200,000 but no authority to issue bills. In 1878 it was reestablished as the Commercial Bank of Selma. Its new president, Richard M. Nelson, won a national reputation as a financial wizard and eventually became the first Alabamian ever to serve as president of the American Bankers Association.

As the nation went through a period of intensive railroad building in the late 1860s, many Alabamians were also convinced that the key to postwar prosperity lay in building railroads. At first the Alabama legislature was willing to vote huge subsidies to almost every railroad in sight, and cities and counties were extravagant in their support. By 1870, however, charges of corruption and incompetence helped to cool public enthusiasm for issuing more bonds to support railroads that were not living up to their initial promise. Dallas County wound up with more lines of track than any other county in the state but Mobile, though all of Dallas County's lines but one were owned by Yankee investors.

Perhaps thinking that battlefield leadership could be translated into business success, four of the five lines launched from Selma named Confederate generals as their presidents. There were plenty of high-ranking Confederate military men to choose from; a reporter for a Cincinnati newspaper made the observation that it was easier to find a general in Selma than it was a private!

The Alabama and Tennessee Rivers Railroad, Selma's oldest, chose Gen. Joseph E. Johnston as its president. Johnston, a native of Virginia, moved to Selma after the war. He succeeded in merging the line with two Georgia railroads to form the Selma, Rome, and Dalton and in securing a $5 million loan to complete the road. Once the railroad was completed to Dalton, Georgia, it would provide the first direct route by rail from New York to New Orleans. By late 1867, however, Johnston was bored with the job and tired of dealing with interfering stockholders. Apparently, he was bored with Selma as well since he both quit his job and moved to Savannah. He was replaced by a New York banker named Frederick H. Delano.

Selma's second-oldest railroad, the Alabama and Mississippi, turned to General

FIGURE 4.3 Gen. W. J. Hardee, president of the Selma and Meridian Railroad; courtesy of Alabama Department of Archives and History, Montgomery, Alabama.

William J. Hardee for leadership. Hardee (1815–73) had served as commandant of cadets at West Point before the war and had composed a classic work on infantry tactics at the request of Jefferson Davis (then US secretary of war). His *Rifle and Light Infantry Tactics* became the standard text used by both sides in the Civil War. When the war came, Hardee followed his native Georgia out of the Union. He was with Pettus at Bentonville, when both Pettus's nephew and Hardee's sixteen-year-old son, Willie, perished in the final battle of the war. After the war, Hardee moved to Marengo County, where his wife owned a plantation. In 1866 he moved to Selma, where he labored earnestly to make his line, renamed the Selma and Meridian, a success. In spite of his efforts, the company was bankrupt by 1870 and two years later was owned by northern investors. Unlike Johnston, he did not find Selma boring but stayed in the Queen City till he died.

Selma's third-oldest railroad, the Selma and Gulf, lay dormant during the war and lost its original president, Col. William T. Minter, in the Battle of Selma. In 1868 the surviving members of its board were approached by the New York and Alabama Contracting Company, which offered to take over the railroad, pay its debts, and start laying track. The board accepted the offer, choosing the New York and Alabama's Dr. D. C. Smyley, a planter from Pleasant Hill, as the Selma and Gulf's new president. Gen. Philip D. Roddey, a Confederate general turned New York merchant, took over as the railroad's "financial officer."

The city, already deeply in debt, tried to rescind its prewar financial commitment to this road in 1870. After Gen. John Tyler Morgan told the city council it had no alternative but to keep its bargain, the council agreed and authorized the issuing of bonds totaling $60,000. The debt Selma incurred on behalf of the Selma and Gulf was to prove a millstone around the city's neck for decades to come. The Selma and Gulf was less successful when it came to getting Dallas County to fulfill its commitment. When the county's lawyer told the county commission that it was obliged to pay the railroad $250,000 approved by a referendum, the commission fired him and got another lawyer. The new attorney told the commission what it wanted to hear, that there was no valid contract; and the Alabama Supreme Court ultimately upheld his argument.

The road reached Pine Apple, forty miles south of Selma, before being overcome by financial problems. It did not help the Selma and Gulf's reputation when its financial officer, Roddey, fled the country in 1875 to escape indictment for his involvement in another matter. By 1876 the railroad was in the hands of the court. Three years later, the Selma and Gulf was purchased by the Louisville and Nashville and renamed the Selma and Pensacola.

The city's newest railroad, the New Orleans and Selma, started out in 1867 with Justice William M. Byrd as its president. It approached the city of Selma for financial support in 1869, but the city's property owners voted down a proposed $10,000 investment. The road had better success with the county, which subscribed for $140,000 worth of stock. It also approached the state of Alabama, which offered a $320,000 endorsement once the New Orleans and Selma could testify that it had completed twenty miles of track on its own. Byrd felt he could not honestly make such a claim and resigned as president. The railroad was able to find a Confederate general, Charles M. Shelley, to take Byrd's place. Shelley (1833–1907) was a native of Tennessee whose family had moved to Talladega when he was three. He had worked as an architect and builder before the war and resumed his trade after moving to Selma in 1866. Shelley was to prove more successful as a politician than as a railroad man, becoming sheriff of Dallas County in 1874 and winning election to the US House of Representatives in 1876. In spite of the generous subsidies from the county and the state, the New Orleans and Selma never reached further than Martin's Station, twenty-one miles from Selma.

While the city of Selma had refused to support the New Orleans and Selma, in 1869 it did vote $10,000 to the railroad being created by Gen. Nathan Bedford Forrest. As president of the Memphis, Holly Springs, and Okolona Railroad, Forrest resolved to create a rail connection between Selma and his hometown of Memphis. He bought majority stock in the Cahaba, Marion, and Greensboro, assumed its presidency, and changed its name to the Selma, Marion, and Memphis. The former grand wizard of the Ku Klux Klan had transformed himself into a "New Departure" Democrat, who granted that black citizens should have the right to vote and eagerly sought their support. When a leading Alabama Klansman (Ryland Randolph of Tuscaloosa) denounced Forrest for associating with Republicans, the general retorted by accusing Randolph of "stirring up strife and discord." Forrest succeeded in winning the support of the majority-black counties of the Black Belt; and when the line reached Greensboro in 1870 amid great rejoicing, one Alabama newspaper hailed Forrest as "the most energetic and enterprising railroad man the country has yet produced." But the outbreak of war in Europe disrupted the stock market and made it impossible for him to raise the capital he needed in New York. His hometown of Memphis turned its back on him, refusing to provide the funds it had promised the railroad; the lone black man on the county court (i.e., county commission) supported him to the end. The railroad never reached his hometown of Memphis and was bankrupt by 1873. Forrest resigned as president in 1874, exhausted, impoverished, and ill.

Jackson's *Story of Selma* expresses puzzlement over Forrest's failure. The author suspects it was due to northern sabotage but confesses that "it is entirely possible, too, that Forrest was a better general than he was a railroad president." Forrest's most recent biographer, Jack Hurst, suggests that the Wizard of the Saddle may have been sabotaged by former Confederates who were outraged by Forrest's willingness to work with Yankees and Republicans to get the railroad built.

In 1878 the Selma, Marion, and Memphis was reorganized as the Selma and Greensboro under the presidency of Dr. Alexander W. Jones. Jones (1840–1916), a native of Tennessee who had served as a surgeon in Forrest's cavalry, proved more successful in railroad management than had his old commander. He laid additional track, connecting the line with other railroads, and, eventually, was able to sell the Selma and Greensboro for a handsome profit. In 1886 Jones became president of a

Figure 4.4 Dr. Alexander W. Jones served as president of two Selma railroads after they went bankrupt; courtesy of Alabama Department of Archives and History, Montgomery, Alabama.

railroad for a second time, when he was entrusted with the New Orleans and Selma, which he renamed the Birmingham, Selma and New Orleans. In 1902 it became part of the Louisville and Nashville system.

Selma benefited from the enterprise of its archrival Montgomery. In 1870 a Montgomery-based railroad, the Western Railroad of Alabama, reached the east bank of the Alabama River opposite Selma. It took the Western till 1872 to complete an iron bridge across the river, but by September 15, 1870, the *Mobile Register* was already expressing alarm: now Selma cotton could be shipped by rail to Savannah instead of down the river to Mobile. This was a serious threat, since "fully one-third of Mobile's cotton crop comes from the territory or basin having Selma for its centre."

While Selma's railroad promoters had a hard time, they did succeed in making Selma a "railroad town." Brewer's *Alabama* notes in 1872 that Dallas County had "about 105 miles of railway in the county, which is a considerable excess over any other county in this [area]" (208). (Montgomery had sixty-seven.) Why did Selma's railroads have such a hard time? The economic conditions of the day played a major role. Most of the cotton crops of the late 1860s did poorly, and the panic of 1873 plunged the entire country into a serious depression, closing down dozens of railroads north and south.

The Politics of Presidential Reconstruction, 1865–1867

To some residents of Dallas County, the bitterness of defeat was so great that they resolved to find another country to live in, one where "true liberty," (i.e., a plantation system based on slaves) could still be enjoyed. Joel Mathews led an expedition to Brazil, where he was welcomed by the emperor. Some of the expedition chose to stay, but Mathews finally returned to his native soil and set up a cotton mill in Selma.

Another fire-eater who had a hard time adjusting to the new order was George W. Gayle. Gayle had run an ad in the *Selma Dispatch* on December 1, 1864, offering, in exchange for $1 million, to arrange for the assassination of Abraham Lincoln, Secretary of State William H. Seward, and Vice Pres. Andrew Johnson. He would gladly undertake this task for "the sum of $50,000.00 in advance." Selmians, knowing Gayle, laughed at this latest example of his wild talk. However, when Lincoln was assassinated on April 15, and Secretary Seward narrowly escaped death after being stabbed by a would-be assassin, a lot of northerners began taking the ad very, very seriously. Gayle was arrested and spent months in a federal prison before his wife was finally able to persuade the government that her husband had nothing to do with Lincoln's death.

Another leading secessionist, Gen. John Tyler Morgan, took a more positive approach to the situation. "We must work as hard for the success of the present regime as we did for the past experiment [the Confederacy]," he wrote to his friend Samuel Dixon on September 9, 1865 (Governor Parsons Papers, Alabama Department of Archives and History [ADAH]). "Honor and good faith demand" no less. For the time being, he felt that people like himself needed to stay out of the spotlight, and let old Unionists like his law partner, William M. Byrd, take the lead. Morgan observed that Dallas County had wisely chosen Judge John Starke Hunter and Thomas M. Mathews as delegates to the constitutional convention to be held on September 12. Hunter and Mathews had both opposed secession and would, therefore, be more acceptable to the US government than men like Morgan, who had spoken, voted, and fought for secession.

For a brief time, Selma's Unionists seemed to dominate the political landscape.

Figure 4.5 Col. John F. Conoley served as probate judge of Dallas County from 1865 to 1874; courtesy of Alabama Department of Archives and History, Montgomery, Alabama.

Alex White's former law partner, Lewis E. Parsons of Talladega, had been named provisional governor of Alabama by President Johnson. Parsons took care to choose old Union men for office: men like Ben F. Saffold, whom he made circuit judge, and John F. Conoley, whom he appointed probate judge of Dallas County.

The Alabama legislature apparently felt much the same way. In December it chose William M. Byrd to be an associate justice of the Alabama Supreme Court. However, the far-sighted Justice Byrd saw what many of his fellow Unionists did not. He wrote to Governor Parsons on July 24, 1865: "The President and Congress will widely differ about the reorganization of the State Governments, and that difference may result in depriving us of our Rights in the Union and in the National Representation [i.e., Congress] during his term of office or at least for several years."

Byrd's words proved prophetic. When Congress met in December 1865, it refused to accept representatives from the states of the old Confederacy. The radicals would acknowledge as "Reconstructed" only those states that would accept the Fourteenth Amendment. President Johnson, however, strongly advised the South not to accept the amendment, which granted US citizenship to African Americans and barred all "traitors" from holding state or national office without a Congressional pardon.

The congressional definition of treason made little distinction between militant secessionists and men like Byrd who had been dragged, kicking and screaming, into secession. In Congress's eyes, anybody who had held any office before the war, no matter how minor, and then gave "aid and comfort" of any sort to the Confederacy was a traitor. Thus, Selma's longtime postmaster, John M. Strong, became a "traitor" simply by staying in office under the Confederacy!

Almost the only Selma Unionists who came up to federal standards were those who fled into Union lines during the war. Among these were Selma lawyer James Q. Smith, who returned as the new US district attorney for north Alabama, journalist John Hardy, who was now a federal marshal, and gardener Edward La Croix, who came back as US assessor of internal revenue.

The Constitutional Convention of 1865 showed how difficult it would be for most white Alabamians to accept the new order. Alexander White, a delegate from Talladega, refused to admit that the question of slavery had been settled by the war. He insisted that the state should appeal to the Supreme Court. The convention finally voted him down 80 to 3. Another delegate from north Alabama wanted to ban black people from entering the state, and Judge Hunter had much to do to talk him out of a proposal both unconstitutional and unwise.

The US Army still had a strong presence in Alabama. Selma served as headquarters for the First Division of the Sixteenth Army Corps, as well as the base for Freedmen's Bureau activities in a ten-county area. The bureau was as close as the North came to providing "foreign aid" to the conquered South. During 1865 it fed thousands of starving Alabamians, both black and white. However, its efforts to help freedmen adjust to their new status, and to protect them from what was deemed exploitation by their former masters, provoked bitter resentment from many white residents.

Mayor Williams, for example, became very irritated when the bureau told him the city could not punish black citizens who had committed minor offenses, such as selling produce without a license, by putting them in chains and setting them to hard labor on the city streets. The hard labor might be permissible but not the chains: they smacked too much of slavery.

Bureau officials were even more alarmed when the Alabama legislature met in December 1865 and passed a series of laws regulating black labor. One of the laws allowed probate judges to take black children away from "negligent" parents and "apprentice" them to their former owners. To many black people, and to bureau officials as well, this seemed like slavery under a new name. Such controversies helped convince the radical leaders in Congress that the South was still in the grip of the "slavocracy" and that Presidential Reconstruction was little more than a farce.

Changes in Religion and Education under the Reconstruction Regime

Anna Gayle Frye's *Memories of Old Cahaba* provides a humorous example of the difficulties felt by Dallas County planters in adjusting to the new order. Her father's slaves had left the plantation en masse with the coming of freedom, so Mr. Gayle went to Selma in search of workers to harvest his crops.

> As he rode into the camp, the first person he spied was an old woman named Patty, one of the slaves inherited from his mother, and the one of all others who had expressed the greatest devotion to her "young master," as she had called him. For years half bent with rheumatism, Patty had not known work, and went hobbling around on a stick but lo! freedom had worked a marvelous change—now, with head erect, she was stepping around as agile and spry as a young girl who had never known an ache or pain. Her master called to her: "Come here, Patty, I want to speak to you." She turned, saw who it was, and flounced off, exclaiming, "Lawd a massie, chile, I ain't got time to fool with you now." This was a novel experience for my father—the first time in his life a negro had ever refused to come at his bidding—and to be answered in this offhand manner, especially by one of his old slaves, was too much to be borne. He concluded to make no further overtures, and returned home. (63–64).

Freedom was indeed "a marvelous change" to men and women like Patty, who now possessed the incredible privilege of leaving the plantation without permission from "young master" and of choosing their own employer. In a sense, they had been kept children all their lives: never sent to school, never allowed to make major decisions about their own lives. Now, they had to grow up overnight, and for many it was an intoxicating experience. Numbers of ex-slaves celebrated their new freedom by changing their names, such as becoming Patty Williams instead of Patty Gayle, and running away to Selma. The black population of Selma more than doubled between 1860 and 1870, jumping from 1,368 to 3,660.

Two areas to which Selma's freedmen devoted most of their energy during the early days were those of education and religion. Politics was to come later.

Most black people had a great hunger for the education that had been denied them under slavery. On December 30, 1865, the *Selma Times* published an appeal from some of the city's leading freedmen to their "dear friends and former masters" for help in getting teachers. They expressed the hope that some of the many "widows and crippled men, who are well educated, and have no employment by which to make a living" might be willing to brave the loss of social prestige involved in teaching blacks.

> Our own people are the people we want to teach us, and we sincerely wish them to do it. And why should they refuse? They raised and taught us all that we know, as carpenters, blacksmiths, stone and brick masons, painters . . . and were not ashamed or backward in performing this service. And why should it be considered a disgrace now to make a living at this business in the South? . . .
>
> If you stand back, strangers [northerners] will come in and take the money from under your hands and carry it away to build up their own country. They are not ashamed to make money from any class of men.

The appeal was signed by prewar freedman Daniel Alexander, blacksmith and Baptist deacon Alex Goldsby, African Methodist Episcopal Zion minister James Wadsworth, and fourteen other freedmen.

Mayor M. J. Williams endorsed their appeal, and a school was set up in the basement of First Baptist. To the dismay of many white residents, the teacher who took charge of the class was Joseph Sears, a "stranger" from Rhode Island who had attended Yale and served in the Union army. According to the tradition preserved by Selma's white Baptists, Pastor J. B. Hathorne met Sears and his students at the church door and chased them off with a gun. The black Baptists' tradition is that the white Baptists generously "bought" the church basement from them by giving them $2,000 with which to build a church of their own on the other side of town. Which tradition should we believe? Probably both. Judging by a contemporary account in the Mobile *Nationalist*, which was reprinted in the April 4, 1866, *Selma Daily Messenger*, there was in fact a confrontation at which local white citizens gave Sears three days to leave town or face the consequences. Sears then applied to the US Army for protection. The bureau intervened, pointing out that since blacks formed a majority of the congregation and claimed to "own" the basement, they had some rights that Hathorne could not ignore. After the white residents calmed down, they decided that it would be wise as well as generous to offer money to the black church members to build their own church. By the end of 1866, most black members of the First Baptist Church had withdrawn to build their own church on St. Philip Street. In 1892 the congregation moved to its present location on Sylvan Street, the street now renamed in honor of Martin Luther King Jr.

Three more schools for black students were established in 1866, one by an ex-slave named Lucy Gee, one by a local white woman named Hubbard, and the third by Rev. John Silsby, a native of New England who had served as a Congregationalist missionary in Siam. Silsby, who was later to play a prominent role in Selma politics, set up classes in a converted carpentry shop, which belonged to a group of black Methodists.

Plantation owners eager to recruit black workers found it wise to establish schools

FIGURE 4.6 Baptist historian Rev. C. O Boothe was later to serve as interim president of Selma University; courtesy of Alabama Department of Archives and History, Montgomery, Alabama.

on their property. Confederate general William J. Hardee, who had settled in Dallas County, wrote to the Freedmen's Bureau in 1867 for help in finding a teacher, "preferably a Southern man," to staff the schoolhouse he was building on his wife's plantation.

Dramatic changes were taking place in Selma's churches. Before the war, American Protestants had split along regional lines; now they split along racial ones as well. Selma pastor C. O. Boothe, author of the *Cyclopedia of the Colored Baptists of Alabama*, tactfully describes the postwar tensions that led to racial separations within the churches. "Ex-master and ex-slave did not quite fit each other in the old 'meeting house' as they had done in days of yore. There was restlessness on one side, and suspicion on the other. The black man wanted to go out and set up housekeeping for himself, while the white man in most cases feared and hesitated to lay on the hands of ordination. We did not know each other. The 'negro preacher' on one side of the river had but little opportunity to know his brother on the other side. Truly our beginning was dark and chaotic."

The Methodist separation seems to have been prompted partly by the arrival of missionaries from two northern-based black denominations, Rev. Godfrey B. Taylor of the African Methodist Episcopal (AME) and Rev. James Wadsworth of the AME Zion. Interestingly enough, the Freedmen's Bureau also played a part. On August

30, 1866, the bureau's assistant superintendent, Samuel S. Gardner, wrote to headquarters in Montgomery asking for financial help for "a society of freedmen under the charge of Elder James Wadsworth of the African Methodist Episcopal Zion Church in this city" in setting up their church and school. On October 3, Gardner wrote to AME officials in Mobile to denounce the other missionary in Selma, Reverend Taylor, as "the tool of those who have been life-long oppressors of your people." Taylor's offense seems to have been that he advised his followers "to continue in the same church with our white brethren, observing all the rules of the church as we did formerly, until we were able to build one of our own." (The *Nationalist* printed the correspondence along with its comments in its December 3, 1866, issue.)

On August 30, 1867, the group of black Methodists who had been meeting in the Broad Street Hotel (later to become the Hotel Albert) voted to break off from the Methodist Episcopal Church South to join the African Methodist Episcopal Church, thereby becoming the first AME church in Alabama. Within a few years, this group had established the congregation now known as Brown Chapel, with Taylor as their first pastor. No doubt the bureau was pleased. Elder Wadsworth had long since set up Zion Chapel on Green Street, an AME Zion congregation now known as Clinton Chapel.

If Goldsby and other black leaders seem to have gotten little help from the town's white citizens in setting up schools, it must be remembered that the white residents were having a difficult time getting Dallas Academy back into operation. Mrs. Johnson, who had founded the school, had retired in 1864, there were no classes at all in 1864–65, and the man hired to replace her had proved unpopular. Moreover, many white people believed that public education was a bad idea for all children: the government had no business teaching people how to read!

In the end, the city was able to establish its public school system for white students only with northern help. A two thousand dollar gift from philanthropist George Peabody of Boston in 1868 made it possible to enlarge Dallas Academy so it could serve both male and female students and to set up a branch school in east Selma. While construction was in progress, male students met in the basement of the Methodist church and female students met in the Presbyterian church.

Perhaps it was inevitable that the black population, also, wound up turning to "strangers" for help in educating their children. Both of the men who came to Selma in 1866 to teach, Joseph Sears and John Silsby, were sincere and dedicated men, but both had served in the Union army (Silsby's son had died in the conflict) and were Radical Republicans. Thus, they were called "carpetbaggers" by conservative white people. The term implied that all northern Republicans who moved south after the war were "poor white trash" who could carry all their possessions in a cheap piece

FIGURE 4.7 Rev. Edwin Silsby, whose father John helped write Alabama's 1867 Constitution and served as acting mayor of Selma in 1873; courtesy of Talladega College Archives.

of luggage made from carpet. Northern immigrants who stayed out of politics, or voted Democratic, were not regarded as carpetbaggers.

John Silsby was chosen as a delegate to Alabama's 1867 constitutional convention. He served on the Educational Committee and is usually credited with the creation of Alabama's state board of education. Sears, elected to the board in 1870, led the fight to create a state college for black students, Lincoln Normal College in Marion, which later moved to Montgomery and became Alabama State University. Sears and Silsby also helped establish the first black public school in Selma, named Burrell Academy after Jabez Burrell of Oberlin, Ohio, who gave a large sum toward its erection. Burrell Academy opened in the fall of 1869 with a full staff of teachers imported from the North by the Congregationalist American Missionary Association but whose salaries would be paid by the Selma city school system. (Silsby's son Edwin later served as principal of Burrell from 1875 to 1885. He and his parents spent the rest of their lives educating the black people of the South.)

Both black and white communities became more diverse after the war. A large number of Irish Catholic workers had come to Selma to work on the railroads dur-

FIGURE 4.8 The Reformed Presbyterian Church was erected in 1875; courtesy of Selma–Dallas County Museum of History and Archives, Selma, Alabama.

ing the 1850s; more came to labor in the war industries during the war; in 1869, they used the stones from the old Confederate arsenal to build the Church of the Assumption of the Blessed Virgin Mary. (The church now known as "Queen of Peace" was thus erected from the stones of war.) Jewish merchants had also been coming to Selma even before the war but did not organize as a group until 1867, when they formed a benevolent society and started a Jewish cemetery. Three years later, they organized themselves into Congregation Mishkan Israel.

Selma's black residents remained Protestant during this period but became more diverse after the arrival of missionaries from the Reformed Presbyterian Church and the Congregationalist American Missionary Association. Both of these groups played a significant role in black education in central Alabama.

In 1874 the Reformed Presbyterians established Geneva Academy, later Knox Academy, on North Avenue (later Jeff Davis and now J. L. Chestnut Jr. Boulevard) and the school was a major institution in Selma until the 1930s, when it was absorbed by the public school system. The Congregationalists both began and helped to staff Selma's black public school, Burrell Academy, at North and Coosa (now Chestnut and Maxey). They ran it in an uneasy, off-and-on alliance with the city until 1889 and then by themselves until the school burned down around 1900. Both denominations attracted small, largely middle-class black congregations.

Congressional Reconstruction: The Rise of the Radicals

By March 1867, it was clear that the radicals in Congress had succeeded in taking the control of Reconstruction away from President Johnson. The South had met presidential requirements, but Congress held these were not sufficient and imposed requirements of its own.

One of the things Congress wanted was for blacks to be allowed to vote. Many northern states still refused to allow black suffrage, which made it evident that for some Radicals the primary concern was less to benefit blacks than to create a "loyal" majority in the southern electorate. Faced with this situation, white Selmians split. Some, like Col. Robert McKee, editor of the *Daily Messenger*, were bitterly opposed to making any concessions whatever to congressional demands. McKee (1830–1903), who had served as secretary of state for his native Kentucky's Confederate government in exile, was fast becoming one of Alabama's most influential journalists. A few people, like Judge Ben F. Saffold and Tom Mathews, were willing to make almost any concession to get Alabama back into the Union. Native Alabamians who took this position and joined the Republican Party were denounced as "scalawags," and conservative Democrats hated them almost as much as they did carpetbaggers. A third group was hesitant and unsure, torn between their anxiety to be part of the Union and their fear of the concessions demanded by the Radicals.

On May 14, 1867, the army installed Ben Saffold as mayor, along with a city council of loyalists. In June, Saffold swore in the first black policemen in the state of Alabama. John Silsby, named head of registration for Dallas County, set about registering both black and white voters. Clearly, a revolution was underway. One effect of black suffrage was to give Dallas County more political weight than it had ever possessed. The county had only been entitled to two delegates to the 1861 and 1865 conventions. For the new constitutional convention to be held on November 5, the county was entitled to five delegates—as many as Mobile. However, white conservatives took no pleasure from the election of these five representatives: transplanted northerners, or carpetbaggers, if you prefer, Gen. Datus E. Coon and John Silsby; ex-slaves Jordan Hatcher of Cahawba and Alfred Strother of Athens; and, of course, Selma's "Military Mayor," Ben Saffold.

Coon (1831–93), a native New Yorker, had been a newspaper editor and a Buchanan Democrat before the war. After Fort Sumter, he raised a company for the Second Iowa Cavalry. He distinguished himself at the Battle of Nashville, winning

FIGURE 4.9 "Carpetbagger" Gen. Datus Coon represented Dallas in both the Alabama Senate and the General Assembly; courtesy of Selma–Dallas County Museum of History and Archives, Selma, Alabama.

promotion to general. After the war Coon decided to try his hand at raising cotton and bought a plantation in Marengo County. In 1867 he turned from planting to politics and began organizing the potential black voters of Dallas County.

Even before the convention opened, the *Daily Messenger* announced, "It matters little to us what this body shall do. It can make no Constitution under which any white man can live." The *Selma Times* took a more moderate line, pointing out that a majority of convention delegates would be prewar residents of Alabama who, surely, would not be too harsh on their fellow Alabamians.

As it turned out, it was the scalawags of north Alabama, many of whom had suffered at Confederate hands during the war, who were loudest in their demands that the "hell-hounds of secession" be punished. Saffold led the south Alabama scalawags in urging a more conservative approach. This split left the carpetbaggers and blacks holding the balance of power. When one black delegate spoke up in support of Saffold's approach, he was denounced by a black carpetbagger, John Carraway of Mobile, as a traitor to his race.

On November 9, the convention voted 50 to 37 to adopt the north Alabamians' suffrage proposal, granting the vote to all adult black males but disenfranchising almost all former Confederate officials. The entire Dallas County delegation voted "no," with Hatcher and Strother being two of the only three black delegates who dared stand up against the extreme radicals on this issue. On other things, such as school integration and racial intermarriage, they took a more militant stance than Saffold, but when it came to mercy toward old Confederates, Hatcher and Strother stood together with their white Dallas County colleagues.

Later, the Dallas County delegation succeeded in having one of the worst features of the suffrage position removed: the disenfranchisement of anybody who failed to vote on the constitution. Still, the constitution of 1867 remained a bitter pill for white Alabamians to swallow. Many former Unionists, such as Alexander White and former governor Parsons, bitterly rejected the constitution. They joined with former secessionists like John Tyler Morgan and Judge William T. Brooks, formerly president of the Secession Convention and now a resident of Selma, to organize a "White Man's Party."

They wanted to defeat the constitution by boycotting the polls. On Parsons's advice, they decided to also boycott the election for state and local offices being held the same day, since the men elected under the constitution of 1865 still had time left in their terms.

Dallas County, with its 80 percent black majority, voted overwhelmingly for the new constitution on February 4, 1868. However, the turnout in most other counties was so small that the constitution failed to receive the support of a majority of registered voters needed for passage. A few months later, Congress arbitrarily changed the rules and declared that Alabama's constitution had been legally adopted after all, and the state was back in the Union under its newly elected Republican government.

As might be expected, this action embittered conservative white citizens even more than they were already. Justice Byrd found himself replaced on the Alabama Supreme Court by Ben Saffold and protested this act as an example of "rule by bayonet."

Alabama conservatives looked to the presidential election of 1868 to get out from under Reconstruction by electing a Democratic president. Dallas County conservatives boldly decided to seek black votes for their cause, urging the former slaves to trust their old masters rather than "strangers." Not all conservatives thought this the best approach. The *Mobile Register* announced its refusal to "stoop" to asking for black votes. Tuscaloosa's *Independent Monitor* suggested using Ku Klux tactics to scare black voters away from the polls.

At a crucial point during the campaign, Benjamin S. Turner and a group of black leaders met with Judge Brooks and the county's Democratic leaders, saying

FIGURE 4.10 Judge William T. Brooks presided over the Secession Convention of 1861 and helped organize the "White Man's Party" in 1867; courtesy of Alabama Department of Archives and History, Montgomery, Alabama.

that black Selmians wanted good feelings between the races and would support the Democrats if the committee could promise they would not lose the right to vote. Judge Brooks replied bluntly that they did not deserve the right to vote because they were incapable of using it properly. (Brooks recounted the exchange in the October 20, 1874, *Selma Times*.)

The judge's candor proved costly to the conservatives. Turner had no intention of using his vote to help end black suffrage, so he influenced his fellow black citizens to support the Republican ticket. On November 8, 1868, Dallas countians cast 5,700 votes for U. S. Grant for president, giving the Republicans a victory in Alabama. Indeed, Dallas County's large black vote made it the "banner county" for the state. Republicans won nationally by a small margin in the popular vote, leading analysts to conclude that the ex-slaves' gratitude for their freedom had put General Grant in the White House.

Grant's election had one startling effect. Alexander White, one of the founders of the White Man's Party, thought things over and decided that an old Union man like himself belonged in the Republican Party. He and his nephew by marriage, George H. Craig, both made the switch. White quickly became a leading spokesman for the radicals and was elected to the US House of Representatives from the state at large in 1872. Craig was appointed sheriff of Dallas County, then city court judge, then circuit judge, and finally, in 1884, was elected to the US House from Selma.

Other former Unionists, like Justice Byrd, stayed with the Democrats. In 1872, Byrd was the chairman of Alabama's delegation to the national Democratic convention, which nominated Horace Greeley for the presidency. Selma's conservative Democrats may have been outnumbered in Dallas County, but they had great influence in the state at large.

Black Power in Old Selma: Turner, Thomas, and Haralson

In some Black Belt counties, the black population seemed to have served merely as puppets of their white Republican leaders. In Dallas County, they were able to assert their independence more effectively and to insist on a better share of offices for themselves. Selma produced three notable black leaders during Reconstruction: Benjamin S. Turner, the first Selmian ever elected to the US House of Representatives; Roderick B. Thomas, the first black judge in Alabama history; and Jeremiah Haralson, Dallas County's first black state senator and, later, Alabama's last black congressman of that era.

Black Selmians asserted their initial political weight within the Republican Party in December 1868, during the first mayoral election held after congressional Reconstruction began. They elected merchant Joshua L. Perkins (1815–85) by a two-thirds margin over wagon-maker William B. Gill, who represented the more conservative wing of the Republican Party. Gill's candidacy had been supported by an all-white slate of old Union men who ran for the city council. Perkins's eight-man slate consisted of three scalawags, including Saffold; three carpetbaggers, including Silsby; and two black members. The first black city council members were Ben Turner and carpenter Ed Northrop. Turner later resigned in indignation when the council decided to start paying its members the handsome salary of twenty dollars a month. He felt the city's financial plight was so desperate that councilmen should be willing to donate their time, effort, and influence.

Other members of Selma's city government obviously felt differently. The tax collector and clerk both mishandled office funds and were driven from office by the mayor. Similar scandals at the state level led Democrats to dub their Republican opponents "the party of fools and thieves."

By mid-1870, the state Republican Party was in serious trouble, rocked by scandals and harassed by the Klan. The radical Republicans of the First Congressional

FIGURE 4.11 Ad for Rep. Benjamin Sterling Turner's livery stable, 1874; courtesy of Selma–Dallas County Museum of History and Archives, Selma, Alabama.

District, which included both Selma and Mobile, decided they needed a candidate who was both known to be honest and able to win black support. To Dr. John H. Henry and other Selma scalawags, the answer was obvious: former councilman Ben Turner. General Coon and other carpetbaggers, who had previously dominated the district, did not like the idea very much. However, the black masses responded to Turner's candidacy with such enthusiasm that he won the nomination easily on the first ballot.

The year 1870 was a bad one for Alabama Republicans. Their governor and senator were both defeated for reelection, and they lost two-thirds of the Alabama House of Representatives. Selma elected a Democratic mayor, who replaced Perkins, in spite of its black majority. Ben Turner won his race, however, by a wide margin.

Turner's platform was one of "universal suffrage and universal amnesty." The first bill he introduced as a representative was to grant amnesty to all Confederate leaders so that the people disenfranchised by the Fourteenth Amendment, about twenty thousand in all, could once more vote and hold office. "Let the past be forgotten," he told Congress in his maiden speech, "and let us all, from every sun and every clime, of every hue and every shade, go to work peacefully to build up the shattered temples of this grand and glorious republic" (Appendix to the Congressional Globe, 42nd Congress, 2nd Session, 530–31).

Turner's bill was sent off to committee to die, but he kept on fighting. "He is a man of brains and will," General Pettus observed during his testimony before the Congressional committee investigating the Ku Klux Klan, "and he means to have his way" (*Testimony Taken by the Joint Select Committee*, 1:395). In May 1872, Republican leaders finally let a limited amnesty bill through Congress. Morgan, Pettus, and all but a handful of top Confederates were full-fledged US citizens once more.

When Representative Turner came up for reelection that fall, some Selma Democrats did not want to oppose him. However, he found himself confronted by two opponents from his own party, one white (scalawag Frederick G. Bromberg) and one black (Philip Joseph), both of them from Mobile. With the black vote split between Turner and Joseph, Mobile County's Democrats insisted that the party take advantage of this golden opportunity by throwing its support behind Bromberg.

In most respects, 1872 was a good year for Alabama Republicans. They won back the governorship and elected a US senator. Turner, however, attacked as he was from both sides, lost his seat in Congress to the candidate supported by the Democrats, "Liberal Republican" Bromberg. The black people of Dallas County turned to young new leaders, the aggressive lawyer Roderick B. Thomas and the flamboyant orator Jeremiah Haralson. Turner never held office again.

About Roderick B. Thomas (1847–87) very little is known except that he was born free in Knoxville, Tennessee, in 1847. Thomas first showed up in Alabama in 1867, when he provoked a near-riot in Mobile by attempting to board a streetcar reserved for white people. He briefly served as one of Mobile's first black policemen before moving to Selma with his mother. In 1870 he won election as clerk of the criminal court of Dallas County. Contemporaries regarded Thomas as "highly educated" but did not tell where he got his education. His aggressive ways infuriated many white Selmians. After Thomas's election to the Selma City Council in 1873, one of his fellow councilmen, Sumter Lea, threw an ink bottle at him. (He missed; the bottle made a dent in the wall and spattered ink over scalawag Eddie Morgan.) The following year Thomas was nominated for judge of the criminal court of Dallas County and elected without opposition.

His term as judge proved very brief. The Democrats had won control of the leg-

FIGURE 4.12 Roderick B. Thomas, Alabama's first black judge; Sketch by Michael Sims, based on a likeness provided by Elena Thomas-Hall.

islature in November 1874, and as soon as the legislature met, a bill was introduced to abolish the court altogether. This bill passed on February 5, 1875, and one year and three days later another bill passed recreating the court under a new name. It would now be called the criminal court of Selma, and its judge would now be chosen, not by the people of Selma but by the governor. The governor chose Jonathan Haralson, who had previously served as judge during the Civil War.

Thomas stayed active in Selma politics for several years. In 1877 he was disbarred by Judge Haralson for allegedly accepting money from both sides in a lawsuit but appealed his conviction to the Alabama Supreme Court, which reversed the conviction. In 1879 he fled Selma after being indicted by a grand jury for intimidating black voters. He spent his last years in Little Rock, Arkansas, where he seems to have won greater acceptance from the white population than he ever did in Selma. When he died in 1887, the Arkansas Supreme Court adjourned in his honor and the local bar turned out en masse for the funeral.

FIGURE 4.13 Rep. Jeremiah Haralson; courtesy of Selma–Dallas County Museum of History and Archives, Selma, Alabama.

Jeremiah Haralson (1846–1916), a native of Georgia who was sold twice before becoming the property of Selma's Jonathan Haralson, was an extremely controversial figure. Called "cotton-stealing Jere" by Democrats, he cheerfully admitted to taking bribes on several occasions. However, Haralson's political skills were such that his black followers would forgive him anything. He campaigned across the Black Belt for the Democrats in 1868—they forgave him. He helped the Democrats get rid of Judge Thomas's court in 1875—they forgave him.

Part of his appeal seems to have been his flair for humorous oratory. Frederick Douglass pronounced Haralson "one of the most amusing, ready-witted, and gifted debaters" he had heard, with "humor enough in him to supply a half dozen circus clowns" (*New National Era*, May 2, 1872). During the 1876 campaign, when the Democrats kept warning about the dangers of racial intermarriage, Haralson delighted his black audience by assuring them he would not marry a white woman unless she was rich. A poor white woman he would not look at twice.

Tradition says that Haralson became a Baptist minister after the war, but no evidence of this survives. He was elected to the Alabama House of Representatives in

1870, became Dallas County's first black state senator in 1872, and was elected to the US House of Representatives in 1874. Since the Democrats won a heavy majority in the House that year, and Haralson's election was being contested, he was afraid the House might refuse to seat him. According to the October 20, 1876, *Alabama State Journal*, Haralson went to see his old master, Jonathan Haralson, and asked him to write a letter on his behalf to the old Confederate veterans in Congress. "Ol' massa" did as his ex-slave requested, and the House Democrats seated Selma's second black congressman.

While in Congress, Haralson followed in Turner's footsteps by voting for amnesty for Jefferson Davis. When some Alabama Republicans criticized him for this vote, he replied in an eloquent public letter which appeared in the January 29, 1876, Mobile *Daily Register*: "I expected before I voted to hear a howl from the hell-hounds below; so say to them all that, God being my help, I will meet with them at Philippi!" (Philippi was where Julius Caesar's ghost vanquished his assassins.)

Haralson reached the height of his influence in 1876. Alabama's Republican Party sent two delegations to the national convention that year, one led by US senator George Spencer, the other by the congressman from Selma. The convention voted to accept Haralson's delegation as the true representatives of the state. When the showdown with his foes came in 1876, however, Haralson found himself opposed from two sides—by the Democratic candidate, Sheriff Charles M. Shelley of Selma, and by the "regular" Republican candidate, former congressman James T. Rapier of Lowndes County. Haralson and Rapier split the black vote between them, and Shelley eked out a narrow victory to become Selma's first Democratic congressman.

Haralson ran again in 1878 and was "counted out." Democratic election officials refused to accept the returns from Selma's two black wards and threw out half the returns from the county, those from Republican beats. This enabled the county to elect a legislative delegation consisting entirely of white Democrats. Haralson accepted a patronage job in Baltimore and left the county for several years, after which he returned to run for Congress again in 1884. By splitting the Republican vote, Haralson helped defeat Republican congressman George H. Craig's bid for reelection. He left town once more, but evidence exists that he returned again as late as 1912.

Selma and Dallas County produced other black leaders during this era of "Black Power"—four on city council, ten state legislators, five county commissioners, a tax assessor, and a coroner. We know very little about most of these men. During the decades that followed, most of the good things accomplished by these men, such as Turner's fight for amnesty, were forgotten, while their mistakes and misdeeds grew into a legend depicting "Black Reconstruction" as a carnival of misrule.

Figure 4.14 Gen. Charles M. Shelley's election to Congress in 1876 marked the Democrats' return to power; courtesy of the author.

Decline and Fall of the Radicals: Dallas County Politics, 1870–1880

The city of Selma went back and forth between the two parties during the early 1870s. Republican J. L. Perkins, who had been elected in 1868, was not renominated by his party in 1870. Instead they turned to Dr. John H. Henry, who had been mayor when the city fell to Union forces. The Democrats nominated Col. James M. Dedman, who had previously served as city marshal and was popular in the black and white communities. Dedman defeated Henry, 895 to 711, and the Democrats won a 6–4 majority of the city council.

James M. Dedman (1826–88) had served as sheriff of Dallas County and as marshal (police chief) of Selma before the war. He is best remembered as the proprietor of the St. James Hotel. His term of office was a difficult one, involving major economies. The city hospital, which had been opened before the war, was closed to save money. The public school system also suffered, and the white school in east Selma had to be closed after property owners refused to approve a new tax to support public education. Justice Byrd, who thought Dallas Academy unconstitutional, was a leading opponent of the tax. Dedman and the city council did find enough funds to appropriate $160,000 toward building a bridge across the Alabama River.

In 1873, John Hardy defeated Dedman's bid for reelection, and the Republicans regained a majority on the city council. Hardy (1823–83), best remembered as Selma's first historian, was a very colorful politician. His prewar unionism won him appointment as US marshal in 1865. He resigned within the year after being charged with using his office to extort money. He then founded a newspaper, the *Alabama State Sentinel*, in Montgomery which served for a few years as the leading voice of the state's radical Republicans. Dallas County elected him to the legislature in 1868, where he was influential in arranging state grants to railroads, allegedly for large bribes. As Silsby lamented in a February 8, 1873, letter to Republican governor David P. Lewis, Hardy did not even pretend to be moral. His term as mayor was relatively quiet. The city hospital was reopened, and official salaries were cut sharply. Hardy himself had serious eye problems and twice turned city government over to substitutes: once to John Silsby and once to Confederate veteran Sumter Lea.

Eighteen seventy-four proved a climactic year for Alabama Reconstruction. The Panic of 1873 had damaged Republican support throughout the country, and the 1874 Civil Rights bill, which outlawed segregation in public accommodations, practically ruined them in the South. North Alabama Unionists, who had been wavering between the two parties for years, now swung heavily behind the Democrats, who won an overwhelming victory in the election of November 1874.

While suffering defeat at the national level, the Republicans carried Dallas County easily enough, in spite of a serious party split. John Silsby bolted the party over the nomination of a tax collector who had been indicted for theft on several accounts. The party machine tried to squelch his rebellion, sending out circulars signed by the county solicitor warning black voters that anybody caught voting for "the bolter Silsby" could be sent to the penitentiary. Such blatant misuse of power, added to other complaints, left the Republicans both divided and discredited.

With firm control of both the legislature and governorship, Democrats set to work to drive all Republican officials from power. They abolished Dallas County's county commission, which had a black majority, and established an all-white court of county revenues in its place. In addition, they redrew Selma's boundaries, removing enough black neighborhoods to create a white majority in the city.

Selma's Republicans, recognizing their failing influence, made no effort to field a ticket in the 1875 city elections. Instead, they threw their support to mayoral candidate and independent Democrat Noadiah Woodruff (1828–81), who received enough votes to defeat the regular Democratic candidate, B. M. Woolsey.

"Regular" Democrats, like "regular" Republicans, accepted the decisions of the

FIGURE 4.15 Noadiah Woodruff served three terms as mayor of Selma; courtesy of Selma–Dallas County Museum of History and Archives, Selma, Alabama.

party convention or machine. Independent Democrats like Woodruff and independent Republicans like Haralson tended to follow their own judgement, even at their party's expense.

The Democrats also called for a constitutional convention to replace the constitution drawn up in 1867. The Republicans, reeling from their defeat, could not agree on how to respond. Alexander White, in what seems a mixed message, urged the party both to oppose the calling of a convention and to support "independent Democrats" rather than loyal Republicans, as candidates for convention delegates. Dallas County followed a portion of White's advice by electing two independent Democrats, Selma lawyer Sumter Lea and Burnsville planter John F. Burns. Both men joined the regular Democratic caucus, and the constitution of 1875, drawn up by a convention with a Democratic majority, further strengthened Democratic control of the state.

Woodruff, a native of Connecticut and a prosperous cotton merchant, was popular enough as mayor that the Republicans nominated him for governor in 1876. Some Selma Democrats, such as Colonel McKee, had been very unhappy with Governor

FIGURE 4.16 Selma's former L&N Station is now the Selma–Dallas County Museum of History and Archives; courtesy of Selma–Dallas County Museum of History and Archives, Selma, Alabama.

Houston's policies, but they closed ranks behind Houston, arguing that it was more important to be "white" than "right." Woodruff carried six Black Belt counties but lost the state by a wide margin. It was several years before the Republicans of Alabama even tried to run another candidate for governor.

Woodruff was twice reelected mayor, in spite of strong opposition from regular Democrats. It was not until the 1881 race, when his health was failing, that the Democratic organization triumphed at last and established firm control of the city. The Democrats' victory in 1881 may have seemed a hollow one a year later when, in December 1882, the city of Selma declared itself bankrupt. In the following year, the Alabama legislature granted the "municipality of Selma" a new charter that tightened up on voting requirements and outlawed the issuing of anything like the railroad bonds that had bankrupted the city.

This began what Jackson refers to as "a new era—one free of the reconstruction political hash that had been served up for nearly twenty years" (*Story of Selma*, 321). It produced a series of one-term mayors: R. J. Davidson in 1883, H. S. D. Mallory in 1885, Simon Maas in 1887, and E. S. Starr in 1889.

In the new era, fewer and fewer Selmians bothered to vote against the nominee of the Selma Democratic convention. In the mayoral election in 1881 1,177 people turned out to vote, only 384 in 1883, and by 1889 only 91 bothered to vote. The conventions were made up of fifty delegates, ten from each of the city's five wards; a two-thirds majority was required for nomination, and balloting could go on for days. It took three days and 379 ballots for E. S. Starr to win the nomination in 1889. The exhausted delegates then resolved, "The peace and harmony of the democratic party will be promoted by adopting the primary system for nominations in the future for the office of mayor" (*Montgomery Advertiser*).

Reconstruction was over. Selma's black residents were free, though still second-class citizens. They had their own churches and schools and a fading memory of political glories. Selma's white citizens had rebuilt and multiplied their organizations and had, at last, regained firm political control. Dallas was still the top cotton-producing county in Alabama, even though its crop had fallen well below the level grown in 1860. Selma was once more a railroad town, having expanded the city's network of railroads at an enormous cost; according to Brewer's *Alabama*, by 1872 Dallas County "had about 105 miles of railway in the county, which is a considerable excess over any other county in this particular" (208).

There was a future to be built, and Selmians turned their attention to it.

5

The Queen City Resumes Her Throne

Selma, 1880 to 1912

When Abraham Lincoln was assassinated, few white Selmians outside the Todd family felt much grief. In fact, the *Chattanooga Rebel* (then being published in Selma) rejoiced that Lincoln "had gone to answer before the bar of God for the innocent blood he has permitted to be shed, in his efforts to enslave a free and heroic people" (reprinted in the April 22, 1865, Montgomery *Daily Mail*).

By 1881, however, Selma's former Confederates were once again feeling themselves part of the Union. When Pres. James A. Garfield was assassinated, a mass meeting was held in Selma to express the city's horror and distress. N. H. R. Dawson and J. W. Lapsley had been on opposite sides back in 1860, but now they joined in drafting the message of sympathy that Dawson, in the name of Selma, would send to Secretary of War Robert Todd Lincoln. Lincoln, son of the only other president to die from an assassin's bullet, responded with appreciation for the city's gesture.

The response to Pres. William McKinley's assassination in 1901 was even more striking. One reason, of course, was that the Spanish-American War had intervened, in which former rebels had flocked to enlist in the American Armed Forces.

The September 22, 1901, issue of the *Selma Times* quotes ex-congressman George H. Craig, himself a former Confederate, expressing his renewed patriotism with some eloquence: "When the tocsin of war between Spain and the United States sounded, the old soldiers on both sides joined hands, and the old Confederates with one accord cried, 'Oh, glorious land of Freedom, we love thee as of yore; we will hoist on high thy Stars and Stripes to pull them down no more; and when our country calls us, our battle cry shall be: One God, one country and one flag, we'll live, we'll die for thee.'" (Craig himself offered his services to the nation, but was not accepted.)

Another Selmian, Lt. John J. Blandin, was involved in the incident that pro-

FIGURE 5.1 Congressman George H. Craig; courtesy of Selma–Dallas County Museum of History and Archives, Selma, Alabama.

voked the war: the sinking of the USS *Maine* in the harbor of Havana, Cuba. Blandin was serving as officer of the deck of the *Maine* on February 15, 1898, when the ship was torn apart by a mysterious explosion. Blandin tried desperately to save some of his fellow sailors, but in vain; some 260 sailors died in the holocaust that followed the explosion.

"I wish to heaven I could forget [the horrors I saw]," he wrote later. "But the reverberations of that sullen yet resonant roar, as if the bottom of the sea was groaning in torture, will haunt me many days, and . . . the reflection of that pillar of flame comes to me when I close my eyes."

"I don't believe the Spanish had anything to do with [the explosion]," Blandin wrote his wife. But the country thought differently. "Remember the *Maine*—and to hell with Spain!" was the battle cry. Congress declared war on Spain on April 25. The war only lasted a few months, but Blandin did not live to see its end. His mind

FIGURE 5.2 Four Spanish-American War veterans from Selma: Todd Atkins, Hal Peterson, Hooper Adams (seated in chair), and Walton Stewart (on floor); courtesy of Selma–Dallas County Museum of History and Archives, Selma, Alabama.

gave way as he constantly relived the horrors of that fatal night. When he died on July 16, 1898, the verdict was "meningitis brought on by shock."

Other Selmians won glory in the conflict. The October 10, 1899, *Times* reported that "a gallant Selma boy," Capt. Marion B. Saffold (1856–99), "distinguished himself [during the charge at San Juan Hill] for his coolness and bravery, coolly lighting a cigarette while at the head of his command." Unfortunately, subduing the Philippines proved more difficult than liberating Cuba; and the forty-three-year-old graduate of West Point was killed during the assault on Noveleta, near Manila. Saffold became the first Selmian to be buried at Arlington National Cemetery.

While Selma's old fire-eaters rose to national prominence, the city bloomed in many ways. It was a time of institution building as Selma's black population concentrated on making the city "the Athens of Black Alabama" and white citizens set up hospitals and a YMCA. The white people were ready to help set up hospitals and schools for black residents, but they were also determined to maintain white supremacy. This determination bore fruit at the Constitutional Convention of 1901, which succeeded in disfranchising over 90 percent of Alabama's black voters.

The first decade of the twentieth century was a golden age of sorts, in which Selma's civic boosters concentrated on building up "the Central City," as they had taken to calling their hometown. The decade saw the erection of some of Selma's most beautiful churches, for both white and black members, and the emergence of new men and new issues. It also saw new forms of segregation being imposed as Selma entered the age of Jim Crow.

The Fire-Eaters Become the Old Guard

The Black Belt was at the height of its political power during the last years of the nineteenth century. In one sense, this power rested on a shaky foundation: the ability to produce Democratic majorities in overwhelmingly black counties. In the early 1880s, this was achieved by throwing out the returns from Republican ballot boxes because of one technicality or another.

In 1882, for example, Republican candidate George H. Craig carried three of the five counties of the fourth congressional district by a good margin, only to see most of his boxes thrown out by Democratic sheriffs. He contested the election and was finally judged to be the winner in February 1885—months after he had already been defeated for reelection! Thus Craig, the last Republican congressman elected from Selma, got to serve only seven weeks of his term.

Congressman Craig's son, William, very sensibly decided to pursue his political career as a Democrat. The younger Craig (1877–1925), a graduate of Cumberland Law School, was elected to the US House of Representatives in 1907 and again in 1909. This made Selma's congressional district one of the very few to have produced father and son congressmen of different political parties.

In 1887, new congressional districts were drawn, and Dallas County was placed in a white majority district that included territory as far northeast as Anniston. With this development, vote enumerators in Dallas County needed to produce as many ballots as possible in order to deflect any challenge by Republican or Populist candidates based in the district's primarily white counties.

Soon, Dallas County was reporting majorities supporting Democratic candidates as massive as those previously supporting Republicans. In 1894, for example, Selma lawyer Gaston Robbins was elected to Congress on the basis of the 5,462 votes he received in his home county. Later, however, a congressional investigating committee decided that only 568 of Robbins's votes had been legitimate!

However shaky the foundations of Black Belt power may have been, the power was real while it lasted. From 1887 to 1907, The Black Belt produced both of Alabama's US senators and, for most of that time, the state's governors as well.

John Tyler Morgan, N. H. R. Dawson, Francis L. Pettus, and Edmund Winston

FIGURE 5.3 John Tyler Morgan represented Alabama in the US Senate for thirty years; courtesy of Alabama Department of Archives and History, Montgomery, Alabama.

Pettus were, in many ways, symbols of Selma's power. Morgan was elected to the US Senate in 1876 and served until his death in 1907. Dawson was elected speaker of the Alabama House in 1880 and named US commissioner of education in 1886. Frank Pettus became speaker of the Alabama House in 1892, and his father, General Pettus, won election to the US Senate in 1896.

By 1880, the old fire-eaters or militant secessionists were part of the established order. John Tyler Morgan was rapidly becoming one of the most respected members of the US Senate. He first attracted national attention shortly after his election in 1876, when he voted to confirm Pres. Rutherford B. Hayes's appointment of black orator Frederick Douglass as marshal of the District of Columbia. Some of his constituents never forgave Morgan for this vote and never understood how much it helped to allay the hard feelings generated by the war and Reconstruction. One of its results was to make it easier for a staunch Republican like Hayes to withdraw all federal troops from the South.

Hayes came to rely heavily on the integrity and judgement of John Tyler Morgan when making appointments in Alabama. There is no record to show that the president consulted his fellow Republican and Alabama's other senator, George Spencer, a carpetbagger widely suspected as corrupt.

Morgan was by no means a liberal when it came to race. He has been called the "most outspoken racial ideologue of his generation" (Upchurch's *Legislating Racism*, 27), defending white supremacy in scholarly articles for national periodicals as well as lengthy speeches in the US Senate. As the *Dictionary of American Biography* observes, "with his extensive learning and subtle logic, [Morgan] was always a power which it was not safe to disregard." Indeed, he served as the leader of the southern bloc in the US Senate when it came to blocking any federal interference with the white South's manipulation of the ballot box. In 1879 Morgan defeated one Radical proposal by conducting a fifteen-day filibuster. And in 1891 he led the Democrats in their opposition to the Federal Elections Bill, which was ultimately tabled by a single vote.

In addition, Morgan never gave up hoping for a massive emigration of African Americans from the South. In 1890, when some black intellectuals began a "back to Africa" campaign, he supported a bill that would have set aside $5 million a year to assist African Americans who wished to emigrate. (The bill did not pass.) After the Spanish-American War, he urged the government to grant land in the Philippines to black soldiers. (The government did no such thing.)

Some Alabamians did not think Morgan was racist enough. The senator protested that Native Americans were not being treated as American citizens. He also campaigned for years to have the US annex Hawaii and make it a state, even though a majority of its citizens were nonwhite. Most southerners strongly opposed Hawaiian statehood, and the *Mobile Register* was so furious it charged that Morgan had "lost the power of forming a clear judgement," that he had gone senile (July 10, 1898).

In 1880, Dawson was elected speaker of the Alabama House of Representatives, the first Selmian ever chosen for that post. In 1881, he became chairman of the state Democratic Executive Committee and held that position for five years. In 1886, Dawson was one of two leading candidates for the Democratic gubernatorial nomination. It says something for his popularity that it was not until the thirty-first ballot that he was defeated by Thomas Seay of Greensboro.

Nationally, the Democrats held the White House for the first time since the Civil War, and, on August 6, 1886, Pres. Grover Cleveland beckoned Dawson to Washington, DC, to become the first Alabamian to serve as US commissioner of education. Some northerners were appalled that a man without an Ivy League education was given so intellectual a post, but Dawson did an impressive job. He took a leading role in establishing the public school system in Alaska and commissioned

FIGURE 5.4 In 1886 N. H. R. Dawson became the first Alabamian to serve as US commissioner of education; courtesy of Alabama Department of Archives and History, Montgomery, Alabama.

a series of studies of state educational systems that became important documents in future planning.

One of Dawson's major projects for US education was strongly opposed by his friend and fellow Selmian, John Tyler Morgan. The federal government had a financial surplus during the 1880s, a very rare problem in our nation's history, and Dawson wanted that money invested in an attack on illiteracy. In 1888, Senator Blair of Vermont introduced a bill, strongly endorsed by Dawson, that would have devoted up to $15 million a year to boosting education in the states where public endeavors were the weakest: in the South.

Many southern leaders were willing to forget their usual opposition to "big government" in order to get help for the hundreds of thousands of children from their area who were growing up in ignorance and poverty. Governor Seay of Alabama,

FIGURE 5.5 Francis L. Pettus served in turn as speaker of the Alabama House and as president of the Alabama Senate; courtesy of Alabama Department of Archives and History, Montgomery, Alabama.

the Alabama legislature and the state's other US senator, James L. Pugh, all endorsed the Blair Education Bill. Morgan, however, despite his commitment to public education, would not compromise. In a January 30, 1888, speech before the US Senate, he warned that allowing black children to spend more time in the classroom and less in the cotton fields would hurt Dallas County's economy. A school year lasting seventy-three days was already "a large item in a cotton country," he asserted. "One hundred and forty-six days would ruin a crop." King Cotton had to come first.

Morgan threw his whole weight against the Blair Bill every time it came before the Senate and later took credit for its defeat. Thus, federal aid to education was postponed until the 1950s, over half a century later.

In 1892, Francis L. Pettus became the second Selmian elected speaker of the Alabama House. At the same time Pettus was elected, Jordan C. Compton, also from Selma, was chosen president of the Alabama Senate. With the Queen City in charge of both houses, it is not surprising to learn that the legislature ordered the Louisville & Nashville Railroad to complete the Selma & Gulf Railroad by building a line from Pine Apple in Wilcox County (which was as far south as the Selma and

Figure 5.6 Gen. Edmund Winston Pettus represented Alabama in the US Senate from 1897 to 1907; courtesy of Alabama Department of Archives and History, Montgomery, Alabama.

Gulf had gotten) to Repton in Monroe County (as far north as the Pensacola Railroad had reached). The renamed Selma and Pensacola was finally completed in 1901.

Young Pettus soon moved up to the Alabama Senate and was serving there when US senator James L. Pugh of Eufaula came up for reelection in 1896. Pugh was looking forward to serving a fourth term, but there were others who wanted his job, including Alabama governor William C. Oates. There were also some north Alabamians who thought their section of the state deserved recognition. However, Selma's representatives succeeded in influencing enough of their peers to elect Frank Pettus's father, Gen. E. W. Pettus, to the Senate. This meant that, for the only time in Alabama history, men from the same town, old comrades and neighbors John Tyler Morgan and Edmund Winston Pettus, filled both Senate seats.

Jackson's *Story of Selma* (398) records the exaltation felt in his hometown following Pettus's election:

> The news flashed like wildfire over the town. The people were so happy that one would have thought that every man in town had been elected instead of only one. General Pettus was in Montgomery, but would be home that morning, and all the people began to make ready to receive him. All business was

> suspended and a general holiday declared. As his train drew into the city every steam whistle was turned loose, the cannon boomed, and the people cheered until it was like bedlam. The general, not expecting such an outburst, did not know what to make of it, and his friends who were on the train with him say that he refused to believe that it was all done because of the election. When he descended from the train and took a carriage to drive to his home, the din and noise of the happy throng was deafening; and then, spontaneously and on the spur of the moment, the young men, as if all inspired by one thought, unhitched the horses from his carriage and themselves pulled him through the streets of Selma to his beautiful, old-fashioned southern home. He sat like one benumbed, scarce believing that all this enthusiasm and love was for him; and when at his home, he tried to thank his fellow-citizens, his tender heart gave way and the tears of gratitude and joy streamed down his rugged face.

Pettus's response was all the more touching in view of his usual reserve. On one occasion, a new acquaintance made the mistake of addressing the senator by his first name. Drawing himself up to his full height, Pettus said, "Young man, some of my friends call me General Pettus, some of my friends call me Judge Pettus, and some of my friends call me Senator Pettus, but damn few call me 'Ed!'"

Pettus and Morgan served together for ten years, working for a wide range of causes, including the creation of a Central American canal, a "soft money" policy to help southern farmers and the South's right to regulate its own affairs (i.e., to maintain white supremacy).

However, their power could do little to ease the sting of the continuing agricultural depression that plagued the United States during the last third of the nineteenth century. Cotton sold for fifteen cents a pound in 1875, ten cents in 1883, and, during the Panic of 1893, prices hit rock bottom at four cents a pound. Other farm products suffered as well—a bushel of potatoes sold for a dime during the Panic—and the South and Midwest felt the pinch badly.

Selma suffered less than other towns because it was a railroad center and a cotton mill town. As an industrial center, however, it was eclipsed by the dramatic rise of Birmingham, whose population tripled between 1880 and 1890. Some of Selma's outstanding young leaders, like ex-congressman Charles M. Shelley, legislator Sam Will John, and future governor Joseph Johnston, moved to Birmingham and devoted considerable energy to building up that city.

One result of the depression was political: a general revolt against the conservatism of the eastern businessmen who controlled both parties. Even a party loyalist like Senator Morgan could not stomach the "hard money" policies followed by Democratic president Grover Cleveland from 1893 to 1897. Cleveland's refusal to appoint Pettus to the Supreme Court did not help relations. "I hate the ground [Cleveland] walks on," Morgan said sourly.

In Alabama, the distress of the small farmers fanned flames of revolt against the Black Belt conservative Democrats who had dominated Alabama politics since Reconstruction. Conservatives like Thomas Jones (governor, 1890–94) and William C. Oates (governor, 1994–96) were staunch supporters of Cleveland's "hard money" policies and generally opposed to reforms. These conservatives came to be known as "Bourbons," after the French royal family that, allegedly, clung blindly to the traditions of the past.

In 1892, "Jeffersonian" Democrats, led by Reuben F. Kolb, bolted from the party and ran an independent slate for state offices. They carried most of north Alabama and the Wiregrass but were defeated by the massive voter turnout in Dallas and other Black Belt counties. Selma lawyer Henry F. Reese later bragged that the sheriffs of the Black Belt had saved the state by their manipulation of the black vote. "You can out-vote us," another Bourbon leader taunted the Jeffersonians, "but we can out-count you!"

Kolb was bitter enough about the vote to suggest publicly that Dallas County Democrats should all be buried face down "so that when they scratch their way out they will find themselves in the right place!" In 1894, Kolb ran for governor again and was, once more, counted out.

Morgan's friend Robert McKee, who had served as private secretary to governors Rufus W. Cobb and Edward A. O'Neal, noted bitterly that the Bourbons had begun by stuffing ballot boxes to save the state from "black rule" and had progressed to stuffing them to save the state from being ruled by poor whites. Electoral fraud had become a vicious habit, one the state needed to break.

Morgan was too much a party loyalist to openly break with the Bourbons, but he joined with Pettus and Joseph Johnston to urge the party to adopt more moderate policies. By 1897, the moderates had largely succeeded; with the return of prosperity, the Populist revolt began to subside. With the Democrats in firm control of the state, Morgan and Pettus felt free to urge Alabama to eliminate election fraud by enacting suffrage reform. Their idea of reform consisted primarily of requiring Alabamians to meet certain educational and financial standards before they would be allowed to vote. These standards would eliminate far more black voters than white ones, even if they were interpreted fairly, and it was clear that in many counties there was little hope of fair interpretation.

The push for suffrage "reform" was fueled in part by the growing racial animosity of the 1880s and 1890s. The April 14, 1882, *Selma Morning Reporter* reported "the first lynching ever to occur in Dallas County" had taken place near Browns. Deputies were guarding two black men who had supposedly confessed to the murder of an elderly white man when forty masked men burst into the room, overcame the guards, and carried the prisoners off to be hanged. The *Times* denounced this "outrageous crime" and lamented, "The lustre of our [county's] fair name has been dimmed indelibly, and utterly without cause."

Dallas's lustre was to be dimmed repeatedly in the years that followed. In 1892 a lynching took place in Selma itself. According to the *Montgomery Advertiser* for February 14, 1892 (no Selma papers survive from that date), "an orderly mob" took Wiley Webb from the Selma jail and hanged the black man for the "diabolical rape" of a white railroad man's wife. A delegation of railroad men came from Montgomery to make sure their Selma brethren did the job "right." More Dallas County lynchings of black people followed in 1893, 1895, 1896, and 1901.

Old Confederate leaders like Morgan and Pettus had always believed in keeping black people "in their place," but they also felt a certain noblesse oblige or paternalistic affection for them. It was due to this type of attitude that Alex Carr, who served as one of Selma's black policemen during Reconstruction, remained in his position into the twentieth century. Similarly, Pettus introduced a bill in the US Congress in 1900 that would have granted all former slaves pensions similar to those enjoyed by veterans. It did not pass.

These leaders were bewildered by the new surge of racial hatred. Former governor and Confederate colonel William C. Oates recalled that during Reconstruction, when black citizens possessed real power, there had been much less hatred. "Why, sir," exclaimed Oates, "now, when the negro is doing no harm, why, people want to kill him and wipe him off the face of the earth!" (*Official Proceedings of the Constitutional Convention of the State of Alabama, 1901*, 4:4141; hereafter *OP*).

Faith and Good Works in the "Central City," 1880–1895

Selma leaders began to refer to their town as the "Central City" because of its location near the center of the state. The term took on extra meaning as the town became not only a commercial center but also a center for religious activities. Selma was an important site not just for black Baptists (because of Selma University) but for white Baptists and for other white people of other denominations as well. The Southern Baptists made Selma their state headquarters in 1880, the same year in which the Jesuits made Selma the base for Catholic missionary efforts in central Alabama. The election of Selma's first Jewish mayor in 1887 showed the growing vitality of the town's Jewish community. First Presbyterian committed itself to missionary work in Africa in 1889. Some projects were too large for any one denomination to handle, like the erection of the city's first YMCA building in 1886 and the open-

FIGURE 5.7 Selma in 1887—A perspective map that shows how much the town had rebuilt after 1865; courtesy of Selma–Dallas County Museum of History and Archives, Selma, Alabama.

ing of Charity Hospital in 1889. The city itself rebuilt Dallas Academy in 1889 and began planning to set up schools for the white and black residents of east Selma.

In 1880 the Alabama Baptist Convention moved its state headquarters to Selma. Judge Jonathan Haralson had been elected president of the convention in 1874 and was to continue as presiding officer until 1891. Haralson (1830–1912), a native of Lowndes County, held a law degree from the University of Louisiana and had been appointed city court judge in 1876, presiding until 1892, when he was elected to the Alabama Supreme Court, where he served until his death. In 1889 he became the first layman chosen to preside over the Southern Baptist Convention, a position he held until 1899. According to Wayne Flynt's history of Alabama Baptists, it was Haralson's skilled leadership and reputation for impartiality that kept the convention from tearing itself apart in the late 1890s. Haralson himself observed wryly, "Southern Baptists are like alley cats. They scream and holler and fight, but in a few months there are more of them" (Caner and Caner, *The Sacred Trust*, 24).

Even after the convention moved its headquarters to Montgomery in 1892, Selmians continued to play an important role in the organization. Selma mayor H. S. D. Mallory served as the convention's president from 1899 to 1904. Mallory led the crusade for prohibition of alcoholic beverages in 1909, at great cost to his political career. Dallas County minister Washington Bryan (W. B.) Crumpton was

FIGURE 5.8 Judge Jonathan Haralson, the first lay president of both the Alabama Baptist Convention and the Southern Baptist Convention; courtesy of Alabama Department of Archives and History, Montgomery, Alabama.

even more zealous than Mallory. Wayne Flynt calls him "the key figure in [Alabama's] energized prohibition movement" (*Alabama Baptists*, 184). A native of Wilcox County and a Confederate veteran, he served as secretary of the Southern Baptist Convention's mission board for a quarter of a century and was elected president of the convention in 1917.

Mallory's daughter Kathleen may have had a more lasting impact on the denomination than either Crumpton or her father. She had to win acceptance for women's work from a denomination in which many of its male leaders regarded such a role for women as unbiblical, and she succeeded.

Kathleen Moore Mallory (1879–1954) graduated from Goucher College in Maryland in 1902 and taught for a year in Demopolis before taking on her life work. A superb organizer and fund-raiser, she played an important role in building up the Women's Missionary Union (WMU), serving as an officer of the state organization from 1909 and of the Southern Baptist Convention after 1912. In 1921 she helped move WMU headquarters from Baltimore to Birmingham, where she led the organization until her retirement in 1948. It is not surprising she came to be known as

Figure 5.9 Kathleen Mallory, "the sweetheart of Southern Baptists," led the Women's Missionary Union through two world wars and the Great Depression; courtesy of Selma's First Baptist Church.

"the sweetheart of Southern Baptists" and that her family was regarded as "the First Family of Alabama Baptists."

In 1880 the Society of Jesus (a society of Catholic priests better known as the Jesuits) took over Assumption Parish and made Selma their headquarters for mission work in central Alabama. The Jesuits remained responsible for Selma Catholics until they returned Assumption Parish to the diocese of Mobile in 1931. For the half century they operated in Selma, the pastor of Assumption was responsible for serving "missions," which ranged from Grove Hill in the south to Anniston in the north. What mattered more for Selma was the Jesuits' resolve to make Selma a center of Catholic education. First they recruited an order of sisters, the Religious of the Sacred Heart of Jesus (better known as "the Madams"), to come to Selma in 1881 to begin a girl's school, Sacred Heart Academy, on Broad Street. The *Selma Times* was pleased at this addition to the city's status as an "educational centre" and let it be

FIGURE 5.10 Sisters of Mercy outside their convent on Broad Street; courtesy of the Edmundite Missions.

known that the Madams had been founded to teach the daughters of the French aristocracy. Then they moved Cahawba's Masonic Hall to Selma and converted it into St. Andrew's High School for Boys. The prep school did not last long, and the Madams left Selma in 1891; but the Sisters of Mercy, who took over Sacred Heart Academy in their place, continued to teach the Catholic children of Selma (and a few non-Catholics as well) until 1971.

The city's Presbyterians were deeply involved in efforts to spread the gospel in Africa. Selma native Samuel N. Lapsley (1866–92) and fellow Alabamian William H. Sheppard were the first two Presbyterian missionaries (one white, one black) to penetrate the Luebo region of the Belgian Congo.

First Presbyterian's Sunday school helped raise the money to build a steamboat, the *S. N. Lapsley*, to aid the two missionaries in their apostolate, and Senator Morgan arranged for Lapsley to meet the king of Belgium. After Lapsley died of a fever in his second year, Sheppard found a new partner, Lucy Gantt, whom he married. The Sheppards served another twenty years. In 1988, the Central Alabama Presbytery chose to honor these early heroes of the faith by taking a new name: the Pres-

Figure 5.11 Rev. S. N. Lapsley, missionary to the Congo; courtesy of Selma's First Presbyterian Church.

bytery of the Sheppards and Lapsley. Other members of First Presbyterian kept up the church's commitment to missionary work in the decades that followed: Dr. Goldsby King and his daughter Annie King established mission hospitals not just in the Congo but in Brazil and China as well.

Some black Selmians shared Lapsley's devotion to missionary work in Africa. Lucius B. DeYampert (1877–1952), who was the first black pastor of Sylvan Street Presbyterian Church, spent sixteen years as a translator and medical missionary in what is now Zaire. After his wife's illness necessitated his return to Selma, DeYampert served for many years as sexton of First Presbyterian Church.

As mentioned above, First Presbyterian joined with other Selma churches in an enterprise of building Selma's YMCA, a venture that was too big for any one of them to accomplish on its own. Selma's YMCA organization had been revived in 1870 and had acquired a paid secretary in 1879 but still had no building of its own. When the noted evangelist Dwight L. Moody visited Selma in early 1885, he gave a stirring lecture on the need for Christian work among young men. The lecture inspired a drive to build "a home for our young men that will be as beautiful and sumptuous as any building in our city" (*Selma Times*, June 20, 1885).

W. B. Gill, president of the Selma Y, donated $5,000 toward the estimated cost

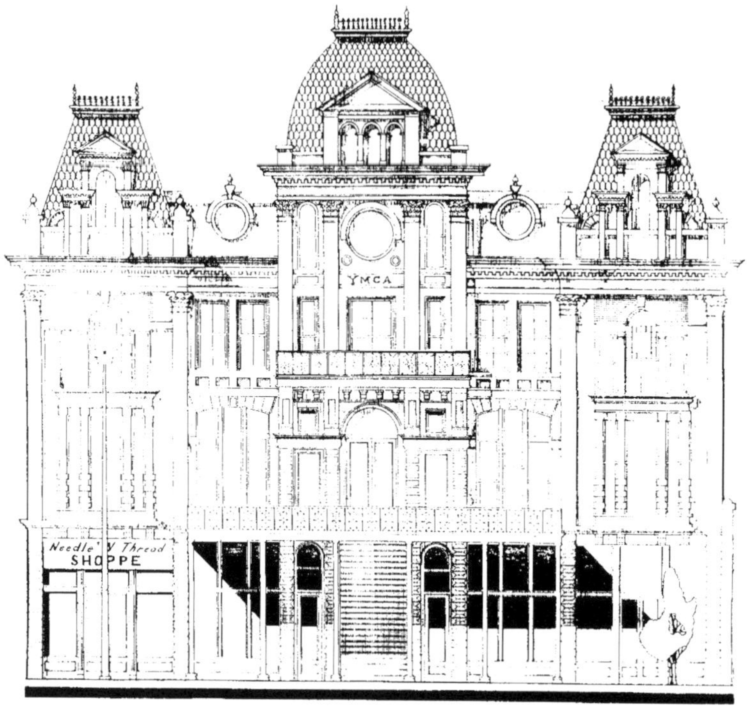

FIGURE 5.12 Selma's original YMCA building, the first in the state, from the *Selma Mirror*, c. 1900; courtesy of the author.

of $25,000, the Armstrong family donated a plot of land on Broad Street, and donations flowed in from Christians and Jews alike to erect the first YMCA building in the state, which was completed in 1886.

During these same years, Selma's Jewish community was growing. Downtown Selma was increasingly dominated by Jewish merchants: Broad Street boasted Lilienthal's, Kayser's, and Tepper's; Alabama Avenue, Barton's, Bendersky's, and Eagle's. The first waves of immigrants were from Germany and worshipped at Temple Mishkan Israel; later waves hailed from Eastern Europe and set up an Orthodox congregation, Congregation B'nai Abraham. In 1887, with no fanfare, grocer and commission merchant Simon Maas was elected as the first Jewish mayor of Selma.

Maas (1843–1906) was a native of Bavaria who came to the United States at the age of ten. Before his election he had served on the Selma City Council and as trustee of the Catholic school. In 1894, Marcus J. Meyer became the city's second Jewish mayor and the first to win reelection to a second term. Meyer (1849–1922) was a native of Mobile and ran a livery stable. Meyer's brother-in-law, Solomon

FIGURE 5.13 Mayor Simon Maas; courtesy of Selma City Hall, Selma, Alabama.

Kohn (1842–98) was even more successful politically, serving six terms as city treasurer. A native of Bohemia, Kohn played an important role in the founding of Selma's Charity Hospital in 1889. "His charity was only bounded by the extent of his means," according to the March 11, 1898, *Morning Times*, "and no deserving call for help ever appealed to him in vain."

Selma's churches joined together again as Jews, Presbyterians, Baptists, Catholics, and indeed members of all the downtown churches joined hands in an effort to set up a hospital for Selma's sick and indigent. The project was launched in 1884 when Mrs. Sally Hardee Roy realized that her own church, St. Paul's Episcopal, could never cope with all of Selma's poverty by itself. She decided to call together a group of ladies from the other downtown churches to see what they could do as a group. Under her leadership, the ladies organized the Society of United Charities "to relieve the sick and destitute in and near said city of Selma, irrespective of race, sex, or religion, and in furtherance thereof, as far and as soon as means will admit, to acquire, establish and maintain a Home, Hospital Infirmary and Dispensary, one or more or all." The board consisted of eight ladies representing the downtown churches and one man, H. L. McKee, representing Alabama Avenue Presbyterian.

FIGURE 5.14 Selma's Charity Hospital and Selma Infirmary, later the Dinkins Training School; courtesy of Selma–Dallas County Museum of History and Archives, Selma, Alabama.

Mrs. Sallie Featherstone Jones donated three acres on Dallas Avenue to the society as a site for the projected hospital on May 14, 1884. It was a while before "means would admit" construction of a hospital, and Mrs. Roy had a real struggle to convince the city fathers that her project was not hopelessly Utopian. Eventually both the city council and the county commission agreed to help, and by the end of 1889 the Charity Hospital and Selma Infirmary was a reality. The hospital had wards for "colored" patients as well as for Confederate veterans. City physician Ira Skinner served as surgeon in charge for years.

St. Paul's rector, R. W. Barnwell (1849–1902), who later became Episcopal bishop of Alabama, had to come to the defense of Mrs. Roy and her coworkers on several occasions when their interfaith enterprise had come under fire. In 1885 he countered charges that the United Charities helped mostly the black poor. In 1893 a group of Selma ministers publicly attacked the ladies of the United Charities for holding a ball on New Year's Day to raise money for the hospital, a ball "unbecoming to Christian conduct and injurious to Christian character." Their attack appeared in the December 29 *Selma Journal*; the very next morning's *Selma Times* printed Barnwell's passionate defense of the ladies, who had demonstrated their "Christian character" by striving to do their duty by the sick and poor. In contrast, Barnwell added, their clerical critics had offered little or no help.

In the long run, the Charity Hospital may have suffered less from the criticism

FIGURE 5.15 Rev. R. W. Barnwell, pastor of St. Paul's Episcopal and later bishop of Alabama; courtesy of St. Paul's Episcopal Church, Selma, Alabama.

of narrow-minded clergy than from the competition offered by private hospitals that began springing up in Selma. Some "men of means" felt it was somewhat disgraceful to be treated at a charity hospital, as though they could not afford to pay, and at least one objected to being treated by a facility that served black patients as well as white ones. When Henry White Vaughan (1842–87) drew up his will, he left eight hundred acres of land to a board of trustees charged with "erecting and maintaining in or adjacent to the City of Selma a hospital for white persons only." In a codicil, Vaughan added that being white would not be enough for admission; the would-be patient would have to be "respectable" as well! The trustees did not succeed in their mission until 1911, when the Vaughan Memorial Hospital (named in honor of Dr. Samuel Watkins Vaughan) came into being.

Bishop Barnwell did not feel the way Vaughan did. When he was struck down by appendicitis in 1901, he insisted on being taken not to a private hospital but to the Charity Hospital he defended and worked to help create. It was there that he died, faithful to the ladies to the last.

In one respect, the board of trustees for the Dallas Academy was also an interfaith enterprise. Its eleven members were chosen from the city's five leading downtown churches. There was always one member from Temple Mishkan Israel and a minimum of two apiece from First Baptist, Church Street Methodist, First Presbyterian, and St. Paul's Episcopal. Assumption Catholic was not represented, since it was regarded as having its own school.

Selma's Methodist, Presbyterian, and Baptist congregations grew during these years, founding new churches in east Selma. There was a Methodist mission in east Selma as early as 1860, and in 1879 Hardy refers to it as doing more good than any other church in Selma. It came to be known as Alabama Avenue Methodist and later moved to Barrett Road. The Methodists were very pleased in 1911 when their state orphanage, later renamed the Methodist Children's Home, moved from Summerfield to Selma, taking over the former Selma Military Institute buildings on Broad Street and First Avenue.

First Presbyterian founded two churches in east Selma: Alabama Avenue Presbyterian for white members in 1872 and Sylvan Street Presbyterian for black parishioners around 1900. The Alabama Avenue church later moved to west Selma and became Crescent Hill Presbyterian, and the Sylvan Street group moved to north Selma and changed its name to Northern Heights.

Members of First Baptist founded Calvary Baptist Mission on Water Avenue in 1896. The mission moved to Sylvan Street in 1900 and became Second Baptist. In 1920 the congregation moved to Alabama Avenue and became Central Baptist. More recently, the peripatetic parish moved to Valley Grande and became Valley Grande Baptist.

Education in Selma, "The Athens of Black Alabama"

Selma became a major educational center for black residents during the years after Reconstruction. By 1890 the city could call itself the Athens of Black Alabama with some justification. It boasted four religious schools serving African Americans: Burrell Academy, founded by the American Missionary Association in 1868; Knox Academy, established by the Reformed Presbyterians in 1874; Selma University, set up by the Missionary Baptists in 1878; and Payne Institute, begun by the African Methodist Episcopal Church in 1889. The Alabama State Teachers Association (ASTA) was founded here in 1882, and two of its first five presidents, George M. Elliot and Richard B. Hudson, were from Selma. In contrast, white Selmians showed little interest in having a college in town for their children to attend. Marion might boast of its Baptist college and Greensboro of its Methodist one, but Selma's well-to-do whites were content to send their children "off" to Tuscaloosa or Auburn or even to

FIGURE 5.16 The Todds, a family of black schoolteachers; courtesy of the Todd family.

out-of-state colleges like Vanderbilt and Davidson for higher education. Ben Turner saw to it that his in-laws, the Todds, became a family of school teachers.

Black Alabama Baptists wanted to begin their own seminary as early as 1872, when W. H. McAlpine preached a strong sermon at their annual convention on the denomination's desperate need for educated clergy.

William H. McAlpine (1847–1905) was a native of Virginia who had been brought to Alabama at the age of three and sold to a Presbyterian minister. He was "born again" during the war and was ordained a Baptist minister. When he enrolled at Talladega College, he was offered a scholarship if he would become a Congregationalist. The offer made him aware how badly Alabama Baptists needed a college of their own, and he resolved to found one.

When the black Baptists first asked advice from their white brethren on the question of setting up a seminary in Alabama, however, they were told that it would be

FIGURE 5.17 Rev. W. H. McAlpine, founder of Selma University and later first president of the National Baptist Convention; courtesy of Selma University, Selma, Alabama.

"folly" to even try. By 1876, however, white Baptists had swung around to supporting the idea. According to C. O. Boothe's *Cyclopedia of the Colored Baptists of Alabama*, the arrival of Harrison Woodsmall, a white minister from Indiana who had dedicated his life to serving black people, proved the necessary catalyst. "We vacillated until Brother Woodsmall appeared," Boothe says. "As the queen bee draws together her wandering swarm and fixes them in settled habitation and orderly toil, so did this saintly man do for the colored Baptists of Alabama" (54).

While Woodsmall set up classes in the St. Philip Street Baptist Church in January 1878, McAlpine and Selma barkeeper William J. Stevens campaigned across the state to raise funds for the school. Woodsmall was later able to persuade the American Baptist Home Mission Society to "adopt" the Alabama Colored Baptist Normal and Theological School, as it was then called, providing an annual subsidy of $3,000. He then resigned as president and devoted himself entirely to teaching theology and let McAlpine assume the position of the school's founder and first black president.

During the early days, although there was a core of theological students, most of the school's enrollment was at the elementary and secondary levels. Many of its

FIGURE 5.18 1889: The first day of classes at Payne Institute; courtesy of Alabama Department of Archives and History, Montgomery, Alabama.

distinguished graduates, like teacher Richard B. Hudson and physician L. L. Burwell, were not ministers but served the community in other capacities.

In 1886, there was a determined effort, supported by McAlpine himself (who had left Selma in 1883), to move the school to either Birmingham or Montgomery. The dispute was settled by a "silver ballot," which meant that each of the three cities was challenged to raise as many dollars as it could for the school, and each dollar counted as a vote. At the 1887 convention, Selma marshalled 873 "votes" to Montgomery's 83. Thus, the school stayed and became Selma University.

Selma's black Methodist college came into existence in much the same way. The AME Convention had discussed the need for a school since the early 1870s, and in 1882 plans were announced for Garfield Memorial University to be established in Montgomery. As year after year went by without concrete action, interested members of Selma's Brown Chapel decided not to wait any longer. On November 4, 1889, minister W. B. Johnson opened Payne Institute, named for AME bishop Daniel Payne, at Brown Chapel with two teachers and eighty-eight students. Selma's citizens supported the effort: the city council contributed a hundred dollars; other groups donated a new organ, a school bell, and record books. When the AME Conference met the following year, it decided to dismiss ideas of a university in Montgomery, and support the already existing school in Selma.

Curiously enough, one of the AME ministers who helped lead the crusade to

FIGURE 5.19 Rev. Mansfield E. Bryant, one of the founders of Payne Institute; courtesy of Alabama Department of Archives and History, Montgomery, Alabama.

establish Payne had to flee Selma a few months earlier. Rev. Mansfield E. Bryant (1852–91) had been publishing a black newspaper, the *Independent*, out of Selma for some time when a fiery editorial touched off an uproar. The editorial, apparently written by an assistant without Bryant's knowledge, predicted a war between the races in the near future and concluded with the hope "that God intends that we [black citizens] will be strong enough to wipe you [white people] out of existence, and hardly leave enough of you to tell the story." The reaction of Selma's white residents can be readily imagined. Colonel Dawson organized a posse to arrest Bryant. Bryant thought that he could explain, but the ladies of Brown Chapel were terrified he might be lynched. So they locked him in the church tower and would not let him out until midnight. Bryant then took their advice and fled town. By the time he was captured in Tuscaloosa, Selma's white citizens had cooled down. Bryant agreed to move to Mobile, and the white Selmians agreed to forget the whole thing.

The year 1889 was also when the city's agreement with the American Missionary Association broke down. The City School Board had been so focused on rebuilding Dallas Academy (which burned down in 1887) that it had failed to keep

Burrell Academy in good repair. The AMA took Burrell back and converted it into a church school, with the result that an entire year went by without Selma having a public school for its black children.

The situation changed after December 10, 1890, when the Selma city schools were turned over to the board of trustees of Dallas Academy. Dallas Academy's board had always been well represented on the city's four-person school board, with George C. Baker and Dr. Courtney Clark serving on both boards. The Alabama legislature decreed that "George C. Baker, Courtney J. Clark, Edmund W. Pettus, William F. Wailes, George Peacock, A. M. Fowlkes, R. M. Nelson, Samuel E. Sterne, Jonathan Haralson, William P. Armstrong, and Hugh S. D. Mallory, who are now the Trustees of Dallas Male and Female Academy, and their successors in office as such trustees be and are hereby incorporated by the name of 'the City School Board of Selma'" (Jackson, *Story of Selma*, 178)

In 1890 the Selma City School Board decided to build two new schools, one for white students and one for black students. Dallas Academy had started a branch school for the white children of east Selma back in 1871 but had to close it after Selma landowners turned down an additional tax to support the schools. Now the growing population of east Selma and the overcrowding of Dallas Academy led the board to divide Selma into two school zones, with Franklin Street the dividing line. Students to the west of Franklin would continue to attend Dallas Academy; those to the east would attend classes in a rented building, "the Green Street School," until a proper building could be erected.

Dr. Courtney J. Clark (1816–93) seems to have been the driving force behind the board's decision to erect what his fellow trustees called the "elegant colored school on Lawrence Street." Clark was a native of South Carolina who served as a US Army surgeon during the Mexican-American War and a Confederate surgeon during the Civil War. His status as a Confederate hero, who had directed hospitals in both Richmond and Montgomery, made his advocacy of black education all the more effective. As president of the City School Board from 1874–89 and as secretary-treasurer of the Dallas Academy Board for many years, he developed a passion for education.

To begin the project for the new school the city rented rooms on Sylvan Street and hired Richard B. Hudson as the principal and tasked him with setting up classes. In 1892, after Hudson's makeshift school had developed a mushrooming enrollment, the board sent school superintendent Richard Hardaway and former mayor H. S. D. Mallory to ask the city council to contribute $5,000, the same amount it had given for the rebuilding of Dallas Academy, toward the erection of a six-room brick building on Lawrence Street. The city did so. Even when confined to his bed by his final illness, Clark continued to take a keen interest in the construction of the

FIGURE 5.20 Dr. Richard Byron Hudson, "Mr. Black Education in Selma"; courtesy of R. B. Hudson Middle School, Selma, Alabama.

new school. Clark did not live to see his dream fulfilled; but when the new school was dedicated on April 22, 1894, it took his name.

Hudson (1866–1931), a native of Uniontown and graduate of Selma University, came to symbolize black education in Selma. He directed Clark School for forty years and was the fifth president of the Alabama State Teachers Association (ASTA). A leading Baptist layman, he served as secretary of the Alabama Baptist Convention from 1897 to 1931 and of the National Baptist Convention from 1903 to 1931. In addition to these activities, he ran a coal business on the side. For almost forty years, Hudson was a dominant figure in Selma's black community, so it was fitting that when the first black public high school was finally established in 1949, it bore Hudson's name.

Public education for the black population received a serious blow in 1891 when the Alabama legislature quietly passed an Apportionment Act that made it legal for Black Belt counties to discriminate between black and white schools in the distribution of funds. The results quickly became apparent in teachers' salaries. In 1889, the average white teacher in Alabama earned $22.04 a month and the average black teacher earned $21.05. Five years later, the average white salary had risen to $24.03, and the average black one had declined to $18.71. By 1902, the average white salary was $10.12 more than the average black one, and by 1908, the average white teacher was making twice as much as his black counterpart: $50.92 a month as opposed to $25.23.

In 1900, black schools in Dallas County were open for one hundred days—roughly five months. Few black children and about 65 percent of white children were in school, while in Mississippi, for example, 53 percent of black children between the ages of ten and fourteen attended school and 75 percent of white children. By 1910, the black school year was down to seventy-six days. Even by southern standards, Alabama was in bad shape.

The grim fact was that in 1918, Dallas County spent $17.35 per capita educating its white children and only $.90 for its black ones. Most Alabama counties spent two to four times more on white children than on black students, but Lowndes and Wilcox Counties seem to be the only ones who spent less than Dallas County.

Dallas County's superintendent of education was one of Selma's most-respected white educators. Darby M. Callaway, or "Boss," as he was called, was born in Mississippi. His father, a Methodist minister, helped in the founding of Southern University in Greensboro. Young Callaway graduated from Southern and came to Dallas Academy, where he taught for two years. After that, he established his own school, Callaway Boys High School, which was patronized by Selma's white elite for decades. It was in 1908, during his almost thirty-year term as superintendent of education, that the state's first public high school was built in Plantersville. Dallas County High was for white students only; Dallas County's black students had to wait till 1930 to be awarded a "training school" for their use.

Selma and the 1901 Convention

In 1892 Selmian Francis L. Pettus launched a campaign for voter reform, which received strong backing from other white leaders during the years leading up to the Constitutional Convention of 1901. Pettus, then speaker of the Alabama House of Representatives, wanted to purge the electorate of uneducated voters, white and black alike. However, his proposal was opposed by not only the Populists, whose supporters were mostly poor whites, but also by some of his fellow Democrats. North Alabama Democrats feared that some of their poor white supporters might lose their votes, and Black Belt Democrats counted on black votes to maintain their control of the state and keep the Populists at bay.

Pettus (1858–1901), a graduate of Davidson College and former clerk of the Alabama Supreme Court, was distressed by the amount of electoral fraud in Alabama.

FIGURE 5.21 Gov. Joseph F. Johnston, the former Selmian who fought disfranchisement; courtesy of Alabama Department of Archives and History, Montgomery, Alabama.

He once told a Mobile audience that the "necessity" of keeping the black vote under control had forced Black Belt whites "to crimes of larceny and perjury and had corrupted the jury, the judge, the solicitor, and others" (*Mobile Register*, January 20, 1900). Senator Morgan shared his distress; the *Selma Times* for May 3, 1899, cites his lament that "as a father he deplores the bringing up the new generation under the influence of this immoral atmosphere that surrounds every recurring election."

By 1896, businessmen and educators were showing more interest in the need for a new constitution. The former hoped for a more business-friendly constitution, the latter hoped to get more state support for schools. The Alabama Commercial and Industrial Association appointed a committee headed by Selma's H. L. McKee to approach the legislature and urge the calling of a new constitutional convention. By 1898 the Populists were no longer seen as a serious threat to Democratic control of the state, and the Alabama legislature voted to call a convention to write a new constitution. Some north Alabama Democrats were still uneasy about the prospect, and one of them was Gov. Joseph F. Johnston.

Joseph Forney Johnston (1843–1913), a native of North Carolina, had moved to Talladega in 1860. After serving in the Confederate Army as a captain, he moved to Selma and took up law. He left Selma for Birmingham in 1884 and became first a banker and then head of Sloss Iron and Steel. He had worked closely with Morgan and Pettus and had enjoyed their support in his campaign for governor in 1896. Now, however, the hope of winning support in north Alabama led him to break with his old allies and call a special session of the legislature to revoke the authority for a convention. The *Selma Times* bitterly denounced Johnston as a "Judas" who had betrayed the Black Belt (quoted in *Montgomery Advertiser* of April 18, 1899).

The race for Morgan's seat in the Alabama Senate became a fight over the wisdom of a new constitution. Starting in the fall of 1899, the two men made a series of joint appearances in which Morgan appealed for "White Supremacy and clean elections," and Johnston warned against a Bourbon conspiracy to disenfranchise poor whites. When county primaries were held in April 1900, Morgan won overwhelmingly, carrying every county in the state but four.

In December 1900, the legislature voted to allow the people to decide whether or not to call a constitutional convention. The state's remaining Republicans and Populists joined with Governor Johnston's supporters in opposing any such convention. Senators Morgan and Pettus, together with former governors Thomas B. Jones and William C. Oates, canvassed the state urging a "yes" vote. When, on April 23, 1901, Alabamians voted on whether or not to hold a constitutional convention, most predominantly white counties opposed the idea. However, Dallas and other predominantly black counties provided the necessary majority for approval. Dallas County, with only 2,360 white voters, somehow managed to approve the convention by a vote of 5,668 to 200.

Five Dallas County lawyers were elected delegates to the Constitutional Convention of 1901. All five were white Democrats from prominent Black Belt families who had served or were serving in the legislature. John F. Burns (1840–1905), a Burnsville native, had studied law under William Lowndes Yancey. Benjamin H. Craig (1835–1907), born in Cahawba, had served as register in chancery through all the convulsions of Reconstruction and "Redemption" from 1863 to 1897. While not a Republican like his brother George, he was easily the most liberal member of the Dallas delegation. Philip H. Pitts (1849–1918), originally from Uniontown, was a graduate of Davidson College and had served fourteen years as solicitor for the Fourth Judicial Circuit. The Pitts family played a prominent role in both Perry and Dallas Counties. Henry Fontaine Reese (1863–1943) came from Demopolis, had studied at Georgetown Law School, and served as president of the Dallas County Bar. His son Henry Jr. was chosen to serve as a page at the convention. Watkins

Figure 5.22 Delegate Benjamin Craig of the Constitutional Convention of 1901; courtesy of Alabama Department of Archives and History, Montgomery, Alabama.

M. Vaughan (1872–1944), a Summerfield native, studied law at Vanderbilt University and composed *Vaughan's Complete Alabama Legal Form Book*. Each of the men had been elected to the Alabama legislature, and two of them, Pitts and Vaughan, were later to serve long terms as probate judge of Dallas County.

It is interesting to note that the oldest member of the delegation had the most liberal outlook. Sixty-six-year-old Craig wanted the new constitution to outlaw child labor and punish lynching. His most radical idea, however, was that Alabama women should be allowed to vote. Craig fought earnestly for most of the convention to gain suffrage for women. His proposal was supported by Senator Morgan but bitterly opposed by Reese and Vaughan. On August 10, the *Times* reported "the convention made Deputy Craig very happy by endorsing his amendment granting women who own $100 worth of taxable real estate [the right] to vote at elections called for the purpose of passing on bond issues." But Craig's triumph was short-lived; the convention retracted its endorsement the next day.

FIGURE 5.23 Delegate John F. Burns of the Constitutional Convention of 1901; courtesy of Alabama Department of Archives and History, Montgomery, Alabama.

John Fielding Burns took a different approach. Lynching? "I deny that any lynching ever took place," he said stoutly (*OP*, 1:882). Let women vote? Out of 155 delegates, Burns cast the only vote against allowing a woman suffragist to address the convention. So far as he was concerned, the convention had been called for one purpose only: "To kill snakes" (that is, get rid of black voters). He was particularly eager to strike at Booker T. Washington, the president of Tuskegee Institute. Burns denounced Washington as "a rattler with his mouth open and his fangs ready" (*OP,* 4:4788). It was a strange metaphor for him to use since his mentor Yancey had considered the rattlesnake an ideal symbol of the white people of Alabama.

Burns's vehement denunciations of black people were made more significant because black voters had elected him to the 1875 convention as an independent-minded Democrat who had served as bondsman for several black elected officials. However, times had changed and, obviously, so had Burns. The younger delegates, Pitts, Reese, and Vaughan, were neither as progressive as Craig nor as stridently anti–black rights as Burns. On female suffrage, Pitts tended to support Craig, while the others leaned toward Burns's attitude.

On May 20, shortly before the convention opened, black leaders from across central Alabama met in Montgomery and drew up an appeal to the delegates. Selma teacher R. B. Hudson served as secretary for the meeting, and the name of Selma minister Charles O. Boothe was the first of the twenty-four signatures on the appeal. The appeal itself, drawn up largely by Booker T. Washington, went as follows: "The Negro does ask . . . that since he is taxed, works the roads, is punished for crime, is called upon to defend his country, that he have some humble share in choosing those who shall rule over him, especially when he has proven his worthiness by becoming a taxpayer and a worthy, reliable citizen" (*OP*, 1:190). The "share" allowed to black citizens was to be humble indeed if the Suffrage Committee's majority report was accepted. The committee majority, which included Selma delegate P. H. Pitts, proposed what later became Article 7 of the 1901 Constitution. It restricted the right to vote to adult males who 1) could read, write, and interpret any article of the United States Constitution, 2) owned forty acres of land or property valued at $300, and 3) had never been convicted of adultery, wife beating, vagrancy, or any other "serious" crime. In addition, voters would be required to pay $1.50 a year for the privilege of casting their ballots. These provisions were clearly designed to eliminate suffrage for most black citizens and a number of poor white ones as well.

Some delegates found the provisions too strict and protested at the number of people who would be disenfranchised by the new constitution. H. F. Reese explained patiently that the property and literacy requirements would not be enough to keep Dallas County's black population from voting since "a great many of these negroes are educated and a great many of them own property." But the poll tax would do the trick, he assured them: "When you pay $1.50 for a poll tax, in Dallas County, you disfranchise ten negroes" (*OP*, 3:3368).

A few delegates felt the suffrage provisions were too liberal. Burns, for example, still thinking of Booker T. Washington, wanted to disenfranchise all illegitimate children of "mixed blood." He made the motion that

> *Whereas*, mixed bloods seldom inherit even the impaired virtues of their progenitors, and in every section of our country are always found among the most vicious and vindictive class of citizens, and, *Whereas*, this Convention was called with the understanding and for the purpose that white boys of Alabama should not be forced to compete with any others, whose only qualification for suffrage lies in their ability to memorize . . . *Be it Ordered*, by the People of Alabama, in Convention assembled, that all bastards . . . not be allowed to register or vote in this State. (*OP*, 4:4429)

Reese supported Burns in his determination to punish illegitimate children for the sins of their parents. When delegates from north Alabama objected, Reese responded curtly, "I do not propose to put my people under the hand of negro rule because it might disenfranchise one or two bastards in the white counties of Alabama. We have none such in our county, we are a moral people, and I say . . . if the gentlemen from North Alabama will conform to the rules of morality adopted in my county they will have no trouble" (*OP*, 3:3276–77) The delegates must not have cared for being lectured about Dallas County morality since they voted Burns's motion down.

The Suffrage Committee did offer poor white Alabamians one concession, known as the "fighting grandfather clause." If their ancestors had fought in the War of 1812, the Mexican-American War, the Civil War, or the Spanish-American War, they would be allowed to vote if they registered by January 1, 1903. The fighting grandfather clause provoked the bitterest opposition, partly because it was so patently racist. Senators Morgan and Pettus both protested strongly against the idea of creating a special class of citizens who would inherit the right to vote. Pettus thought it unconstitutional; Morgan thought it positively un-American. In his eyes, "the American Revolution was not so much a redress of grievances, as it was a struggle to abolish heredity in government. . . . To make blood the medium of translating the electoral power from father to son, is to uproot from its foundations, the whole system of democratic government, and to reinstate the system and the form of regal government" (*OP*, 3:2863). Ex-governor Oates pointed out that some black citizens had served the Confederacy loyally, even though forbidden to bear arms in its defense, while some white citizens had deserted. Burns, a leader in the United Confederate Veterans, replied indignantly that Oates was insulting the memory of the South's heroic dead. Oates, who had fought in twenty-seven battles and lost an arm for the Confederacy, was forced to defend his record.

In the end, the pleas of Morgan, Oates, and the other old Confederate leaders were of no avail. On July 30, 1901, the fighting grandfather clause was approved by a vote of 109 to 23. Dallas County's delegates all voted with the majority. Alabama, which in 1819 had enjoyed probably the most liberal suffrage in the South, now adopted the most restrictive provisions in the nation.

It is worth noting, however, that most of the Dallas County delegates voted against an August 15 proposal aimed at crippling black education. Delegate Tom Heflin of Randolph County, who was later elected to the US Senate, led the fight to apportion taxes according to race, so that no "white" taxes would go to support black schools. The *Selma Journal* strongly endorsed this proposal.

Booker T. Washington and other black leaders protested that black schools "would virtually be blotted out" by such a policy. The *Mobile Register* agreed, saying in its June 7, 1901, issue that "we must not disenfranchise the Negro on account of his ignorance and then refuse him help to escape from his ignorance." Heflin responded indignantly that the black population was too educated already and that book learning ruined them as field hands.

Ex-governor Thomas B. Jones fell back on the religious argument, saying black people had souls and deserved to be taught, at least how to read the Bible. He also assured the convention that Robert E. Lee would have wanted them to be generous to their former slaves (*OP*, 4:4301–2). This twin reference to God and General Lee seems to have won the day: while Burns supported Heflin's proposal, Pitts, Reese, and Vaughan joined the majority in voting it down 90 to 31.

Unlike most disfranchising conventions, Alabama's 1901 convention allowed the people of the state to decide whether or not they wished to accept the new constitution. A host of newspapers, afraid that the constitution would be rejected, urged the Democratic delegates to forget about their promise to let the people vote on the issue. But Reese insisted that the delegates keep their promises, and he prevailed. A bitter campaign developed, with ex-Selmians like Governor Johnston and ex-congressman Shelley leading the fight against the proposed constitution. Senator Morgan maintained a grim silence for most of the campaign, waiting until the last days before endorsing the document.

On November 11, 1901, the predominantly white counties of north Alabama and the Wiregrass voted against the constitution, but their protest was drowned under the sea of "yes" votes from the Black Belt. Over half the margin of victory came from Dallas, Perry, and Hale Counties. If one is to believe the official returns, thousands of Selma's black voters raced to the polls on November 11 to vote for their own disenfranchisement.

The three white Democrats appointed to serve as Dallas County's board of registrars (one by the governor, one by the state auditor, and one by the commissioner of agriculture) were Daniel B. Edwards of Polk, Gilbert Nicholson of Selma, and W. L. Sheppard of Safford. The March 8, 1902, issue of the *Selma Times* reported that the registrars were "discharging their duties in a straight-forward, business-like manner, and every person not entitled to register under the constitution is promptly informed of the fact, no matter who recommends them or testifies to their good character. Likewise every white man who applies is speedily enrolled, and given his life certificate."

The results were striking. In 1900, there had been 9,871 black men who were eligible to vote in Dallas County. Only fifty-two were left after the new constitution went into effect. In the state as a whole, only 3,654 black voters remained of the 181,471 who had been registered in 1900. While 205,278 white voters succeeded in registering, the new tax kept many poor white Alabamians from polling places.

FIGURE 5.24 The lobby of the newly completed Hotel Albert reflected Selma's prosperity during its "Golden Age"; courtesy of Selma–Dallas County Museum of History and Archives, Selma, Alabama.

THE "GOLDEN AGE": 1898–1912

As cotton prices rose in the late 1890s and early 1900s, the long agricultural depression ended at last and Selma saw a return of prosperity. The city's downtown still shows ample architectural evidence of its new wealth. Dallas County laid the cornerstone for its new courthouse on October 9, 1900. The city's administrators moved into a new city hall on Franklin Street (now the police department) on October 1, 1904. Selma's new Carnegie Library (now the Centre for Commerce) opened its doors in January 1905.

Selmians may have taken particular pride in the newly completed Hotel Albert, which was modeled on the Doge's Palace in Venice. The Albert had been the Broad Street Hotel when begun in 1861. The war had interrupted construction, and it was reborn as the National Hotel in 1867, completing its first two floors before its owners ran out of money. Banker Albert Gallatin Parrish led the campaign to have the hotel's top two floors completed in the 1890s, and the finished hotel took his name out of gratitude. Parrish (1850–1934), a native of Greensboro, later became president of the City National Bank and chairman of the Selma School Board.

The St. James Hotel closed its doors that same year, signaling almost too neatly that Selma was now more dependent on its railroads (the Southern Railway and the Louisville & Nashville) than it was on the Alabama River.

Some of the city's most impressive downtown churches were completed during this period. The Jewish community, which had been meeting in the Methodist church for worship, moved into Temple Mishkan Israel in 1899. Church Street Methodist finished erecting its new building (complete with a baptismal font donated by its Jewish friends) in 1901. And the imposing High Gothic First Baptist Church raised its towers on Lauderdale in 1904.

East Selma also showed signs of prosperity in this new era. Baker Elementary School was erected at the corner of Washington and Dallas, replacing the inadequate Green Street School, in 1902. It took the name of George Baker (1828–91), a native of Philadelphia and a leading Selma merchant who had served for a time as the head of the Selma School Board. In 1903 a Canadian minister named W. C. Matthews set up a branch of the YMCA ("The Railroad YMCA") on Alabama Avenue to serve the young men of the area. In addition, two impressive new churches appeared in east Selma, both on Alabama Avenue: Alabama Avenue Methodist (formerly Water Street Methodist) in 1904 and Alabama Avenue Presbyterian (formerly Oldside Presbyterian and now Crescent Hill Presbyterian) in 1908.

Before the end of the decade, the city's east end had acquired two additional schools, thanks to two determined ladies, one black and one white, Sophia Kingston (1856–1934) and Frances Claypool Thomas (1845–1917). Mrs. Thomas, the wife of railroad engineer J. J. Thomas, asked the school board to set up a school more convenient for the white children who lived east of the railroad. The board refused. When she returned with a petition signed by thirty parents, they agreed to hire a teacher—but only if she would find a location. Mrs. Thomas then appealed to Mayor Atkins, who persuaded the city council to pay rent on a house on Florence Street. In December 1908, the Alabama Avenue School (later to be renamed the Frances Thomas Elementary after Mrs. Thomas) opened its doors for the first time.

Sophia Kingston didn't bother with either the school board or the city council. A native of Summerfield who taught at Knox Academy, she was concerned for the black children of East End. So she recruited Knox's shop class, marched them across town to Shelley Avenue, and had them erect a building for her there. She ran East End Academy from 1904, when it was set up, till 1922, when the city finally took steps to provide the children of the East End with a public school. After East End Elementary was ravaged by a flood in 1990, the school was rebuilt on Selma Avenue, just one block from the former site of Francis Thomas Elementary (which closed after integration). In 2005, East End also took the name of its founder, becoming Sophia Kingston Elementary.

The city's population grew by 56 percent during the first decade of the twentieth century, rising from 8,713 in 1900 to 13,649 in 1910. Two new banks were opened

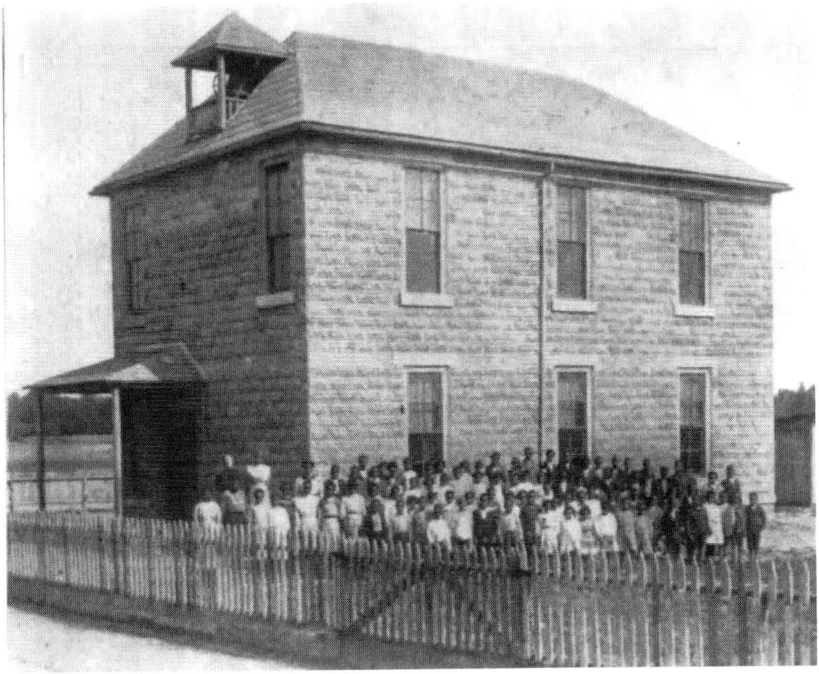

FIGURE 5.25 East End Academy was set up by Sophia Kingston in 1904; courtesy of the Reformed Presbyterian Church, Selma, Alabama.

to serve the growing population. In 1902 Charles M. Howard (1863–1920) founded the People's Savings Bank, which a few years later became the Peoples Bank and Trust Company, with offices on the corner of Broad Street and Water Avenue. Edward Carlisle Melvin (1870–1954) established Selma National Bank in 1904 and was its chief executive officer until his death. He later began the Selma Trust and Savings Bank, which is now a branch of First Alabama Bank.

Selma's black community also shared in the new prosperity. Under the leadership of Charles S. Dinkins (1856–1901), Selma University was finally able to get out of debt. Dinkins, a native of Mississippi with degrees from Roger Williams in Nashville and Newton Theological in Massachusetts, was able to complete the erection of a women's dormitory, Susie Stone Hall, and raise the pay of his teachers.

Payne Institute also got the money to build a girls' dormitory in 1904. And in 1908 a striking new Brown Chapel AME Church was erected on Sylvan Street (now Martin Luther King Jr. Boulevard). In 1911 a branch of the Alabama Penny Savings Bank, then the second-largest minority bank in the United States, opened on Franklin Street with Henry Boyd as vice president and R. B. Hudson as cashier.

FIGURE 5.26 Rev. Charles S. Dinkins served as president of Selma University from 1893 to 1901; courtesy of Selma University.

The success of this institution was dramatic evidence of the growth of Selma's black middle class.

Dallas County's black community also benefited from a sharp decline in lynching. The new constitution made county sheriffs responsible for preventing lynching, and Sheriff Frank Doherty took his responsibility seriously. In 1904, the *Selma Times* reported that Ed Bell, a black man from Sardis, had been arrested for murdering a fellow black man. The three white men who were supposed to bring him to Selma for trial reported that a mob of masked black people had overpowered them and taken Bell off to be hanged. The *Times* thought their story "preposterous," and Sheriff Doherty agreed. The three "well known citizens of south Dallas" found themselves in jail awaiting possible trial while Doherty scoured the county for witnesses. He found evidence that the lynching had in fact been a biracial affair, with the deputies pretending to resist but actually directing their black accomplices how to tie the noose around Bell's neck. The grand jury refused to indict the men, to the indignation of the *Times*; but enthusiasm for lynching declined markedly thereafter.

FIGURE 5.27 Hospital founder Dr. Goldsby King; courtesy of Sturdivant Hall, Selma, Alabama.

Between 1895 and 1910, Selma became a medical center for west central Alabama. Four private hospitals sprang up to compete with the Charity Hospital that the ladies had worked so hard to establish. The Goldsby King Sanitarium opened in 1896, Union Street Hospital in 1901, DuBose Sanitarium in 1904, and Burwell Infirmary (Selma's first black hospital) in 1907. The biracial Charity Hospital itself closed in 1907, leaving the buildings to be occupied by Dinkins Academy, a private school for white boys.

Dr. Goldsby King (1860–1920) founded Selma's first private hospital on December 6, 1896. King, a native of Selma, had earned his medical degree at the Medical College of Charleston, following it with postgraduate work at Johns Hopkins Hospital and at Heidelberg. He hid his tender heart behind a brusque manner and kept his charitable donations (like the mission hospitals he helped to found in Brazil and the Congo) as quiet as possible. After his death, King Sanitarium on Mabry Street became King Memorial Hospital. Its buildings later housed the Dunn Rest Home.

Selma's second private hospital was opened a few years later on Union Street by a group of doctors led by Dr. Samuel Gay and Dr. John Furniss, former Confed-

FIGURE 5.28 Hospital founder Dr. F. G. DuBose; courtesy of the Vaughan–Smitherman Historic and Civic Building, Selma, Alabama.

erate surgeon and son-in-law of N. H. R. Dawson. This same group of physicians assisted in the establishment of the Alabama Baptist Hospital here in 1922.

Dr. Francis Goodwin DuBose (1873–1941), who claimed Maplesville as his native town, began DuBose Sanitarium in 1904. With a medical degree from Tulane University, DuBose did postgraduate work in New York, Baltimore, Philadelphia, and Chicago and became an outstanding surgeon. When the sanitorium burned down in 1910, DuBose and his group decided not to rebuild on Lapsley but to accept the terms of Henry White Vaughan's bequest to establish a hospital for respectable white patients in what is now the Vaughan-Smitherman Building. Thus the Vaughan Memorial Hospital was born.

Dr. Lincoln L. Burwell founded Selma's first black-administered hospital in 1907. Burwell (1867–1928), a native of Marengo County, earned an MD from Leonard Medical College in Raleigh, North Carolina, in 1889 and that same year passed the Alabama State Board examination. He established his practice here, opened a drugstore on Franklin Street, and, later, set up Burwell Infirmary on Philpot Avenue.

FIGURE 5.29 Hospital founder L. L. Burwell; courtesy of Selma University, Selma, Alabama.

The *Times-Journal* explained in its centennial edition (November 2, 1927) that "at the time the infirmary was founded the Union Street Hospital and the [DuBose Sanitarium] both had houses in their yards for negro patients, but the Burwell met a necessity for an exclusively negro establishment and at the beginning commanded attention in hospital circles throughout the South owing to its work and high character of its staff."

However, even the marvels of modern medicine could not keep Selma's "Grand Old Men," Senators Morgan and Pettus, going forever. In 1906, the state legislature reelected them to additional terms but voted to hold a popular election for "alternate senators": men they could appoint when Morgan and Pettus died. Morgan, with his usual humor, referred to the proceedings as "the pallbearers' election" (Fry, *John Tyler Morgan*, 255–56).

John Tyler Morgan died in Washington, DC, on June 11, 1907. He had lived to see work begun on his dearest project, an Isthmian Canal. He would have much preferred to have the canal cut through Nicaragua and never really forgave Pres.

Theodore Roosevelt for having the canal dug in Panama. Morgan's remains were returned to Selma for burial next to the tomb of Vice President King who, like Morgan, had spent three decades in the Senate. Prominent visitors from across the country attended the impressive funeral, and a huge obelisk was erected to mark his grave.

On July 27, Edmund Winston Pettus also died. He, too, was brought to Live Oak Cemetery for burial. Pettus had left firm instructions that his ceremony be quiet and his gravestone modest. In death, as in life, he was obeyed.

Selma's two senators were replaced by two north Alabama "pallbearers," ex-governor Johnston of Birmingham and John H. Bankhead of Jasper. This event symbolizes almost too neatly the passing of political power from the Black Belt to the northern and more industrialized section of the state. The Black Belt continued to exercise a great deal of influence in the legislature, however, usually in concert with the "Big Mule" industrialists in Birmingham and Mobile.

New Men and New Issues

New issues emerged with the new century. On December 19, 1906, the *Selma Morning Times* reported that a "bombshell" had gone off at the regular meeting of the city council. The bombshell was a petition presented by Rev. Edward W. Gamble to Mayor V. B. Atkins and the city council asking them not to grant any liquor licenses. Gamble (1869–1958), a native of Tallahassee and pastor of St. Paul's Episcopal, flatly charged that the white saloons, like the black ones, were "dens of vice" that needed to be closed. His petition was endorsed by the Ministers' Union, which included every white Protestant clergyman in town.

Gamble was followed by Dr. W. W. Harper, who presented a similar petition endorsed by most of the doctors in town. Harper (1869–1941), a Dallas County native who had studied medicine in Edinburgh, London, and Paris, was later to serve as president of the Alabama Medical Association. Last of all came Judge Daniel Partridge (1873–1915), who warned of all the crimes associated with drinking. Mayor Atkins and the city council listened politely but went on to grant licenses to a dozen local establishments. The *Times* announced that a major new reform movement had been launched, and the paper was quite correct.

Victor Boardman Atkins (1863–1915), a native of Hale County, had come to Selma at the age of sixteen and started making his mark in business. By 1890 he was head of V. B. Atkins Grocery and Commission Company and in 1893 he was elected to the Selma City Council. Ten years later he was mayor, and in Jackson's words "carried all before him and with him" (*Story of Selma*, 414). In the years to come he would prove a staunch opponent of prohibition.

FIGURE 5.30 Mayor Victor B. Atkins; courtesy of Selma City Hall, Selma, Alabama.

The Alabama legislature proved easier to persuade than the Selma City Council; in 1907 it passed a law outlawing the manufacture and sale of beer, wine, and whiskey in the state of Alabama, to take effect at the close of 1908. The "dries" were not content with a mere law and demanded an amendment to the Alabama Constitution "forever prohibiting the manufacture, sale, and keeping for sale, of alcoholic and malt liquors and other intoxicating liquors and beverages." Mayor Atkins warned that that the loss of revenue might make it necessary to raise taxes, and state representative A. D. Pitts voted against the amendment.

When the amendment came up for a statewide vote on November 29, 1909, there was a battle royal in Dallas County. The *Selma Journal* heartily endorsed the amendment, while the *Selma Times* strongly opposed it. Selma lawyer H. S. D. Mallory, who was widely regarded as a future governor of Alabama, and other leading "dries" supported the amendment with great energy. Mayor Atkins led the forces opposed to the amendment and had the satisfaction of seeing it voted down both in Dallas and in the state at large.

In the following year Mallory ran for governor as the choice of Gov. B. B. Comer and the "progressive" wing of the Democratic Party. H. S. D. Mallory (1848–1920), a native of Talladega with a law degree from the University of Virginia, had served ably as president of the Alabama Baptist Convention, grand master of Alabama

FIGURE 5.31 Mayor H. S. D. Mallory; courtesy of Selma City Hall, Selma, Alabama.

Masons, chairman of the Alabama Democratic Executive Committee, and mayor of Selma. Atkins and other Selma "wets" loyally supported him, but Mallory's identification with Prohibition hurt him badly in the big cities, and he lost to Edward O'Neal, the "conservative" candidate from north Alabama.

It is ironic that Dallas County's success in disenfranchising its black population probably cost its favorite son that election. The "Plumed Knight of Dallas," as the *Selma Times* called Mallory, had been a notable friend of black education, serving as a trustee of Alabama State University for many years. He would probably have received enough black votes to carry him to victory, had a significant number of black citizens still been able to vote.

6

The Decline of the Cotton Kingdom

Selma, 1912–1939

IN THE EARLY 1910S, BEFORE THE coming of the boll weevil and the outbreak of World War I, Selma's life was rather untroubled. However, the decades that followed brought striking changes in the Queen City of the Black Belt.

Among the notable events were the great flood of 1916, Alabama's entry into World War I, the decades-long battles over Prohibition and women's suffrage, the revival of the Ku Klux Klan in the 1920s, the trauma of the Great Depression and the coming of the New Deal. All these changes, however, began after the boll weevil had shaken the Black Belt's Cotton Kingdom to its foundation.

In 1914, the year the boll weevil reached Alabama, the state's cotton crop amounted to 1,751,375 bales. In 1915, production dropped to 1,050,000 bales and, by 1916, it had fallen to only 525,000 bales. In Dallas County, the crop plunged from 64,230 bales in 1914 to 14,230 bales in 1917.

In the years that followed, Dallas County farmers had to make serious adjustments. Some switched to crops like cattle, soybeans, and timber; others learned the modern, costly methods to keep the boll weevil in check; and many left farming altogether. The local chamber of commerce began referring to the city as part of the "Clover Belt," trying to promote the use of its rich prairie soil for crops other than cotton. As bad as things were, Dallas County somehow managed better than most of the rest of the state. As late as 1970 it still ranked among Alabama's top cotton-producing counties—the only Black Belt county to do so. Today many of those cotton farms have been transformed into pine plantations due to the proximity of paper mills. In west Dallas the prairie soil has given rise to hundreds of acres of catfish farms.

It would be difficult to accurately assess the boll weevil's cost to human morale. Most of Selma's large landowners survived, but large numbers of small farmers were wiped out. The Alabama Penny Savings Bank failed in 1915, leaving many middle-class black citizens without their savings. When the Alabama River flooded in July 1916, it seemed the last straw.

Selmians responded generously to the suffering occasioned by the flood, which left hundreds homeless and caused property damage estimated at close to $1 million. The July 10 *Selma Times* reported that "Mayor [Louis] Benish, Julian Smith, Frank Milhous and others left the town immediately, carrying with them every available boat and began the work of rescue." Meanwhile, Truman L. McGill, president of the Rotary Club, called a meeting at the courthouse to raise money for the relief of flood sufferers. McGill (1872–1936), a native of Louisville, Kentucky, came to Selma in 1900 as secretary of the YMCA and later became a partner in the jewelry store of Hobbs & McGill. The General Relief Committee included bankers Houston C. Armstrong and E. C. Melvin, merchant Albert Kahn, Rabbi Isadore Isaacson, and lawyer Hugh Mallory.

That same day, two other groups held separate meetings in response to the crisis. Selma's black leaders set up a committee headed by Dr. L. L. Burwell, Rev. J. D. Jessell, and Rev. Solomon Kingston. Later in the week they held a mass meeting at Rev. Kingston's church (Reformed Presbyterian) to coordinate with Chairman Armstrong on how they would help those in need. The ladies of the Selma Suffrage Association also threw themselves into the effort, appealing for clothing and household goods to be brought to their headquarters at the Hotel Albert. According to the July 10 *Selma Times*, "Mrs. [Carrie] Parke and Mrs. [Anna] Converse were busy with the telephone wires this morning organizing the committee and furthering the work of relief as much as possible." (The well-known author and storyteller Kathryn Windham told the author that she thinks this was "the most popular thing Selma's suffragettes ever did.") Rev. Edward W. Gamble, the pastor of St. Paul's Episcopal, agreed to take charge of distributing the clothes to those most in need.

It was at this point that the "Great Migration" began. "Dozens of negro families will shake the soil of this section from their feet this year never to come back," observed the *Selma Times* of August 11, 1916. Northern industries had expanded to meet the growing demands created by war in Europe, and thousands of black southerners moved north to the ghettoes of Chicago, Detroit, and other midwestern cities. Some of the industries even sent recruiters south to enlist black workers. The steady flow continued for decades, until the black population of Dallas County, which had once been 80 percent of the total, declined to 55 percent.

FIGURE 6.1 Dallas County women and children picking cotton; courtesy of the Edmundite Missions.

POPULATION OF DALLAS COUNTY

	White	Black	Total
1910	9,890	43,511	53,401
1930	14,227	40,867	55,094
1950	19,694	35,576	55,270

It was usually the black men who left for the North, often leaving wives and children behind with the promise that they would send for them when (and if) they found work. The loss of so many adult male laborers caused some panic among Dallas County landowners. The *Selma Times* insisted that in the long run the exodus would be good for the South, leading to a more diversified economy.

In the short run, however, US involvement in World War I drained off still more men, both white and black, out of the fields. Selma businessman Lloyd McKee Hooper, the director of the Alabama Defense Council during World War I, described "the scarcity of farm labor" in a June 12, 1918, letter to the National Council of Defense:

> Our cotton and corn crops are universally "in the grass." Young men of high school age are not fit to chop cotton and corn and plow the same. We are pro-

> posing to use them largely in the harvesting of the crop, but it is not practicable to use them now in cultivating the crops.
>
> Women choppers who in previous years received 40 or 50 cents a day for their services are now being freely paid from one dollar to one dollar and fifty cents per day, and refuse to work over ten hours.

He suggested that it might be necessary to start importing workers from Mexico.

The "Central City" Goes to War

In 1917, when the United States was drawn into the "Great War," later renamed World War I, Selmians threw themselves into the war effort. Eleanor Gray Hooper (1864–1938), the president of the Alabama Federation of Women's Clubs, became head of the Women's Divison of the Alabama Council of Defense. "Nellie," as she preferred to be called, took charge of mobilizing the women of Alabama to conserve food, clothes, and raw materials for the war effort. Selma educator Arthur Harman (1875–1948), the former president of the Alabama Education Association, took on the responsibility of designing a program to teach the state's illiterate recruits to the army how to read and write.

Selma businessman Lloyd McKee Hooper (1869–1923) was asked by Gov. Charles Henderson to take over the Alabama Defense Council itself. Hooper was the son of a leading Selma grocer and had business interests including cotton, oil, timber, and a soft drink named Chero Cola. When Hooper took charge of the council on January 5, 1918, he discovered that the Alabama legislature, which met only once every four years at that time, had failed to provide money for operation of the council. Hooper raised $20,000 with personal appeals and set up the council headquarters in Selma. The governor finally persuaded Hooper to move his headquarters to the state capital, promising that the legislature would eventually pay his expenses.

A number of Selma's young white men were already in uniform when the United States entered the War on April 6, 1917. The National Guard's Fourth Alabama had been called into national service in June 1916 because of tensions along the Mexican border. In March 1917 the Fourth was called back from Arizona to serve as home guards; in August the Fourth was renamed the 167th Infantry and sent to Camp Mills, New York, to prepare for service in France. The 167th became part of the 84th Brigade of the 42nd ("Rainbow") Division and was sent into battle under the command of Gen. Douglas MacArthur.

Other Selmians enlisted once the conflict was underway, choosing to serve in the army, navy, or marines. Still others waited to be called up by Selective Service as "selectmen" (the term "draftee" came later). All had the opportunity to risk their lives for their country.

FIGURE 6.2 Lloyd McKee Hooper, director of the Alabama Defense Council during World War I; from Albert B. Moore's *History of Alabama and Her People*, 2:102–103, American Historical Society, 1927.

Dallas County's black community got caught up in the war effort as well. "Selma Ablaze with Patriotism," Montgomery's black newspaper the *Emancipator* reported on March 22, 1918, describing the excitement generated by the departure of 160 black selectmen for training at Fort Dodge, Iowa. A mass meeting was held at Tabernacle Baptist to plan a reception to be held at Selma University Friday night and the religious service Sunday morning in honor of "the Flower of Central City Youth" as they prepared to go "over the top."

> Never in the history of the city have the colored people made such extensive demonstration of loyalty to the cause of the Allies as were witnessed when 160 Colored Selectmen boarded Pullman Sleepers here Monday for Camp Dodge to begin training to face the Kaiser in France. They left among cheers of five thousand People, many of whom were white.
>
> Monday morning the 160 soldiers assembled at the courthouse . . . where a procession was formed with the Knox band leading, followed by Mayor Benish, the Draft Board and members of the four schools [Clark, Knox, Payne and Selma University], and the patriotic procession took up its march to the

FIGURE 6.3 John T. Melvin, the first American naval officer to die in the war, as a cadet; courtesy of Alabama Department of Archives and History, Montgomery, Alabama.

> union station, where each selectman received a bouquet from the ladies comprising the Red Cross Auxiliary. A Bible was presented to each of the draftees, a gift from the schools of the city.

It need hardly be added that Selma's black physicians helped the draft board by examining recruits for free, that Selma's black ministers helped raise money for the War Appeal, and that its black families aided in every drive to support the troops.

The first Selmian, and the first American commissioned naval officer, to die in the war was Lt. John Tillman Melvin. Melvin was a graduate of Annapolis and the son of one of Selma's most prominent families. He was killed on November 5, 1917, when his ship, the USS *Alcedo*, was torpedoed off the coast of France by a German submarine. A monument to his memory stands at the corner of Alabama Avenue and Lauderdale Street. (Another son of Dallas County, mess steward Ernest Harrison of Tyler, went down with the *Alcedo*. No monuments were erected in his honor, and his name was left off the war memorials erected by the Ladies Memorial Association and the American Legion.)

For some, Melvin's death early in the war evoked memories of Noble Leslie DeVotie,

FIGURE 6.4 1st Lt. William H. Dinkins, later president of Selma University, was one of the few blacks to achieve officer status in World War I; courtesy of Selma University.

the Selma minister who became the first casualty of the Civil War when he drowned in Mobile Bay. Two of the city's prominent Baptist leaders followed Devotie's example of embracing military service. Rev. John Davison, the pastor at First Baptist, resigned his pulpit and joined the YMCA units serving America's sons abroad. William H. Dinkins (1890–1977), the dean at Selma University, enlisted in the army, serving as a second lieutenant. Both were more fortunate than Devotie; Davison sur-

FIGURE 6.5 Medic Dr. Monroe Maas was one of seven Selma doctors to serve as medics during World War I; courtesy of Selma–Dallas County Museum of History and Archives, Selma, Alabama.

vived the war to serve as pastor at First Baptist once more during the Second World War, Dinkins to serve as president of Selma University as his father had before him.

Selma's medical men also contributed to the war effort. Dr. Drayton Doherty (1883–1969) served as a doctor with the British and was awarded the British Military Cross for his "attending the wounded in the open under very heavy shell fire, with utter disregard for personal safety." Dr. W .W. Harper and his son, W. F. Harper, both enlisted; the senior Harper, who had trained at a hospital in Paris, wound up back in France as a captain in the medical corps. Drs. W. W. Burns, Pressley Y. Donald, Monroe Maas, and Marcus Skinner also served as medics. Dr. Maas's brother, Corp. Charles S. Maas, was singled out by Selma historian Walter Jackson for the awards he won. Corporal Maas and Lt. James Rowan were both awarded the Distinguished Service Cross for risking their lives to rescue their commanding officer, who had been wounded.

FIGURE 6.6 Prince Phillips was the first black Selmian buried in Arlington National Cemetery; courtesy of Alabama Department of Archives and History, Montgomery, Alabama.

The first Selmian to die in France was Sgt. Aaron Frazier, who succumbed to pneumonia on January 18, 1918. His death was typical in that more of the forty-one Dallas County boys who died in World War I were brought down by disease than by German bullets, and that most of them (like Frazier) were black.

Even after the Armistice was declared on November 11, 1918, the Spanish flu continued to ravage the American troops. One of the last Selmians to die was Prince

Phillips, who succumbed on March 27, 1919. His mother had been a slave of the Phillips family; he became the first black Selmian to be buried in Arlington National Cemetery. His death passed without any notice in the Selma papers.

After the war, the ladies of the Selma Memorial Association erected a small monument in Live Oak Cemetery "dedicated to the memory of the Dallas County boys who died in the world war defending the principles of true democracy." The monument lists eighteen names, all of them white. Apparently "true democracy" did not require the ladies to add the names of the twenty-three other "boys" who died in the war. (The American Legion later added the names to their monument in New Live Oak.)

The Women's Suffrage Movement, 1912 to 1922

Following the 1901 Constitutional Convention, when Selma delegate B. H. Craig was defeated in his efforts to secure the vote for women, the women's suffrage movement seems to have gone into hibernation. However, on March 29, 1910, the movement was brought back to prominence by a small group of ladies who met at the Carnegie Library to establish the Selma Suffrage Association.

The five original members of the group included Mrs. Aimee Nelson DuBose, wife of one of Selma's leading physicians; Mrs. Mary Amelia John Watson, daughter of Selma mayor J. R. John and a leader in the establishment of the library; Mary Howard Raiford, soon to become business manager of the *Selma Times*; and the Partridge sisters, Mrs. Julie P. Hatch and Mary Winslow Partridge.

Miss Partridge (1881–1958), a legal secretary, was chosen president of the group. Like her pastor, Reverend Gamble, and her brother the judge, she was a firm believer in Prohibition. She felt that Alabama would never accept Prohibition until women got the vote. In 1912, she led a delegation from Selma to Birmingham where, with other women of like mind, she organized the Alabama Equal Suffrage Association (AESA). Miss Partridge was chosen first vice president and state organizer. By January 1913, she could boast of having launched a chapter in Montgomery and was busy carrying the crusade to other Black Belt cities.

On January 29 of that same year, the first AESA state convention met at the Hotel Albert in Selma, and delegates resolved to begin lining up members of the Alabama legislature to promote a referendum on the question of female suffrage.

Selma's women did their work well. When the legislature met in 1915, all three of Dallas County's representatives—Joseph W. Green, Sam Will John, and John Lapsley—were pledged to support the referendum. Representative Green, whose support of Prohibition had endeared him to many of the suffragettes, had asked for and been granted the privilege of introducing the bill.

However, Selma's male population began to grow uneasy. They could not deny that leaders of the Selma Suffrage Association were above reproach: all white, middle-class churchgoers, primarily Presbyterians and Episcopalians, and all descended from Confederate veterans. Still, the movement struck them as subversive. When they discovered that one of the Birmingham leaders was married to a Republican, their worst fears were instantly confirmed: women's suffrage was simply another northern plot to destroy the southern way of life!

A group of nameless lawyers, probably led by Selma judge James B. Evans, produced an anonymous pamphlet, *A Protest against Woman Suffrage in Alabama*, and had it placed on the desk of every member of the legislature. The pamphlet began: "Women's suffrage is the most dangerous blow aimed at the peace and happiness of the people of Alabama and white supremacy since the Civil War. . . . It strikes a blow at the cleanest, highest and most beautiful civilization on earth." The pamphlet went on to challenge the patriotism of anyone foolish enough to endorse so radical a proposal. Congressman Tom Heflin had already questioned the manhood of any male who supported female suffrage, so prosuffrage legislators found themselves accused of being both sissies and subversives.

Some of the legislators panicked. Joseph Green, who had introduced the bill, made a speech denouncing it. His "somersault" won him the derisive nickname, "the Dallas County acrobat." Selma's two other representatives, J. W. Lapsley and Sam Will John, stood by the bill; Sam Will, whose sister Mary Amelia had been one of the founders of Selma's suffrage organization, made an eloquent speech in support of the bill, but it was to no avail. The bill fell short of the two-thirds majority vote needed for passage.

The ladies did not give up. They simply reset their sights on the 1919 meeting of the legislature. At the next Alabama Equal Suffrage Association convention, on February 12, 1916, Mrs. Carrie McCord Parke (1862–1939), daughter of one of Selma's pioneer families and wife of a wealthy merchant, was chosen president and announced plans to move the state headquarters to her home city of Selma. Mrs. Parke proved a formidable spokeswoman for the group.

The forces opposed to suffrage were also busy. Judge Evans had called on "the good women of Alabama to organize" in opposition to "this insidious attempt" to drag them into the corruption of politics. Now his sister-in-law, Nellie V. Baker, answered the call by agreeing to serve as president of the newly formed Alabama Association Opposed to Women Suffrage. According to the February 12, 1916, *Birmingham Age-Herald*, Baker was "one of the richest women in Selma," as well as a leader in the Daughters of the American Revolution. She was joined in her fight for "Home Rule, States' Rights and White Supremacy" by the widows of two delegates

FIGURE 6.7 Selma legislator Joseph W. Green; courtesy of Alabama Department of Archives and History, Montgomery, Alabama.

to the 1901 Constitutional Convention: Mrs. Eugenia Clay Burns, whose husband John had been strongly opposed to women's suffrage, and Mrs. Cola Barr Craig, whose husband Ben had fought valiantly to secure the vote for women.

During the years when Carrie Parke led the prosuffrage movement, one group after another—the Alabama Education Association, the Farmer's Union, and the Alabama Federation of Labor—fell in line to support female suffrage. In January 1918, Pres. Woodrow Wilson announced that the service provided by American women during the war made them fully entitled to vote.

The men of Dallas County, however, were not convinced. When legislative elections were held in August 1918, they elected a solidly antisuffrage delegation. Sam Will John, who had been an outstanding legislator for decades and an eloquent champion for women's suffrage, was defeated for reelection, while Joseph W. Green was triumphantly returned to office. John Lapsley wisely chose not to run. When a former resident of Dallas County, US senator Kenneth D. McKellar (D-Tennessee), joined President Wilson in endorsing suffrage, Judge Evans was so outraged that he

FIGURE 6.8 Selma legislator Sam Will John; courtesy of Alabama Department of Archives and History, Montgomery, Alabama.

sent McKellar a telegram: "The people of Dallas County Alabama, especially the women, regard you as their Judas Iscariot." Evans went on to explain that "they are unalterably opposed to letting an inferior race participate in the election of their officers or in the making of their laws" (*Selma Journal*, September 9, 1918). Selma insurance agent Martin L. Calhoun shared Evans's passionate opposition to women's suffrage, making speech after speech and writing letter after letter to rally the Black Belt against this nefarious Yankee plot to degrade southern womanhood.

On June 5, 1919, Congress approved the Nineteenth Amendment (also referred to as "the Susan B. Anthony Amendment") giving women the vote and sent it to the states for ratification. When the amendment was presented to the Alabama legislature in July 1919, J. W. Green led the opposition in the house, and Dallas County's James B. Ellis did the same in the senate. Ellis (1862–1934) was a native of Orrville and president of the Union Iron Works. He was a particularly effective leader, and his parliamentary expertise led to his later selection as president of the state senate.

When Carrie Parke was allowed to state her case to the legislature on July 16, she said: "We feel we are your equals, and we want our right to vote to count at the polls. Women have been too long treated as irresponsible children, and now they want to share in the things that are going on." Her pleas were in vain, and both houses of the legislature rejected the amendment by a decisive margin: 60 to 31 in the house, and 19 to 13 in the senate.

The *Selma Journal* showed where its sympathies lay by reporting Parke's and other prosuffrage speeches in ordinary type, and the antisuffrage ones, made principally by women from Montgomery, in large, bold type. (One of the leading antisuffragists was Selma's Cola Barr Craig, who was then serving as vice president of the Southern Women's League for the Rejection of the Susan B. Anthony Amendment.) The *Selma Times*, which supported suffrage, calmly noted that the Nineteenth Amendment, giving women the vote, had already been passed by Congress, approved by numbers of states, and would be the law of the land within a year. The *Selma Times* was right and, in November 1920, the women of Selma voted for the first time.

In 1922, women in Birmingham and Mobile tried to gain seats in the legislature but were defeated. In Selma, however, Harriet Hooker Wilkins ran for the Alabama House of Representatives against Joseph Green and won. Mrs. Wilkins (1875–1949) was a graduate of Peabody College, had taught for three years prior to her marriage to the president of American Candy, and was an active supporter of women's suffrage. At election time, Green carried the county boxes, but Mrs. Wilkins's four hundred–vote margin in Selma gave her the distinction of becoming the first woman ever to serve in the Alabama legislature.

Mrs. Wilkins served only one term before stepping down. By then Joseph Green had made peace with the ladies of Selma, and the "Dallas County acrobat" landed on his feet once again, taking Mrs. Wilkins's place in Montgomery. In 1928, the unity of the women's movement was shattered by conflict between the Women's Christian Temperance Union (WCTU), which bolted the Democratic Party in protest over the nomination of Al Smith, and the League of Women Voters, which supported Smith. The old suffragists were in such disarray that the task of heading the Democratic Women's Club of Dallas County was entrusted to Cola Barr Craig, formerly a fierce opponent of female suffrage.

Twenty years passed before another woman succeeded in being elected to the legislature, and it was 1980 before Rita Sims Franklin became the first woman elected to the Selma City Council. However, one strong suffrage leader, Mary Howard Raiford (1876–1959), played an influential part in state politics for decades. When Selma's two papers merged in 1920, Mary Raiford and her husband, Frazier Titus Raiford, assumed the responsibility for the *Selma Times-Journal* and, together, ran

FIGURE 6.9 Harriet Hooker Wilkins, the first woman elected to the Alabama legislature; courtesy of Alabama Department of Archives and History, Montgomery, Alabama.

it until Frazier's death in 1936. Mrs. Raiford, the only female publisher in Alabama, continued to direct the paper alone for twenty-three years longer.

Ironically enough, it was Joe Green's grandson, Selma lawyer Cecil Jackson, who became chief of staff for Alabama's first female governor, Lurleen Wallace.

Politics, Prohibition, and the Klan

Selma was also of two minds about Prohibition, and its division was reflected in the attitudes taken by its two daily newspapers, the *Selma Journal* (founded 1890) and the *Selma Times*. The *Journal* strongly supported Prohibition, sharply criticizing the *Times*'s insistence that the issue was not one of morals but of business. If Birmingham, Mobile, and Montgomery allowed alcohol to be sold within their city limits, the *Times* felt that Selma had to meet the competition by doing the same.

When the issue came before Alabama legislature in 1911, Dallas County's delegation split down the middle; while Sen. Victor B. Atkins and Rep. A. D. Pitts both voted for local option, Joseph W. Green and Samuel A. Fowlkes voted to make the

FIGURE 6.10 The Klan's showmanship and its "100 percent Americanism" won it a national following in the 1920s; courtesy of Alabama Department of Archives and History, Montgomery, Alabama.

whole state "bone dry." The dries lost that vote, but when the next legislature met in 1915, Benjamin F. Ellis of Orrville had replaced Atkins as senator, and the county delegation had a "dry" majority; J. W. Lapsley was the only holdout. By 1919 Dallas's delegation was unanimous in its support for Prohibition. When the US Congress passed the Eighteenth Amendment establishing nationwide Prohibition, Joe Green introduced the joint resolution ratifying the amendment, which the Alabama legislature passed almost immediately.

The dispute over Prohibition came at a time when racial and religious tensions were on the rise dramatically across the nation. The Ku Klux Klan had been revived in 1915 but did not become a major force until after the close of World War I. The war had made many Americans distrustful of anything "foreign" and anyone who could be portrayed as less than "100 percent American;" and the movie *Birth of a Nation* made the Klan seem glamorous and attractive. In 1919 there was a wave of lynchings and riots across the country. The new Klan held as much animosity for Catholics and Jews as it did for blacks. Many rural Protestants were so uneasy about changes in the United States that their support for national Prohibition, imposed by the Eighteenth Amendment, was based partly on their fear that urban corruption and immorality were causing America to "lose its soul." Their fears made such people susceptible to the Klan's warning against the "Catholic menace," and the Klan quickly won a national following, which, among other things, allowed them

FIGURE 6.11 Rep. William B. Craig launched the drive to keep the Klan out of Selma in 1923; courtesy of Selma–Dallas County Museum of History and Archives, Selma, Alabama.

to influence the election of a governor in Indiana and have Catholic schools outlawed in Oregon.

In fact, most Selmians regarded the Klan's crusade to impose Protestant morality by terror and the lash with a cold eye. The notion of excluding Jews from the new country club or Catholics from the new YMCA building struck them as ludicrous. They were amused by the convent inspection bill passed by the Alabama legislature in 1919, marveling that anyone might think the Sisters of Mercy were torturing Protestants in a secret dungeon under their convent on Broad Street. "There's no room for bigotry in America," said the *Selma Times-Journal*. "Let's laugh the Ku Klux Klan out of America," William B. Craig urged the members of Kiwanis on January 10, 1923 (*Selma Times-Journal*).

Later all four of the city's civic clubs joined with the American Legion (G. Claiborne Blanton, commander), the Selma Bar (Edmund W. Pettus, president), and the Selma Medical Association in issuing a "Statement in Opposition to a Ku Klux Klan in Selma," which ran as a full-page advertisement in the May 18, 1923, issue of the *Selma*

Times-Journal. The paper followed up with a May 20 editorial proclaiming, "Selma has no room within her confines for that ugly, malevolent institution of the devil known as Ku Kluxism, and her citizenship has risen almost as one man to speak in thunder tones against this nursery of suspicion and hate gaining a foothold in her midst." By May 29, the Selma City Council had passed an ordinance prohibiting the wearing of masks, clearly aimed at the Klan.

The Klan's supporters responded indignantly that their enemies were fuddy-duddies who were holding back civic progress. By December a "provisional" chapter of the Klan had been organized in Dallas County. On September 14, 1924, the *Times-Journal* was forced to report that the Klan had initiated two hundred new members in a ceremony on Orrville Road. The minister who presided bragged that the Klan consisted solely of native-born white Protestants who were "100 percent American." The *Times-Journal* account closed with the acid observation that surely the speaker did not think "that the 9,000 young Americans, who themselves or their fathers were foreign born, and who now sleep in Flanders fields, having given their lives as a sacrifice for their country, were not '100 percent American.'"

By 1926 the Klan was at the height of its influence in Alabama, having succeeded in electing two of its members to high office: Gov. Bibb Graves and US Senator Hugo Black. Alabama's other senator, Tom Heflin, already had a national reputation for his opposition to education for blacks, female suffrage, and the Catholic Church. With sublime arrogance, the head of the Alabama Klan actually considered attacking the American Legion for not being "100 percent American" after the legion chose Moritz Frohlich, a Jewish lawyer from Selma, as Alabama's representative on the national executive committee.

The Klan's hour of power was to prove brief. The *Selma Times-Journal* and the *Montgomery Advertiser* joined in pointing out the many atrocities committed by hoodlums wearing hoods. When some readers protested that the papers were ruining Alabama's public image, the *Times-Journal* responded in a November 28 editorial that the scandal came from "the acts of the hooded mob at war with all constituted authority and not from the publicity and exploitation growing out of this lawless activity." By December 2, 1927, the *Times-Journal* thought it saw signs of "The Gradual Extinction of the Klan." The paper's only fear was that "the Klan will experience a new birth of enthusiasm and enlist many new members if Al Smith should be given the democratic nomination for the presidency."

The *Times-Journal* opposed Gov. Bibb Graves for his association with the Klan. Along with many conservative Selmians, it also criticized his economic policies in general and in particular his proposed $20 million bond issue for education. After the legislature submitted the bond issue to a vote of the people, businessman Ernest

FIGURE 6.12 Rev. Edward Gamble served as pastor of St. Paul's Episcopal from 1903–37; courtesy of St. Paul's Episcopal Church, Selma, Alabama.

Lamar, lawyer Hugh Mallory, and banker E. Carlisle Melvin organized the opposition. Mallory founded the Alabama Taxpayer Defense League, which warned that such a bond issue would inevitably mean higher taxes. Lamar and Melvin, who both served on the Selma School Board, made it clear that the schools of Selma were unlikely to benefit from the bond issue. When the referendum was held in January 1928, Dallas County and the state voted it down by an overwhelming margin.

The paper's fears proved prophetic. The Democrats did nominate the governor of New York for president. It was bad enough that Smith was a devout Catholic; the fact that he was also an ardent critic of Prohibition, came from New York City and had long been associated with the city's political machine, Tammany Hall, made him anathema to many southern Protestants.

To many of Selma's most progressive Protestants, the problem with Smith was not his faith but his lack of support for Prohibition. Rev. Gamble was the president of Selma's interracial committee, but he was also vice president of the Alabama Anti-Saloon League. On August 24, Gamble sounded the alarm that Prohibition was in danger. At a gathering of Masons from central Alabama, he called on his fellow

FIGURE 6.13 Ed Pettus rallied the loyalists in support of Al Smith; courtesy of Alabama Department of Archives and History, Montgomery, Alabama.

Masons to vote against Smith. Forget about the race issue for now, he said; we can vote Republican this once without endangering white supremacy!

On September 7, Selma dentist W. E. Allen presided over the public meeting called to organize "the anti-Smith Club of Dallas County." The principal speaker was Judge Hugh Locke, a Klansman from Birmingham. Ernest Lamar, a leading Baptist layman, drew up the resolutions opposing Smith's candidacy and Martin L. Calhoun was elected treasurer.

Other Selma Democrats rallied to their party's banner during this crisis. Selma lawyer Edmund Winston Pettus (1884–1945), son of Frank L. Pettus and grandson of General Pettus, was chairman of the state Democratic Executive Committee. He and other Black Belt leaders like Hugh Mallory of Selma, Lister Hill of Montgomery, and Judge Benjamin Meek Miller of Wilcox County worked feverishly to hold Alabama in line for Smith. Mallory and Miller were both staunch "dries" whose loyalty to the Democrats outweighed their support for Prohibition. Mallory's status as a member of the "First Family of Alabama Baptists" gave him the credibility to assure Alabama Christians that God had created the Democratic Party to maintain white supremacy.

The *Selma Times-Journal* printed editorial after editorial denouncing the anti-Catholic slander being spread by Heflin and the Klan. On September 8, 1928, for example, the paper lashed out at "those Poison-Spreaders who are gumshoeing through our rural communities with their bogus Knights of Columbus oath and other scurrilous propaganda to fan the prejudices of the unintelligent." (The oath in question, which appears in *Congressional Record*, supposedly bound all members of the Knights, a Catholic men's organization, to "make and wage relentless war against all heretics, Protestants and Masons . . . to extirpate them from the face of the earth.")

Four of Dallas County's rural precincts did go Republican, but Selma went for Smith, 1,347 to 431, and the county as a whole provided the Democrats with an eight hundred–vote margin, enabling them to carry the state for Smith. Alabama was one of only six southern states that stood out against the national landslide for the Republican Party candidate Herbert Hoover.

The coming of the Great Depression in 1929 proved a severe blow to Hoover's Alabama supporters, to the Klan, and to Prohibition. In 1930, Pettus and other loyal Democrats blocked Heflin and other "Hoovercrats" from running in the party primary. In addition, they supported Judge Miller, a Smith supporter and a noted foe of lynching and the Klan, for governor. Miller's campaign was managed by Judge Sam Hobbs of Selma and enthusiastically supported by the *Selma Times-Journal*. The "Hoovercrats" (or "Jeffersonian Democrats," as they preferred to call themselves) bolted the party once more to support Heflin for the Senate and Judge Locke for governor; but both their candidates lost Dallas County and the state by a solid margin, signaling that the Klan's glory days were over.

Samuel Francis Hobbs (1887–1952), Miller's campaign manager, moved on to national prominence. A graduate of Vanderbilt and the Alabama School of Law, he had served as judge of the Fourth Judicial Circuit from 1921 to 1926. In 1931 he was appointed by President Hoover to chair a commission studying the Muscle Shoals project, which later became the Tennessee Valley Authority (TVA). Two years later, Pres. Franklin D. Roosevelt asked him to serve as chairman of Alabama's National Recovery Administration (NRA) committee. In 1934, Hobbs ran for the US House against five-term congressman Lamar Jeffers of Anniston. The *Anniston Times* endorsed Hobbs, explaining that "the interests of the Democratic Party and the nation will be better served though election of a Congressman who is wholly in accord with President Roosevelt and the New Deal" (reprinted in the March 4, 1934, *Times-Journal*). Hobbs won election to the US House of Representatives, becoming

FIGURE 6.14 Rep. Samuel F. Hobbs represented Selma in the US House from 1934 to 1950; courtesy of the Hobbs family.

the eighth Selmian to serve in that body. His sixteen-year tenure was longer than that of any predecessor.

During his first term, Congressman Hobbs's judicial background won him the dubious honor of managing the impeachment of a federal judge in south Florida. In all US history to that point, Congress had removed only three federal judges from office. Following Hobbs's skillful presentation of the evidence, the US Senate voted 56 to 28 for conviction.

Hobbs continued to distinguish himself in Congress. He later broke with President Roosevelt on a number of issues, but he always made sure that Selma got its share of federal funds. The Edmund Pettus Bridge, A. G. Parrish High School, now Selma High, and the Colored Community Center, now the George Wilson Building, stand as reminders of Hobbs's continuing interest in his hometown.

Prohibition's days were also numbered, though its supporters kept fighting with all their strength. After Pres. Franklin D. Roosevelt called for special state conventions to consider the Twenty-First Amendment (which essentially repealed the Eighteenth Amendment establishing national Prohibition), Dallas County "wets" fielded a ticket headed by V. B. Atkins Jr. (whose father the mayor had been a staunch opponent of Prohibition), and on July 18, 1933, the Atkins ticket carried the county by 1,450 votes to 750—almost a two-thirds margin.

Even though national Prohibition was repealed in 1933, it was four years after that before Alabama counties were allowed the option of deciding whether or not to legalize alcoholic beverages within their own boundaries. Dallas County's "dries" did their best to keep the county dry. One of Dallas County's legislators, Reuben Hamner (a native of Northport who had previously served as sheriff of Dallas County) spoke for the "dries" when he thundered, "The only things that can come from liquor are money and hell. It will bring only poverty, destruction and misery." His fellow representatives James A. Hare Jr. and George P. Quarles must have disagreed since they both voted for local option. Dallas County finally had the opportunity to vote itself "wet" on March 10, 1937. The WCTU held a prayer vigil at First Baptist Church on Lauderdale all that day, but in vain. The county voted in alcohol 1,362 to 964, and Selmians have been downing their legal drinks ever since.

Church, School, and Hospital "Between the Wars"

Shortly after the close of World War I, a man who was to emerge as one of Selma's outstanding youth workers, Paul M. Grist (1899–1982), arrived in Selma.

Grist, a native of Atlanta, came to Selma as physical director of the YMCA in 1919. He brought about a dramatic increase in Y membership, going into the schools to teach the importance of regular exercise and initiating a summer program at the camp he established on Mulberry Creek. In 1925, a new YMCA building was erected at the corner of Broad and Furniss. In 1934, he took over the directorship of the entire YMCA program and continued in that position for thirty years. His wife, "Miss Tiny," served as camp dietitian for most of that time and his brother-in-law Clifford Morrison served as the Y's receptionist. "Son, don't wait to be a great man," he counseled generations of youngsters. "Be a great boy!" Grist's devotion to "his" boys became legendary in the area, and a number of them, including Auburn coach Ralph "Shug" Jordan, went on to win state and national recognition as athletes or coaches.

Three of Selma's four private hospitals—the King Sanatorium, the Union Street Private Hospital, and Burwell Infirmary—underwent significant changes during the years between the two World Wars. (The DuBose Sanitarium had already transformed itself into the Vaughan Memorial Hospital back in 1911.)

After Dr. Goldsby King died in 1920, Dr. Marcus Skinner and Dr. P. B. Moss

FIGURE 6.15 Paul M. Grist with YMCA team; courtesy of the Selma–Dallas YMCA.

assumed the administration of the sanitarium, which they renamed the King Memorial Hospital. Dr. Skinner won statewide recognition for his work with crippled children. King Memorial Hospital was an important part of Selma's medical community until Skinner's retirement in 1953.

In 1921, Selma beat out Birmingham to become the site chosen by the Alabama Baptist Convention for the erection of a state hospital. The city offered a site and an investment of $80 million, an offer the convention apparently could not refuse. In 1922, the Alabama Baptist Convention opened two new hospitals in Selma. The Alabama Baptist Hospital on River Avenue, housed in what later became the Department of Human Resources building, received white patients from the Union Street physicians group, whose black patients were taken to Good Samaritan Hospital on Voeglin Avenue, in what was the former home of dentist H. S. Sullivan. Thus, Selma became one of a few Alabama towns with two black hospitals—Good Samaritan and the Burwell Infirmary. Nurse Mamie Norris, a graduate of Tuskegee Institute, presided over "Good Sam" for twenty-two years until World War II, when its administration was assumed by a Catholic religious order. Dr. Burwell's head nurse Minnie Anderson took over the Burwell Infirmary after his death in 1928 and ran it for decades with her husband Marius J. Anderson, a funeral director.

Selma gained not only two Baptist hospitals in 1922 but also a Lutheran college.

FIGURE 6.16 The original Good Samaritan Hospital; courtesy of the Edmundite Missions.

Lutheran missionaries had come to the Black Belt in 1916, in response to an appeal from Wilcox County teacher Rosa Young.

Young (1890–1971), a graduate of Selma's Payne Institute, had appealed to Booker T. Washington for help after her own denomination failed to help her. Washington suggested she apply to the Lutherans, who were doing good work among the black residents of New Orleans. The Lutherans responded to her appeal by launching an apostolate in Wilcox. Since many of the Lutheran clergy were of German descent, they were met with suspicion from the authorities. It took Rosa Young's producing the letter from Booker T. to satisfy the authorities that they were not dealing with spies for Kaiser Wilhelm.

After establishing a number of parishes in Wilcox, the Lutherans saw the need for a college. On November 13, 1922, the Lutherans opened Alabama Lutheran Teachers Training School on First Avenue, with two teachers and ten pupils, all girls. Rosa Young served as matron. Three years later, the school moved to its present site on Green Street and became Alabama Luther College, providing a high school education that would prepare their graduates to serve as preachers, teachers, and missionaries in the Lutheran Church. By 1932, the school newspaper, the *Eagle Annual*, could boast, "We began with ten students, and now we have . . . about one hun-

FIGURE 6.17 Rosa Young, the "founder" of Concordia College; courtesy of Concordia College, Selma, Alabama.

dred and forty. We began with two classes, and now we have a four-year standard high school program, and a two-year normal as well as an elementary program." The elementary school was a separate entity under Trinity Lutheran Church. (Richard Dickinson's *Concordia College Selma: The Miracle on Green Street* [St. Louis, n.d.], 26). Rev. Robert O. Lynn served as the first president of the school, but Rosa Young (who served as matron) has come to be regarded as the true founder.

Selma thus gained a Lutheran college at a time when it was very close to losing its Methodist college. The AME had been unhappy about Payne Institute's location at least since 1918, when the state conference expressed concern about the Selma campus's "health conditions." In 1921 a rival AME college, Bethel University, was set up in Montgomery. By 1925 the conference resolved to close Bethel and move Payne's college program to Birmingham, leaving only the high school in Selma.

Selma's black citizens did acquire a new secondary school during this period. The Southern Presbyterians sponsored Ford Industrial School in Selma, which was administered by Rev. W. J. Bishop, the pastor of the Sylvan Street Presbyterian Church.

The US Department of the Interior had issued a lengthy report in 1916 that noted "while [Selma's] one public school for colored people is above the average in quality of work, it is entirely inadequate for the city, accommodating only about one-third of the children 6 to 14. The existence of three private schools, with elementary departments having an aggregate attendance of 1,196, has doubtless relieved the public officials of a proper feeling of responsibility for developing an adequate school system" ("Negro Education," Washington, DC, 1917, 2:43–44).

In the years that followed, the city erected several additions to Clark: a two-story annex in 1917 and a one-story brick building in 1921. And in 1922 it set up a branch in the East End, replacing Sophia Kingston's "Little Knox" with "Little Clark." But as late as 1929, more black Selmians were enrolled in private schools—Alabama Lutheran, Ford Industrial, Knox Academy, Payne University, and Selma University—than in Clark, the only public school provided for them. Clark had 1,300 students, Knox 700, Selma University 400, and Payne 350.

There were six public schools for white Selmians. They included not only Baker, Byrd, Dallas Academy, and Francis Thomas but also the city's first high school on Tremont Street, which was erected in 1912; and its first junior high school on Washington Street, built in 1924. In addition, there was Sunset Village School, which had been built for the children of Sunset Mills's employees. Since the mill workers primarily attended Sunset Mills Methodist Church, they seemed to live in a world mostly apart from other Selma residents.

Depression and the New Deal

During the early twenties, Selma prospered and expanded under the leadership of Dr. William B. Hall (mayor, 1920–24) and Thomas (T. J.) Rowell (mayor, 1924–32). William Bonnell Hall (1866–1946), a native of Lowndes County, is remembered as "Selma's most educated mayor." He had served both as a physician at Bryce Hospital and as vice chancellor of the University of the South (better known as Sewanee) before moving to Selma in 1914. He was the first mayor elected to a four-year term, and he served only that term. It was during his term that Selma began expanding west of Valley Creek, acquiring the land that was to become new Live Oak Cemetery and Valley Creek Park (now Bloch Park).

When Hall announced his candidacy for mayor in 1920, neither of the city's major political factions cared to oppose him. Instead, the "People's party," consisting mainly of employees of the Southern Railway, and the "Democrats," consisting largely of businessmen, fought it out for seats on the city council. The Democrats succeeded in electing their entire ticket, including T. J. Rowell as president of the council.

Thomas Joseph (T.J.) Rowell (1871–1934), a native of Carlowville who founded a shoe store in Selma, succeeded Hall as mayor and carried on his programs. During his two terms in office Dallas Avenue was extended out to the County Club area and the city erected a baseball and athletic field in the Valley Creek Park, naming it Rowell Field in his honor. Rowell was reelected without opposition in 1928, along with most of the council.

One of the city fathers' major projects that year was raising money to build a "New Hotel to Outdo Anything of Its Kind in Any City in the State of Alabama." They envisioned a seven-story hotel to be erected at Washington and Dallas, to be christened "the Morgan-Pettus" (*Selma Times-Journal*, March 21, 1928). Their vision never came to pass. The stock market crashed the following year, and during the Great Depression that followed Selma found itself struggling to maintain the institutions it already had rather than striving to erect new ones.

When Mayor Rowell came up for reelection in 1932, the city was in debt. He was defeated for a third term by his president of the council, Lucien Burns, who called for "strict economy."

The Great Depression changed the lives of many Dallas County citizens, as it did people throughout the country. Selma's three banks survived, but the Bank of Orrville and sixty-two other Alabama banks were not able to weather the Depression. The jewelry store of Hobbs & McGill, which had survived the Civil War, went under during the Depression. Even worse, two of Selma's major employers, Alabama Textile Mills and Sunset Mills, both closed down, leaving hundreds of Selmians without jobs.

A restaurant sign from that era poignantly describes the situation in the city. It offers hot meals for a quarter, adding, "Come in & eat before we both starve." The earlier mentioned roadside sign proclaiming Selma the "fastest growing city in Alabama" fell to the ground and was never replaced.

One early effect of the Depression came from the Alabama Baptist Convention, which resolved at its 1930 convention "that the Baptist Hospital at Selma be closed not later than March 31, 1931, unless in the meantime it should have been leased or sold." In response to this crisis, a group of Selma doctors organized the Physicians and Surgeons Society (Eugene Callaway, president; Monroe Maas, vice president) on February 28, 1931, "for the purpose of operating without profit . . . hospitals for both white and colored in Selma, Dallas County, Alabama" (Dallas County Corporation Record, stored in Dallas County Court House, 5:484–85). The group leased the two hospitals for ten years, in hopes that it could eventually raise the money to buy them outright. (A. H. Reid, *The Baptists of Alabama*, Montgomery, AL, 1967)

Selmians rallied to face the Depression just as they had rallied to deal with the Great Flood of 1916. The February 12, 1931, *Times-Journal* provides a grim catalogue of the work being done by the Selma Relief Association:

FIGURE 6.18 Selma during the Depression; courtesy of Selma–Dallas County Museum of History and Archives, Selma, Alabama.

> During the month of January $1,177.25 was spent for relief among white families of Selma, and $1,005.21 among colored families of Selma and Dallas County. Food was issued during the month to 132 white families and work was provided for many white men who applied for food, with $350 paid out for wages for cutting wood at the city airport. A total of 727 negro families was cared for in city and county. Since January 23 the Red Cross has taken over the relief work among county negroes, and at present between 300 and 325 rations are being issued to negroes of Selma by the Selma Relief Association. The Association expects this number to continue to increase during the month of February.

The article noted that Rev. E. W. Gamble was in charge of relief for blacks, with able assistance from the Colored Relief Association headed by P. L. Lindsey of Selma University. Gamble stressed that "the colored employees of the Selma Manufacturing Company of which Mr. J. F. Ames is president, have authorized Mr. Ames to deduct ten cents of their wages each week to be given to the Selma Relief Association."

The city, the county, the local churches, and the local post of the American Legion were also making regular contributions. Isidore Kayser (1875–1951), a department store owner and one of the town's leading philanthropists, led the Selma Relief Association. He was named "First Citizen of Selma" that year and richly earned the title during the Depression.

Selma's well-to-do also came up with a new way of raising money to help the unfortunate with the founding of the Charity League in March 1931. The league held beauty contests and follies to raise money. In its first year, the league undertook to provide lunches for the students at Baker School.

The Charity League was not the only organization that stepped forward to provide school lunches to needy children. The school board's minutes, which are stored at the old Baker School, for June 9, 1932, provide a catalog of the church and civic groups involved:

> At the Frances Thomas School the Council of Jewish Women fed at least 100 children, (and) had taken care of the dental defects of approximately 70 children. . . . The Session of the Broad Street Presbyterian Church had furnished 2 gals. of milk at this same school. At the Baker School, the Charity League had fed about 50 children daily, the Broad Street Presbyterian Session furnished 2 gals. of milk per daily and the Rotary Club had furnished 1 and ½ gallons per day. At the Dallas Academy money to the amount of $195.50 had been furnished by the various religious organizations and by the American Legion to feed the under privileged children. At the Byrd School [St. Paul Episcopal's] Altar Guild furnished $40.00 for lunches for the underprivileged children.

Elsewhere we learn that the Missionary Society of Church Street Methodist was feeding the children at "the black school" (Clark).

Selma's public school system had to tighten its belt drastically in the face of a sharp drop in income. In May 1931, the city school board voted to cut teachers' salaries by 10 percent for the coming year. A year later, the board had to borrow from local banks to meet its payroll and was seriously discussing opening the schools for only four and a half months in 1932–33.

To make things even worse, Selma's religious schools began to falter under the impact of the Depression. Selma University's enrollment fell from 700 to 291 and the school had to sell property to raise the money to stay open. The Lutherans actually closed down their college department in Selma, reducing the school to junior high level. And on July 26, 1932, the leaders of the Selma School Board (Houston Armstrong, W. I. Bloch, Ernest Lamar, and A. G. Parrish) heard grim news from a delegation of black residents, led by W. J. Bishop, Rev. Solomon Kingston, Rev. C. T. Hayes, and Dr. N. D. Walker. The Reformed Presbyterians were closing down Knox's elementary section. The Southern Presbyterians were cutting back on their subsidy to Ford Industrial, and the school might not survive. The city needed to step forward to meet this crisis. Specifically, they pleaded "that the negro citizens

Figure 6.19 Gov. B. M. Miller led the fight for a state income tax; courtesy of Alabama Department of Archives and History, Montgomery, Alabama.

of the community be given a school on the north side of the Southern Railroad." The school board responded by approaching Payne Institute, which readily agreed to provide three classrooms rent-free to serve the black children of north Selma.

By January 1933, the board was telling its employees that their contracts would terminate on February 1. Fortunately, the city council loaned the schools $5,000 to help them finish the school year; but they could do so only by paying its employees in "certificates of indebtedness" (i.e., IOUs) instead of cash. By May even more cuts become necessary; black teachers' salaries were cut an average of 16.6 percent and white teachers' by an average of 21 percent. Superintendent Munro offered to take a 60 percent cut in his own salary, but the board refused his self-sacrificing offer and only reduced his pay by 40 percent. By this point things were so bad that even a staunch conservative like Governor Miller was campaigning for a state income tax to raise enough money to keep the schools open.

After Governor Miller came out for an income tax, Selma's conservative leaders hoped to repeat their earlier success in defeating Governor Graves's bond issue. On January 30, 1933, school board members E. Carlisle Melvin and Lamar called for a mass meeting in Selma to oppose the proposal and summoned the county's legislators to instruct them to vote "no." Lamar explained that the board had cut the Selma schools' budget by 40 percent and the state should follow their example. Sen. John W. Lapsley and Rep. John Morgan Burns both vowed to cut government spending rather than raise taxes. When state representative William P. Mollette showed up at the rally, however, he struck a different note. Much as he hated all taxes, Mollette could not bear to see the schools close. (The state senator from Wilcox, John Miller Bonner, had seriously proposed that Alabama close four of its colleges and sell the property.)

In the end, Burns joined Mollette in voting for a state referendum on the income tax amendment proposed by Governor Miller. Lapsley and Rep. Walter C. Givhan both voted against the referendum, but in vain. Lawyer Harry Gamble launched a local campaign in support of the tax. And when the vote came, Dallas County and the state voted for the tax.

To Paul Grist's distress, the YMCA almost lost its new building in 1934; Isidore Kayser took over as chairman of the Y's finance committee and succeeded in renegotiating its mortgage. The Selma Y suffered an additional blow when a 1938 flood destroyed Camp McGee.

In 1937 the Reformed Presbyterians found themselves unable to continue their support of Knox at all and offered to turn it over to the city school system. Once again the school board rose to the occasion, and Knox became the city's first black public high school, going as far as the tenth grade. For the first time in the city's history, education of black children would no longer be primarily dependent on the churches or northern charity.

Another missionary group arrived in 1937 for the sole purpose of ministering to the black people of Selma. The Fathers of St. Edmund, a community of Catholic priests and brothers from Vermont, were asked by the pope to undertake a special apostolate to black southerners, and they made Selma their base of operations. According to J. L. Chestnut, they were "the first whites who ever addressed my parents as Mr. and Mrs." (*Black in Selma*, 41). Some local whites suspected the fathers of being Communists, and a few black leaders scorned them as "white trash."

From their headquarters on Broad Street, the Edmundites moved out to found missions from Anniston to the Mobile Bay area. Like the Lutherans before them, they opened a school, St. Elizabeth's, in 1940, which was presided over by the Sisters of St. Joseph from Rochester, New York.

Money provided for public works by Roosevelt's New Deal became available for the erection of public buildings in the city. In 1936, the Works Progress Administration (WPA) allotted $81,000 for the construction of a new city hall and county

FIGURE 6.20 Mural from the old community center depicting the agriculture of the Deep South; courtesy of Selma–Dallas County Museum of History and Archives, Selma, Alabama.

jail for Selma. The city had to put up an additional $100,000. In 1937 plans to construct a new bridge across the Alabama River were announced. In 1939, a new high school for white students was constructed on Broad Street to replace the building on Tremont. The name Parrish High School was given the structure in honor of longtime president of the school board, Albert G. Parrish.

Parrish already had his first name affixed to the city's leading hotel, the Hotel Albert. The hotel had been started before the Civil War, but its final story was not completed until 1892, when Parrish spearheaded the drive to raise the funds needed.

In May 1940, the city celebrated the opening of the Edmund Pettus Bridge across the Alabama River. During that same year, a Colored Community Center was erected on Franklin Street. Black leaders, like assistant county agent Samuel W. Boynton and notary public Charles J. Adams, had long felt the need for a downtown building where the hundreds of black shoppers who crowded into Selma every Saturday could go to sit down or use a restroom. However, Adams and Boynton were both "race men," or militants, who were active in the Dallas County Voters League and, therefore, too controversial to win white support for a community center that would serve their race.

In 1938, Dr. E. W. Gamble of St. Paul's Episcopal Church agreed to "run interference" for the project. As a result, the city donated the land, the WPA provided $40,000 for construction, and a two-story building was erected on Franklin Street, which was then Selma's main thoroughfare for black residents. The building was erected by black labor working under black contractor George Wilson. This structure, located between Alabama and Water Avenues, had on its second floor murals depicting black life, which are a noteworthy example of 1930s art (the murals are now on display at the Old Depot Museum). One of the murals depicts black scientist George Washington Carver presenting the South with the peanut as a new cash crop—showing that the Cotton Kingdom was no longer the absolute monarchy it had once been.

On September 26, 1940, a group of black leaders approached the Selma School Board (Dr. E. A. Wilkinson, chairman) about a matter they considered more important than the new community center. "We, the negro citizens of Selma," said the Colored Civic League, "do appeal to the progressive white people of Selma and do petition the Selma School Board to provide an accredited high school for negroes in Selma and construct a building for a high school that will not be a constant hazard to the lives of the children." The school board did respond to the petition; but the new high school, like the new YMCA camp, would be pushed aside by the coming of the Second World War.

7

World War II and After

Selma, 1939–1963

In some respects, World War II had greater impact on Selma and Dallas County than any other conflict since the War between the States. In large part this was because, in 1941, an air force training base was established here. The base provided an enormous boost to the city's economy, making it possible for Selma to grow and to expand.

But the war also rekindled the Great Migration with black people leaving the farm more than ever, now that there were jobs in the cities once again. In 1930 black farmers cultivated over half of Dallas County's farmland; by 1950 the percentage had declined to 15 percent. Many moved inside the city limits; while only 15 percent of Dallas County's black population had lived in Selma in 1910, 43 percent did so in 1950. Frederick Douglass has said that town slaves were "half free," and black Selmians were now better educated, better organized, and more inclined to resent white supremacy. Others moved to the big cities of the North, taking jobs in defense industries and becoming part of the northern Democratic coalition.

World War II brought changes to Selma; the postwar years were to bring still more. The nation became more concerned about black rights. President Truman ordering the integration of the armed forces in 1948 meant that black pilots would ultimately be trained at Craig Air Force Base. Leading white citizens realized that the only way to preserve segregation was to provide facilities for the black population that were "equal" as well as separate. Selma's black residents finally were blessed with a new high school. The city became more prosperous, more urban, and a better place for black people to live. A religious revival that began during the war produced a Catholic hospital, athletic programs for black youth, and a brace of new

Figure 7.1 Mayor Lucien P. Burns; courtesy of Selma City Hall, Selma, Alabama.

churches. There was a sustained effort to make "separate but equal" less unequal. As J. Mills Thornton has pointed out, the number of registered black voters in Dallas County tripled between 1944 and 1954.

After the Supreme Court decision outlawing segregation in public schools, Selma whites began circling their wagons in defense of "the southern way of life." The city gave birth to Alabama's first Citizens' Council, also known as the White Citizens' Council, which used its economic power to clamp down hard on any signs of dissent. Black citizens began finding it much, much harder to register to vote; Dallas County's board of registrars approved only fourteen new black voters between 1954 and 1961.

The Acquiring of Craig Air Force Base

Mayor Lucien P. Burns and chamber of commerce official Harmon Hunt Frazier led the campaign to have Selma considered for the installation of Craig Air Force Base.

Burns (1889–1959) was a native of Selma who earned his bachelor's at Howard College (now Samford). After a year of postgraduate study at Washington and Lee,

FIGURE 7.2 Chamber of commerce manager Harmon Hunt Frazier; courtesy of the Selma–Dallas County Chamber of Commerce.

he came home to join his father in the wholesale grocery business. First elected to the City Council in 1916, he moved up to Council President in 1924 and to mayor in 1932. He was to win reelection as mayor four consecutive times, serving longer that any of Selma's previous mayors.

Frazier (1893–1947) was a native of Elmore County who had been a teacher at Marion Military Institute (MMI) before he became manager of Selma's chamber of commerce in 1923. His success at the chamber paved the way for his election to the Alabama legislature in 1943.

By Frazier's own account, the intimate friendship he formed with MMI's commandant of cadets, Gen. Walter B. Weaver, helped open the doors for Selma to be chosen as a site. When Weaver later became the officer in charge of locating sites for possible airfields in the southeastern United States, he listened sympathetically to Frazier's argument that Dallas County offered "an ideal tract" for pilot training. The tract he had in mind was located about four miles southeast of Selma, adjacent to the Western of Alabama Railroad and near Highway 80. It was ideal because of its "soil and topography, that it was a turtle-back plateau and would drain perfectly." As Frazer tells the story in a later interview,

> Early one Saturday morning . . . General Weaver called me and said he was leaving for Washington Sunday and wanted a statement from the City Fathers that they would give the property to the Government if the Government would put an airfield on it. We called in the City Council and the Chamber of Commerce on Saturday afternoon, and Sunday morning the Mayor and I carried a letter from the City saying they would donate the property. The Mayor and I left Sunday afternoon for Washington to meet General Weaver there to assist in any way we could. It took the entire week to get the approval of the Chief of Air Corps and the War Department. Friday at noon we were advised by telephone from General Weaver that the matter was settled for Selma. (Interview with Harmon Hunt Frazier, October 4, 1943, on file at Craig Field Museum)

The mayor promptly called the *Selma Times-Journal*, which rushed into print with the news, "Selma has been approved by the Air Corps and the general staff of the United States Army for an Air Corps Pursuit Training School with an original personnel of 300 officers and 800 men" (June 21, 1940).

The city purchased two thousand acres of agricultural land from four white and four black property owners for $140,000 and then leased them to the government for a dollar a year. On August 4, 120 men from the Sixty-Seventh Group Detachment arrived to establish "Selma Army Air Base," and by August 15 construction had begun on what was later to become almost 175 acres of runways, taxiways, parking aprons, and other things necessary for an air base. Construction of the base began on August 10, 1940, and eight months later it began operations. The first class of sixty cadets arrived in time to hear Mayor Burns proclaim May 29, 1941, "Flying Cadet Day."

Five days after "Flying Cadet Day," Selma native Bruce Kilpatrick Craig (1914–41) was killed when the bomber on which he served as test engineer crashed at San Diego, California. Craig had already earned his wings by the time he graduated from Selma High in 1931. He earned his bachelor's in aeronautics from Georgia Tech in 1935 and enrolled in the Infantry Reserve. Craig had applied for a commission in the army air force before the crash, and he was named "lieutenant" posthumously. The plane he was testing was meant for the British, who were already at war with Nazi Germany.

To the *Times-Journal*, Craig "gave his life for the preservation of democracy and its ideals just as surely as if he had been shot down by an enemy raider or had been felled by a bullet upon the field of battle" (July 23, 1941). Thus it seemed appropriate that the new training school in Craig's hometown should be named in his honor.

Bruce Craig had been one of "Grist's Boys," who had a close relationship with the YMCA director. He was not the last of Grist's boys to perish in the war; fifteen more would perish in the service of their country before the war was over. Thus, the

FIGURE 7.3 Col. Victor B. Dixon, first commanding officer at Craig Field, raises the flag over the tent city that would later become Craig Army Air Force Base; courtesy of Selma–Dallas County Museum of History and Archives, Selma, Alabama.

FIGURE 7.4 Lt. Bruce K. Craig; courtesy of the Craig Field Museum, Selma, Alabama.

city that had once been the Arsenal of the Confederacy became a training school for the Allies. Between 1941 and 1945, Craig trained some 11,402 pilots—6,000 Americans, 4,000 French, 1,392 English, and 10 Dutch. A housing development built next to Craig Field was named Nathan Bedford Forrest Homes in recognition of Selma's Civil War defender.

Selma in World War II

Within a month the Dallas County United Services Organization (USO) had launched a drive to raise the money to set up a recreation center for the soldiers to be trained at Craig. The new Colored Community Center was quickly adapted for use by African American soldiers and sailors, and the old YMCA was converted into a USO for white members of the armed forces under the direction of Paul Grist and Mrs. Helen Anderson (1896–1963).

According to Jean Thompson Martin, the curator of the Old Depot Museum, the cadets made a big impression on the young women of Selma. "They all had convertibles and crewcuts and dark tans, and they all wore those wraparound sunglasses," she recalls. "We stood on Broad Street and watched them come over the bridge in their convertibles. It was very exciting" ("Alabama's Airfields," *Alabama Heritage*, Summer 2010, 30).

Craig Field had been in operation only a few months when war came in earnest. Following the attack on Pearl Harbor by the Japanese Air Force, Selma's sons and daughters once again went off to fight and, once again, there was an early death that brought home the tragic loss of life that comes with any war. On June 24, 1942, Selma learned that Lt. Leonard Wilson Thornhill, USN, was missing after his plane went down during the Battle of the Coral Sea. Thornhill (1915–42) had been president of the senior class at Selma High School, a camp leader for the YMCA, and a youth leader at First Presbyterian. He graduated from Annapolis in 1938 and was commissioned in the navy. He maintained close ties with his friends in Selma. Wilson (as most people called him) was serving on the USS *Lexington* when the airship carrier became engaged in the Battle of the Coral Sea. The *Times-Journal* printed his last letter to his widowed mother: "Mother, if anything happens to me, I hope you will be happy and proud to know that my life was not in vain—it was given for a purpose as worthy as any I can conceive of. However, I believe that a thousand shall fall at my side, and ten thousand at my right hand, but it shall not come nigh me, if God so will it. All my love, Wilson." In many respects the Second World War recalled the First. Once again Selma's sons in the Alabama National Guard were already in uniform when fighting broke out, having been called up November 26, 1940.

Once again ministers followed their parishioners and doctors their patients into

FIGURE 7.5 The Rotary Club of Selma's success in raising money for the war effort was rewarded by having its name on a plane; courtesy of Selma–Dallas County Museum of History and Archives, Selma, Alabama.

the service. Rev. Freeman B. Parker of Alabama Avenue Presbyterian was the first Selma clergyman to be called up (May 6, 1942 *Selma Times-Journal*); but there were others to follow, including Selma's lone rabbi, Samson Levey, who took a leave of absence from Temple Mishkan Israel to serve. Dr. Josiah H. Smith, later to be chief of staff at Vaughan Memorial, was one of several doctors who enlisted in the army medical corps.

Once again Selmians pulled together in civilian defense. Rev. Josiah T. Mangum (1887–1947), a retired Methodist minister, was appointed chairman of the Dallas County Defense Council. Lawyer Harry W. Gamble served as chairman of the Alabama War Chest for five counties; timber man Lloyd W. Morgan headed up the drive among the county's white community, with grocer Mark Thomas leading the campaign among the black population. The Rotary Club of Selma raised so much money for the war effort that it had its name painted on the fuselage of a fighter jet.

Even the school children joined in the war effort. Selma Junior High collected

FIGURE 7.6 2nd Lt. Kitty Driskell Barber; courtesy of Selma–Dallas County Museum of History and Archives, Selma, Alabama.

so much scrap metal (persuading the county to donate the old Cahawba Bridge, the Clarence Agee Bus Company to donate an old bus, and the railroad to donate a locomotive and some track) that it was allowed both to name the Liberty Ship being built in Mobile (the USN *William C. Gorgas*) and the student who would christen the ship (fourteen-year-old Betty Rives Allen, who had spearheaded the drive) on January 4, 1943.

Another Selmian, Gertrude Carlisle Bailey, went to Kearney, New Jersey, in October 1943 for the launching of the destroyer USS *Melvin*, named after her great uncle, John Tillman Melvin, the first naval officer to die in World War I. Within a year the Melvin family was to lose another member, also named John Tillman Melvin (1924–44), who drowned in a freak accident in September 1944 when his plane crashed and his parachute landed him in a lake.

Once again Selma's daughters followed the troops as nurses; this time, one of them was to perish in the struggle. Kitty Driskell (1919–1944) had trained at Touro School of Nursing in New Orleans and joined the army nursing corps two months before Pearl Harbor. Her first assignment brought her back to Selma to serve at Craig Field Hospital, where she met and married a soldier from Vermont named

FIGURE 7.7 Capt. Mac Ross of the "Tuskegee Airmen"; courtesy of Randy Williams.

Wendell Barber. Her second assignment was overseas; a month after her marriage, Kitty Barber was sent to Sardinia. She died in a plane crash in October 1944; hers is the only woman's name listed on the monument outside Memorial Stadium.

The women of Selma were serving not only as nurses but as members of the Women's Army Corps (WACs) and WAVES (Women Accepted for Voluntary Emergency Service) as well. Rosa Miller Hobbs, the congressman's daughter, was one of the city's first WACs and served as a recruiting agent. Future Selmian Frances Xavier served as a marine.

Black people also served their country in ways not permitted in World War I. Of course, their training for the army air force had to take place at a separate facility; work began on the Tuskegee Army Air Field on June 23, 1941. It was there that Dallas County native Mac Ross (1912–44) became one of the first black pilots to earn his wings and serve as one of the famous "Tuskegee Airmen." Ross's family had been part of the "Great Migration" to the north, settling in Dayton, Ohio, in the late 1920s. Ross graduated from West Virginia State College in 1940. In 1942 he

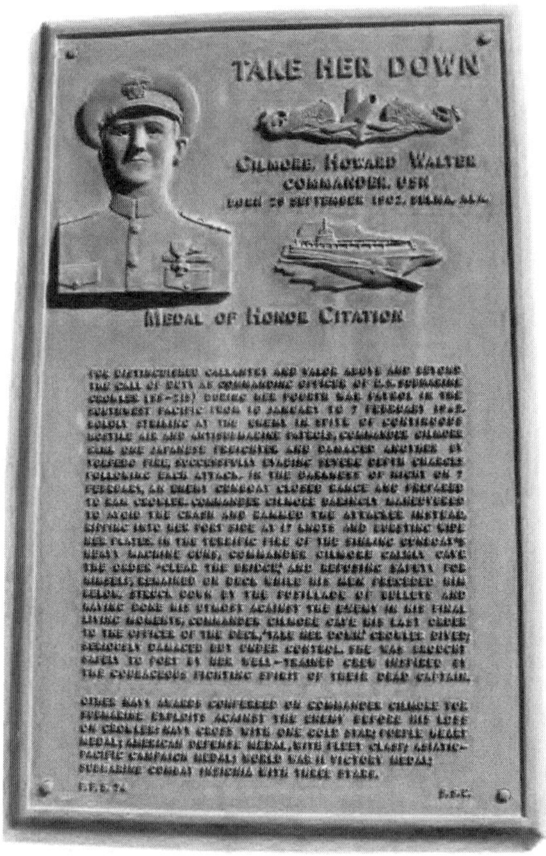

FIGURE 7.8 Monument to Comm. Howard K. Gilmore outside Selma's Memorial Stadium; courtesy of the author.

was commissioned a second lieutenant and named commanding officer of the One Hundredth Pursuit Squadron. The squadron was sent to Italy, where Ross (now a captain) flew fifty combat missions and earned a Distinguished Flying Cross before crashing and dying on July 10, 1944. His body lies in the American Cemetery in Nettuno, Italy, not far from that of Kitty Driskell Barber.

The most famous of Selma's casualties was Comm. Howard W. Gilmore. Gilmore (1906–43), a Selma native and an Annapolis graduate, was commander of the submarine, the USS *Growler*, which was on war patrol in the South Pacific during early 1943. What happened to him can best be told in the words of the Congressional Medal of Honor citation.

> In the darkness of night on 7 February, an enemy gunboat closed range and prepared to ram the Growler. Commander Gilmore daringly maneuvered to avoid the crash and rammed the attacker instead, ripping into her port side at 17 knots and bursting wide her plates. In the terrific fire from the sinking gun-

> boat's heavy machine guns, Commander Gilmore calmly gave the order "Clear the bridge," and refusing safety for himself remained on deck while his men preceded him below. Struck by the fusillade of bullets and having done his utmost against the enemy in his final living minutes, Commander Gilmore gave his last order to the officer of the deck, "Take her below." Growler dived; seriously damaged but under control, she was brought safely to port by her well trained crew inspired by the courageous fighting spirit of their dead captain.

Eighty-four other Dallas Countians perished during the war. In 1949, their names were inscribed on a monument outside Memorial Stadium, where they remain as a reminder of the sacrifice of some of the area's youths and their families. Originally there had been talk of separate monuments to honor the city's black and white soldiers who died in the war. In the end, however, Selma Post No. 20 of the American Legion (Sam O'Hara, commander) and Selma Post 3016 of the Veterans of Foreign Wars (Norborne Powell, commander) built one marker to honor the war dead of both races. Methodist minister Dr. John Frazer proudly noted as much at the dedication on November 11, 1949. "On this block of granite are the names of the heroic band of Dallas County men, both white and colored. Let it be known that here, in the Deep South, we honor them impartially. They were each and all true Americans. They each and all wore the uniform of their country. They each and all died defending our rights. They each and all will be remembered with sorrow and pride." However, the "colored" names are listed separately from the white ones.

Postwar Progress and Upheaval, 1944–1954

Frazer's speech exemplifies one of the changes that followed the war: a broadening of horizons that provided Selma's black residents with a greater place in the sun. The war itself brought about changes in Selma, and more changes followed its close. The changes included an expansion of church ministries, new medical and educational facilities for black citizens, and a growing rebellion against the national Democratic Party.

During and after the war, Selma enjoyed a revival of interest in religion. Under the leadership of Rev. John Davison, First Baptist Church began three missions, which quickly developed into West End Baptist Church (1943), Northside Baptist Church (1943), and Water Avenue Baptist Church (1945). In 1946, Central Baptist Church, which had originally been a mission of First Baptist, organized Selmont Baptist Church to serve people living south of the Alabama River. In 1952, members from First Baptist Church formed Elkdale Baptist Church, and Central Baptist Church encouraged some of its members to establish Fairview Baptist Church. Thus, the city gained five new Baptist congregations in less than fifteen years.

This same period saw a dramatic expansion of the Catholic presence in Selma's black community. In 1940 the Edmundites recruited the Sisters of St. Joseph from Rochester, New York, to set up a parochial school for black children; St. Elizabeth's School offered a first grade class that fall, and added a grade every year after that. The sisters were not content with merely teaching school; they also opened a library for Selma's black community (who were not allowed to darken the doors of the public library) and urged the Edmundites to do something about the sick poor of Selma. In 1943 the missions set up Holy Infant Inn, a nursing home for black people, on Union Street; and in 1944 they purchased Selma Good Samaritan from the doctors who owned Selma Baptist. In the years that followed, they began systematically converting the run-down facility into a modern hospital.

Two medical missionaries joined the staff of "Good Sam" in 1944—Dr. Isabel Dumont from Germany (1908–85) and Joan Mulder (1913–86) from the Netherlands. Dumont was a surgeon, Mulder an artist who doubled as a medical technician. The two women had been training in Birmingham for missionary work in Africa when they were recruited by the Edmundites. Their dedicated service to Selma's black community earned them a reputation for sanctity, a reputation they found amusing. "Actually, we're having fun," they insisted. When Miss Joan arrived at their office one morning in 1950 to find a sign warning, "THE K-K-K IS WATCHING YOU," she took out a pen, scribbled "Keep Watching!" on the sign, and went merrily to work. In the end the Klan left them alone.

Along with the religious revival, Selma's citizens manifested an increased humanitarian spirit. On July 6, 1944, YMCA general secretary Paul Grist and four Selma businessmen (accountant John Furniss, cotton broker Irving Hohenberg, merchant Isidore Kayser, and timber man Edgar Sheffield) met to organize the Community Chest of Selma and Dallas County. The Community Chest, with Irving Hohenberg as its first chairman, planned to raise money for eight organizations: the Salvation Army, YMCA, Boy Scouts, Girl Scouts, Crippled Children's Clinic, anticancer and antituberculosis groups, and the "Alabama War Chest." The Community Chest continued its work until 1952, when it dissolved itself after a series of unsuccessful campaigns. However, it was reborn two years later as the United Community Services of Selma and Dallas County, forerunner of the United Way program, with R. B. McKenzie serving as its first president. By this time, the concept of payroll deductions as a more effective way of raising money had been developed, and the organization continued to prove successful for many years.

The leading pastor in the black community during this period of time was Davis V. Jemison. He became pastor of Tabernacle Baptist Church in 1902, a position he held off and on for almost four decades. Jemison (1873–1954) was a zealous minister who "even preached in the pool rooms," and he quickly rose to prominence within

FIGURE 7.9 Medical missionaries Dr. Isabel Dumont and Joan Mulder with their first patient; courtesy of the Edmundite Missions.

his denomination. Beginning in 1917, he served as president of the Alabama Colored Baptist State Convention and, from 1941, was president of the National Baptist Convention as well. A staunch supporter of Selma University, he insisted on having the school shed its elementary division and focus on seeking accreditation for its college. The president of Selma University, Dr. W. H. Dinkins, opposed the change and resigned in 1950 rather than agree to it. In the year before his death, Jemison was elected as vice president of the Baptist World Alliance. Dr. Jemison's son, native Selmian Theodore Jemison, later helped to found the Southern Christian Leadership Conference (SCLC) in 1957 and won election to his father's former post as president of the National Baptist Convention in 1982. J. L. Chestnut's *Black in Selma* notes Jemison's conservatism and contrasts it with the outlook of two outstanding clergymen who began working among Selma's black youth during the war years and soon thereafter.

FIGURE 7.10 The logo of the Don Bosco Boys Club; courtesy of the Edmundite Missions.

Rev. Claude C. Brown and Father Nelson B. Ziter were both struck by the lack of organized recreation for black youngsters at a time when most black schools and churches had no such programs and the YMCA was all white. The Edmundites had attempted to set up a "savings and athletic club" for young males as early as 1942, but it was not until Ziter's arrival in 1947 that their program really took hold. Ziter, (1920–2000), a short, bustling Lebanese American, had a devotion to youth not unlike Paul Grist's. He laid out a basketball court, set up a clubhouse, and founded the Don Bosco Boys Club (named after an Italian saint). Claude Brown (1912–75), a Selma native who took over as pastor of Reformed Presbyterian in 1942, responded by setting up the Ralph Bunche Club (named after an outstanding African American diplomat); the two clubs competed fiercely for years. (There was also a Don Bosco Girls Club under the tutelage of Joan Mulder, who designed the club's logo.) The Bunche Club was accepted as a branch of the YMCA in 1956 and ultimately became the Claude C. Brown Branch.

Ziter urged his "sons" to get college educations and arranged for them to receive scholarships at various Catholic colleges around the country. He lived to see several of his protégés make good: Moses B. Anderson Selma's first Catholic bishop; Ernest J. Harrell its first air force general; and Nathaniel Walker its first black judge since Reconstruction.

Brown also helped youngsters win admission to higher education but did not live long enough to see one of his protégés, George Evans, elected mayor of Selma.

FIGURE 7.11 Rev. Claude C. Brown and Louvenia Brown were pillars of Selma's black community; courtesy of the Reformed Presbyterian Church, Selma, Alabama.

Ziter left Selma for another assignment in 1961, returning ten years later to take on the challenging task of merging Selma's two Catholic parishes into one happy integrated family.

Claude C. Brown's influence was not limited to his own race or denomination. He was a Reformed Presbyterian but served on the Home Mission Board of the United Presbyterian Church and, for a time, supervised their schools in Wilcox County. According to J. L. Chestnut, Brown did more for Selma University than most Baptists. His wife, Louvenia Ransom Brown (1917–2011), served as head librarian at Hudson High and started libraries at Selma's other black public schools. The two of them both knew how to work with white people on behalf of their own.

In 1947 the Edmundites completed a two-story brick wing for Good Samaritan Hospital. In 1948, they set up St. Elizabeth's Library on Broad Street, to provide local black residents with a place they could check out books. In 1950, they opened the Good Samaritan Hospital School of Practical Nursing— the only school of its sort in Alabama open to black students. In that same year the fathers helped Edwin L. Moss start the Elks Credit Union, creating virtually the only financial institution in the city independent of white control. Moss (1915–2005) a veteran and graduate of Alabama State, was a staunch Methodist who served as head of the state Elks as well as production manager for the Edmundite Missions. He became a leading figure in Selma's black community.

Public education for black youth also began to improve in the years following the Depression. As late as 1930, Dallas County spent $51 a year on each white student, as opposed to $7 on each black one. By 1950, per capita expenditures had risen to $103 for white children and $58 for black ones. In Selma, the disproportion was less. By the 1940s, it was evident that the city's school board intended to make the "separate but equal" slogan less of a farce.

In 1946, a survey by the state board of education pronounced all of the city's black schools "should be abandoned" and that Knox in particular "is inadequate and unsafe for school use. . . . A new high school building consisting of approximately 22 classrooms and other auxiliary rooms should be constructed at the earliest practicable date" (*Report of a Partial Survey of the Selma City School System*, 15). In the following year, the school board asked the city council to float a three hundred thousand–dollar bond issue to improve the city's rundown schools, with the construction of a new high school for black students the top priority. (Knox Academy was rapidly deteriorating.) The council responded by voting for two bond issues—one for the schools and one to build a stadium and launch a citywide recreation program. In 1949, a four hundred thousand–dollar high school building was erected on Summerfield Road for black students. The new school, which was named for educator R. B. Hudson, generated a great deal of pride in the city.

Harris Wofford's "Preliminary Report on the Status of the Negro in Dallas County, Alabama" (Yale Law School paper, 1953) notes the various reasons offered for the change. One white leader asserted that the war had made more white people conscious of black needs. Black Selmians rejoiced that there were now some "real Christians" on the school board. Some whites felt that the initiatives taken by some "real Christians" who were not on the school board—the Edmundites—were having an impact. There were a few cynics, like "the Negro who pointed to the new city high school and said, 'That's what the Supreme Court did!'" (30). The Court was yet to attack segregation directly, but it had become increasingly insistent that "separate but equal" needed to be genuinely equal.

The school board had ambitious plans to erect two new schools, one to serve the new subdivisions recently annexed by the city and one to serve north Selma. But it took pains to match each new school for white students with another for black students. Thus in 1956, when the new Knox and Edgewood Elementary Schools were built, the school board stressed that the two buildings had "identical floor plans." And when Meadowview was built in 1961 to serve the white population living west of Valley Creek, a completely renovated East End Elementary was opened as well. Selma's black children, previously served by only one public school, now enjoyed four elementary schools, Clark, East End, Knox, and Payne, in addition to R .B. Hudson High School.

Less than a year after Hudson was opened, North Korean troops invaded South Korea and the United States found itself at war once more. Craig Air Force Base quickly assumed a dual role: conducting advanced single-engine pilot training both for US student pilots and those from allied nations and training both military and civilian flight instructors for duty at other flight schools around the United States. During the course of the war, Craig saw seven hundred American and Allied pilots earn their wings and more than four thousand airmen trained as flight instructors.

The December 5 *Selma Times-Journal* reported the "First Casualty from This City," Lt. Grady P. Mitchell. Mitchell, a native of Chattanooga, had joined the marines in 1944 while a student at the University of Alabama; he missed being sent to Okinawa by only three days. He survived World War II and spent some years working on a degree at the University of North Carolina before reenlisting. Mitchell took part in the Inchon landing, which turned the tide of the war, but perished himself during the fighting that followed.

Other deaths were to follow. But this war was not like World War II, which involved the whole community and ended in triumph. For one thing, it was technically not a war but a "police action" under the command of the United Nations.

Jeff Ratcliffe, a World War II vet who was recalled to duty as an army medic, spoke for many Selmians when he said, "I hated the term ["police action"]. It was to be a bloody war" (*Korea, As I Saw It as a Combat Medic*, 1.) As the *Times-Journal* later observed, "The rallies, parades, war bond efforts were apparently missing. . . . The American people had anticipated so long an end to the conflict in Korea that the truce itself is so much in the nature of an anticlimax and rejoicing is restrained" (July 28, 1953). One of the last prisoners of war to be released by the Communists was Selmian Lt. Jack Taylor. Taylor, a veteran of World War II and an Auburn graduate, had been missing since May 21, when his plane was shot down over North Korea.

The Korean conflict became "the Forgotten War," and thirty years passed before a monument was erected to Dallas County's dead from that struggle. Ratliffe said that the war had made him a pacifist; he still loved his country but would not take up arms again "until the enemy is about to cross Jones Creek [a stream flowing through West Selma]" (*Korea, As I Saw It as a Combat Medic*, 31).

The frustration generated by the Korean stalemate helped to solidify a political revolution against the national Democratic Party that had been slowly taking shape since the New Deal. Some leading Selmians, like Congressman Sam Hobbs

FIGURE 7.12 1st Lt. Jeff Ratcliffe served as a medic during the Korean War; courtesy of the Ratcliffe family.

(1887–1952) and *Times-Journal* managing editor Edward B. Field (1903–63), had been unhappy with the national Democrats ever since the late thirties. Hobbs had opposed President Roosevelt's 1937 proposal to "pack" the Supreme Court and protested against his support of labor unions. However, what had been rumblings of discontent under Roosevelt became open rebellion under Truman, whose adoption of a strong civil rights program in 1948 resulted in southwide indignation.

The Alabama Democratic Party was split by the controversy between "states' righters" and "loyalists," much as it had been split in the 1850s by the struggle between William Lowndes Yancey's "chivalry" and William Rufus King's "hunkers." Dallas County state representative Walter C. Givhan was one of the leading states' rights Democrats and Sen. Lister Hill served as chief of the loyalists.

Givhan (1902–76) was a native of Perry County and grew up in Marengo County. He was elected to the Alabama House from Dallas County in 1931, and again in 1943, 1947, and 1951. In 1954 he moved up to the Alabama Senate, where he served

FIGURE 7.13 "Dixiecrat" Walter C. Givhan represented Dallas County for thirty-eight years, first in the Alabama House and then in the Alabama Senate; courtesy of the Givhan family.

until his death, serving as a linchpin of the alliance between the Black Belt and the "Big Mules" of Birmingham and Mobile. He was dedicated to fighting integration and "Folsomism," the policies supported by Gov. Jim Folsom, both of which he saw as forms of Communism. Givhan represented the cause of Black Belt conservatism in the Alabama legislature with great skill and determination.

In 1948, Givhan and his allies won control of the Alabama delegation to the national convention in Philadelphia. When the convention approved a civil rights plank, most Alabama and Mississippi delegates walked out—just as they had done in 1860! Mayor L. P. Burns, who attended the convention, "felt deeply the scorn and the lack of consideration leveled at the South." The seceding delegates then met in Birmingham to organize a southern rights, or "Dixiecrat," Party, and nominated Gov. Strom Thurmond of South Carolina for president. Mrs. F. T. Raiford, the publisher of the *Times-Journal*, was reminded of "another great moment— . . . the stormy and determining discussions which marked the Abolitionist movement back in 1844" (July 14, 1948).

Since Truman's name was not allowed on Alabama ballots, the selection of "Dixiecrat" electors, including Givhan, met with little opposition. Selma's conservatives were both astonished and disgusted when Truman was reelected without the votes of the Deep South.

During the early 1950s, an era began coming to an end. Selma's last Confederate veteran, James William Moore (1852–1951), who had for some years been commander-in-chief of the remaining handful of United Confederate Veterans, died quietly in March. In 1952, ex-congressman Samuel F. Hobbs died, severing another link between Selma and its Democratic heritage.

Most of the Black Belt returned to the Democratic fold in 1952, when the national party nominated Sen. John Sparkman of Alabama for vice president (much as it had nominated William Rufus King a century earlier). Selma followed a different path, casting its votes for Republican presidential candidate Dwight David Eisenhower. The *Selma Times-Journal* endorsed the Republican candidate for the first time in its history and ran one front-page editorial after another denouncing "Trumanism." While John H. Blanton tried to rally the troops for Adlai Stevenson, Judge William B. Craig led Citizens for Eisenhower. The city had remained fiercely loyal to the Democrats during the Populist revolt of the 1890s and again during the uprising of the "Hoovercrats" and the Klan in 1928, but now Selma cast its votes for "Ike," 1,385 to 1,189. Dallas County went Republican for the first time since Reconstruction. It was one of only three Alabama counties that did so. This was a choice it repeated in 1956, 1960, and in 1964, when it gave Barry Goldwater an astonishing 83 percent of its votes.

In one respect, Selma was returning to its antebellum politics, when the "Whigs and nullifiers" rebelled against Andrew Jackson's policies. Harry Truman's economic policies did not suit Selma's business community, and his support for civil rights angered the city's segregationists. Opposition to the policies espoused by such leaders of the national Democrats as Harry Truman, Adlai Stevenson, John Kennedy, and Lyndon Johnson began to make Selma, especially in the national political arena, look more and more like a bastion of Republicanism.

On the surface, the town's economic future seemed bright. The city was continuing to expand, with housing subdivisions springing up in west Selma. In 1954, the city acquired a fourth bank to serve its needs: Citizen's Bank and Trust, later a branch of SouthTrust and now part of Wells Fargo. In 1955 the city expanded dramatically, annexing 9.53 square miles and almost tripling its size. In 1956 the city fathers rejoiced over the news that Alamet was setting up a $7 million magnesium plant, with a projected payroll of $1 million.

But there was a dark side to the picture as well. The railroads were in decline across the country; they had 538 employees in Selma in 1950, but within ten years

FIGURE 7.14 Dr. Philip P. Moss Jr. led the crusade to build a new city hospital in 1956; courtesy of the Moss family.

that number had fallen to 223. In 1959 Union Station closed, so that the city lost passenger service for the first time since the Civil War. Selma's wholesale grocers, who once supplied the plantations of the western Black Belt, were also in decline. There were twelve wholesalers in Selma in the 1920s; only two were still operating in 1959. The *Times-Journal* lamented in an October 16, 1956, editorial that "from its once proud status of fourth city in Alabama, Selma gradually slid back to eighth and it seemed that virtual stagnation was to be its fate, despite the great value of Craig Airbase as a community asset."

It was in this context that the city fathers responded to the closing of the city's oldest private hospital, King Memorial, in 1953. The closing of King Memorial touched off a move to set up a new general hospital for the city. The Dallas County Medical Society (president, Dr. Philip B. Moss Jr.) called for the creation of a $3 million 189-bed general hospital to replace the city's two remaining white hospitals, 84-bed Selma Baptist and 40-bed Vaughan Memorial. (Black patients would be treated in a separate wing.) In a sense, Moss was carrying on a family tradition; his father had helped establish King Memorial back in 1920. A graduate of Tulane Medical School, Moss was a deeply public-spirited person who served as president of the YMCA board for years.

The proposed facility would cost $3 million, with $2 million in federal money and $1 million to be paid for by a one-cent sales tax. The Selma Ministerial Association endorsed the plan, saying "no greater service can be rendered mankind than the care of its sick and suffering" (*Selma Times-Journal*, October 9, 1956). The *Times-Journal* also endorsed the proposed tax, though from less idealistic reasons: a new facility would help to maintain the city's status as the medical (and trading) center for the area.

One might have expected the city's political leaders to be as eagerly supportive of the move as they had been of the earlier campaign to establish a state Baptist hospital in Selma in 1921. But Mayor Heinz "went on record as bitterly opposing a one-cent sales tax to be used for the erection of a Hill-Burton general hospital here" (*Selma Times-Journal*, October 8, 1956), and Probate Judge Bernard Reynolds later joined him in opposition to the hospital. Fears that the new hospital would be integrated and under federal control helped to bring about a major turnout of voters, with 748 more votes being cast in the referendum over the proposed tax than were cast in the presidential election being held on the same day. The proposal lost by a wide margin, with 2,235 votes in favor and 3,412 against.

In the wake of this defeat, Dr. Josiah Smith and the other physicians at Vaughan Memorial went ahead on their own, launching a drive to raise enough private donations to build a medium-sized hospital. Cotton broker Charles Hohenberg donated land on West Dallas Avenue, Hill-Burton came through with matching funds, and in 1960 the new Vaughan Memorial opened its doors. Lovely as the 60-bed new Vaughan was, it was not the 189-bed ultramodern facility that the County Medical Society had hoped to see, one that they hoped would attract specialists to practice in Selma.

The Old Order under Siege: 1954–1963

The wave of postwar progress in race relations was slowed and then stopped by reaction to the 1954 US Supreme Court decision in *Brown v. Board of Education,* which declared "separate but equal" schools unconstitutional. The justices directed that schools should begin racial integration "with all deliberate speed." White Selmians reacted with shock and indignation. "It was like hearing about the firing on Fort Sumter," recalls Judge Miller Childers, a young lawyer at the time. Selma quickly became a center of opposition to any move to implement the decree in Alabama.

Even before *Brown v. Board of Education*, the Fikes case had shocked and outraged the city's white community. On April 26, 1953, the *Times-Journal*'s front page reported that a black man had broken into the home of Mayor Heinz's daughter and attempted to rape her. She had been able to fight off her assailant, who then fled into the night. There had been a similar incident a month earlier, when an intruder had succeeded in breaking into the home of an air force wife and assaulting her. In the months that followed, nine similar incidents occurred, bringing the town to a fever pitch of anxiety. Respectable black groups like Ed Moss's Elks and Mark Thomas's Veterans of Foreign Wars joined in offering rewards for the capture of the criminal. On May 16, a retarded young garage attendant named William Earle Fikes was arrested and persuaded to confess.

In 1893 an alleged serial rapist like Fikes might well have been lynched on the streets of Selma. But in 1953 things were different. Fikes was quickly taken out of the city for safety's sake. And when Fikes was brought to trial that June, Circuit Judge Walter E. "Jack" Callen assigned two lawyers from old Selma families, Sam Earle Hobbs and Hugh Mallory Jr., as defense attorneys. Hobbs and Mallory conducted an aggressive defense, raising serious questions about Fikes's confession. It took the jury eighteen hours to reach a verdict, but in the end (to the amazement of the town and the indignation of the *Times-Journal*) they sentenced Fikes to ninety-nine years in prison rather than to the electric chair.

James Hare, the prosecutor in the case, did not give up his attempts to have Fikes convicted for a capital crime. When he brought Fikes to trial for a second sexual assault in October, however, Hare found himself facing two new lawyers provided by the NAACP: black attorneys Peter Hall and Orzell Billingsley. Hall was less interested in defending Fikes than in indicting the system: Why were there no blacks on the jury? He called on local blacks like county farm agent Sam Boynton, Baptist minister J. D. Hunter, and retired grocer Mark Thomas as witnesses that no blacks had served on Dallas County juries in living memory. He succeeded in forcing Judge Callen to add five hundred names (about half of them black) to the jury rolls. However, the case still wound up with an all-white jury; and this time the jury wasted little time in sentencing Fikes to the electric chair. (The US Supreme Court overturned the verdict in 1957, deciding that Fikes's confession was involuntary.)

The Fikes case had a marked impact on Selma's black community, generating a host of new memberships in the NAACP. Among the blacks who crowded into the courtroom to watch Peter Hall challenge the system was a young student at Howard Law School named J. L. Chestnut Jr. Chestnut had been thinking about starting a law practice in New York City; now he decided that the South was "where the action was" and that he would return home to become Selma's first black lawyer since Reconstruction.

The response in Selma's white community was very different. Mayor Heinz un-

Figure 7.15 Alston Keith founded the first Citizens' Council in Alabama; courtesy of the Keith family.

derstandably felt that any organization that defended the man who had assaulted his daughter was the enemy of everything that was decent; and he came to feel the same way about the NAACP and the US Supreme Court. Prosecutor Hare (who succeeded Callen as circuit judge in 1954) later asserted that the Fikes case had been the opening gun in the integrationists' war against Selma. It was no wonder, then, that Selma's white leaders responded as they did when Selma attorney Alston Keith called for the organization of a Citizens' Council to unify the white community in total opposition to integration.

On November 29, 1954, Marshall Alston Keith presided over a mass meeting of white Selmians at the Dallas County Courthouse. Some four hundred people promptly joined what is usually considered the first Citizens' Council in Alabama. "Colonel" Keith (1904–79), longtime chairman of the county Democratic Executive Committee, had studied law under his father, noted attorney Chambliss Keith. He shared his father's distaste for the Klan with its anti-Semitism and anti-Catholicism. In February 1956 when some north Alabama councils began distributing pamphlets blaming the Jews for integration, Keith issued a stern protest, "There is no place for prejudice . . . in this movement." When the Klan bombed an Atlanta synagogue in 1958, Keith had the Dallas County chapter donate money for a reward to catch the bombers. His idea of the council was that it would seek to prevent integration by strictly legal and nonviolent means. As one early leader put it, the council intended "to make it difficult, if not impossible, for any Negro who advocates desegregation to find and hold a job, get credit or renew a mortgage" (*Selma Times-Journal*, November 28, 1954).

In August 1955 the council had its first chance to flex its economic muscles. Rev. John D. Hunter and twenty-eight other black parents of school-aged children signed a petition to the Selma School Board calling for immediate integration of the schools. Eight of the twenty-nine lost their jobs immediately, and another eight shortly thereafter. Five retracted their signatures, saying they had completely misunderstood what the petition was about. Hunter, carpenter Ernest Doyle, and barber Henry W. Shannon were among the very few petitioners who were able both to stand up to pressure and to stay in Selma.

Economic weapons could cut both ways; many black Selmians stopped patronizing Cloverleaf Creamery after it fired Joseph Holmes, an employee for nine years, for signing the petition. When Cloverleaf sent a white lady to investigate why its sales had fallen off so dramatically at John Smitherman's grocery, the black grocer made the mistake of giving the lady his phone number and asking her to call him later. The lady told her friends that Smitherman must be interested in her sexually; and the friends (who included a couple of Selma policemen) decided to take action. On October 17, police officer William D. Bailey set fire to the home next to Smitherman's; learning of his mistake, he returned the next night and fired two shots into the house, wounding Smitherman's wife.

But Selma was not "Bombingham"; police chief Ed Mullen found out what was going on and slapped the rogue officers in jail. Bailey was so shaken to discover that his actions did not meet general approval that he committed suicide a few days later. The grand jury let his accomplices off the hook, just as the grand jury in 1904 had refused to indict the lynchers of Ed Bell. Smitherman wisely sold his grocery and left town.

In 1956 Alabama attorney general, and later governor, John Patterson launched a series of legal attacks on the NAACP, forcing the organization to stop operating in Alabama. Selma's black community responded to the outlawing of the NAACP by organizing a new group to represent the interests of their community. In a meeting held at Tabernacle Baptist on August 21, 1956, P. L. Lindsey, director of public relations for Selma University, was chosen as president of the Dallas County Civic League. While Lindsey took pains to make it clear that the new organization was not linked with the NAACP, Mayor Chris Heinz announced that it would be "a waste of time" for him to meet with the new group.

In 1957 there was a revival of the Ku Klux Klan across Alabama. On November 15 the *Times-Journal* reported that this was "the first time in some 30 years that the robed and hooded organization had shown its head here" by burning crosses on every main approach to Selma. The paper called the Klan "Unwelcome Here," recalling that Black Belt leaders like Gov. B. M. Miller and *Selma Times-Journal* editor F. T. Raiford had led the crusade against the Klan in the 1920s and 1930s. In a November 17 editorial, the paper warned that "this impetuous element only can be expected to undo many of the effective things which already have been done to guard our way of life, by creation of a force which easily could get out of hand and lose friends where we need them the most." By December the paper reported the existence of "a local Klavern, with 39 members and a newly-elected cyclops or kleagle." The Grand Dragon of the US Knights of the Ku Klux Klan, Robert Shelton of Uniontown, disavowed the violent tactics of some north Alabama Klansmen, much as Alston Keith had disavowed the anti-Semitism of some north Alabama councils (*Selma Times-Journal*, December 1, 1957).

The Selma Klan went in for intimidation rather than violence. Its favorite tactic in the years that followed was to conduct nighttime parades through Selma's black neighborhoods. Martin Luther King's visit to Selma in the summer of 1958 to speak at the Baptist Sunday School and Training Union Congress prompted an evening motorcade of fifteen horn-blowing cars on July 31. The *Birmingham World* noted that the Baptists had been unable to obtain a parade permit from the city and that no city official had shown up for the program welcoming the delegates to Selma. On August 27, the Klan returned with "fifty auto loads of robed Klansmen from four counties" to have "a high time riding around the Negro sections and chasing a lone *Times-Journal* photographer" (*Selma Times-Journal*, August 28, 1958). The city had refused to issue the Klan a parade permit, but police chief Ed Mullen decided that the motorcade was not really a parade, since it did not include a marching band. A year later, the "High Place Klaverns 110–47" chose to erect "welcome signs" on entrances to Selma, "signs, painted on sawmill blades . . . which gave the appearance of blood dripping from their teeth" (*Selma Times-Journal*, July 17, 1959). To erect such signs on state property was against the law, but Gov. John Patterson had been elected with Klan support and made it plain that he did not care to have the signs removed.

Most white Selmians felt so confident of the Citizens' Council's ability to maintain segregation by legal means that they felt no need for the Klan's antics. After all,

FIGURE 7.16 A 1963 ad for the Selma Chapter of the Citizens' Council; courtesy of Selma–Dallas County Museum of History and Archives, Selma, Alabama

the Citizens' Council included a quarter of the county's adult white males, including all its elected officials and most of its bankers, lawyers and prominent businessmen.

Dallas County's state senator, Walter Givhan, helped organize Citizens' Councils across much of the Black Belt. At a mass meeting in Linden, Marengo County, he assured his audience that the NAACP'S true aim was "to open the doors of our white women to Negro men." As if the spectre of interracial sex were not terrifying enough, Givhan went on to warn that once integrated into the schools, blacks might assassinate the president and take over the country (*Time*, December 20, 1954). In 1958, he succeeded Sam Englehardt of Macon County as president of the state organization, and moved the headquarters from Montgomery to Selma.

Another major opponent of integration became circuit judge of the Selma district in the same year integration became law. Judge James A. Hare Jr. (1906–69) was a native of Browns in Dallas County, and a graduate of the University of Alabama Law School. He served two terms in the Alabama House of Representatives before becoming solicitor for the Fourth Judicial Circuit, which includes Bibb, Hale,

FIGURE 7.17 Judge James A. Hare Jr., "the man the moderates feared most"; courtesy of the Selma–Dallas County Library, Selma, Alabama.

Perry, Wilcox, and Dallas Counties. Gov. Gordon Persons appointed him judge of the circuit in 1954 and then appointed Blanchard McLeod as solicitor in his place. According to Selma mayor Joseph T. Smitherman, "Judge Hare was the man the moderates feared most. He was a blueblood with a brain, someone they could neither patronize nor hope to control."

Blanchard LeBaron McLeod (1912–93), the scion of a prominent Wilcox County family, shared Hare's antipathy to integration. Chestnut recalls him as "the only court solicitor I ever knew who came to court wearing a big pistol on his hip" but adds that McLeod was always enough of a "Southern gentleman" to not want black women to be mistreated in jail (Chestnut and Cass, *Black in Selma*, 211).

As events developed, however, it was not Keith, Givhan, McLeod, or even Judge Hare who emerged as the symbol of white Selma's resistance. Instead, it was a native of Coffee County who owned a cattle farm near Browns. The man, whom Jim Folsom appointed sheriff of Dallas County as a political reward in 1955, was James G. Clark Jr. His appointment was roundly applauded since he was not one of the coun-

FIGURE 7.18 Sheriff James G. Clark Jr.; courtesy of the Selma–Dallas County Library, Selma, Alabama.

ty's political insiders. Clark proved a colorful sheriff; he wore a uniform of his own design and recruited a "posse" to help him maintain order during a labor dispute.

Sheriff Clark was opposed in the 1958 election by Wilson Baker, a police captain with seventeen years' experience and the support of some of Selma's oldest and most influential families. Clark ran as the "county" candidate, denouncing the Selma "machine." He carried the rural precincts by a good margin and amassed enough votes in the city to be returned to office. Ironically enough, Selma's few black voters (roughly 140) almost certainly voted for Clark since the *Times-Journal* had mistakenly identified Baker as a member of the Klan.

Early in 1960, Clark decided to organize a group of volunteer deputies as a "posse" to fight integration throughout the state. "We must meet force with force," solicitor McLeod told the members of the posse at their formal swearing in. "The day of pas-

FIGURE 7.19 NAACP leader Rev. John D. Hunter, one of the few bold critics of white supremacy; courtesy of the National Voting Rights Museum and Institute, Selma, Alabama.

sive resistance has passed" (*Selma Times-Journal*, March 13, 1960). In the following year, Clark's posse rendered valuable assistance to the black victims of a flood. For the most part, however, Clark used the posse in ways that made it highly unpopular with black citizens. For example, Clark took the group with him to Birmingham in 1963 to stand with police commissioner Eugene "Bull" Connor in his clash with civil rights demonstrators. "The posse was made up of some fine people, a few real fine people," according to Wilson Baker, "and then some run-of-the-mill people, and then a lot of Ku-Klux-Klan types. And Clark's excuse for having them in his posse was that if he had the Klan there, he could control them, but he couldn't" (Howell Raines, *My Soul Is Rested*, New York, 1977, 200).

Clark was not the only person in Dallas County ready to fight for segregation across the South. When rioting broke out at the University of Mississippi on September 30, 1962, after the registration of the school's first black student, Senator Givhan wanted to organize a motorcade of Selmians to drive to Oxford, Mississippi, in support of Gov. Ross Barnett's efforts to block the integration of "Ole Miss." He and industrialist Earl Goodwin flew to Oxford in a private plane to offer their

7.20 Tabernacle Baptist Pastor L. L. Anderson, one of the few bold critics of white supremacy; courtesy of the National Voting Rights Museum and Institute, Selma, Alabama.

services, only to find out that the US Army had blocked all access to the city. The Selmians returned home full of indignation, and the *Times-Journal* lashed out at the Kennedy administration and "the growing prospect of a Shanty Irish dictatorship" (October 2, 1962).

There were a few black people who dared to openly challenge segregation like John D. Hunter, L. L. Anderson, and Samuel and Amelia Boynton.

Hunter (1917–2003), a native of Macon County, was an insurance salesman as well as a Baptist minister. It was he who persuaded the state NAACP to intervene in the Fikes case in 1953, and he who got up the petition to integrate the Selma schools in 1955. He served as president of Selma's NAACP chapter until the organization was driven out of Alabama.

Louis Lloyd Anderson (1920–99), a native of Steubenville, Ohio, was also a Bap-

FIGURE 7.21 Samuel W. and Amelia Platt Boynton (*left*), along with their son Bruce (*right*), were considered the "first family" of Selma protests for decades; courtesy of the Boynton family.

tist minister. Unlike Hunter, who served two tiny country churches, Anderson was the pastor of one of Selma's largest and most influential black churches: Tabernacle Baptist. His dynamic preaching had enabled him to succeed Jemison as pastor of Tabernacle Baptist. A graduate of Western Theological Seminary in Pittsburgh and a former army chaplain, Anderson was part of a new generation more inclined to protest injustice. Segregationists soon came to regard him as a potential troublemaker. When he was involved in a traffic accident that killed a bystander in 1959, a grand jury indicted him for second-degree murder and an all-white jury sentenced him to ten years in jail. (The Alabama Supreme Court upheld the verdict, but in 1961 the US Supreme Court overturned the decision.)

Samuel W. Boynton (1901–63) and Amelia Platt (1911–2015) were both Georgia natives and Tuskegee graduates who were assigned to Selma by the Alabama Extension Service, he in 1928 as a county farm agent and she in 1930 as home demonstration agent. They married in 1936. "Dallas County is fortunate in having the services of a farm agent of Boynton's ability," asserted the September 22, 1940 *Times-Journal.* Together with his white counterpart John Blake, Boynton "had managed to achieve an amazing amount of rural betterment." Later his activism made him unpopular with Selma whites, and he resigned to join his wife in setting up the Boynton Insurance Agency.

FIGURE 7.22 Samuel W. Boynton, the leader of the Dallas County Voters League, did not live long enough to see the triumph of the movement he helped launch; courtesy of the Boynton family.

The Boyntons' son, Bruce, became famous while still a law student at Howard University by bringing a lawsuit, *Boynton v. City of Richmond*, that led to the Supreme Court's 1960 decision to outlaw segregation in interstate travel. The state of Alabama responded by barring Boynton from practicing law in Alabama for several years.

In 1958 the US Civil Rights Commission met in Montgomery to hold hearings on voter discrimination. Judge Hare blocked the commission from access to the voter registration rolls of Dallas and Wilcox Counties; and Judge Reynolds took the commission a doctor's excuse so that registrar Ruth Horne would not have to testify. Six black Selmians—Sam and Amelia Boynton, nursing home operator Susie B. Anderson, Frank Gordon, Dr. Sullivan Jackson, and Ruth K. Lindsey—defied the Citizens' Council by daring to testify. The *Times-Journal* noted that "the Anderson woman, 32, wife of an undertaker, the Lindsey woman, 61, wife of the public relations director of Selma University, and Gordon, 77, originally from Lowndes County, all told the court of futile efforts to vote in Dallas County"(December 10, 1958). In sharp contrast, the minister from Camden whom the commission staff asked to testify about Wilcox County practices fled the state in terror (Fleming, *In the Shadow of Selma*, 133).

Despite Dallas County's reputation as a citadel of white supremacy, Selma itself could be called "liberal" by Black Belt standards. It is clear, for example, that the county made more effort to apply the voter registration laws fairly than did some of its neighbors. Even though it is true that only about 3 percent of Dallas County's potential black voters were registered, as opposed to 66 percent of its whites, in both Wilcox and Lowndes Counties, 90 to 100 percent of potential white voters were registered and not a single black person.

The Justice Department brought several suits against Dallas County's board of registrars and sheriff during the early sixties, asking the courts to order the board not to discriminate against black applicants. A suit was filed in April 1961 before federal judge Daniel Thomas, the judge for the Southern District of the US Fifth Circuit. Thomas, a native of neighboring Autauga County, finally heard the case in May 1962. Circuit solicitor Blanchard McLeod defended the county by offering to "show proof that Negroes are (in) general morally unqualified to vote and that a high rate of illiteracy exists within the county" (*Selma Times-Journal*, May 6, 1962). The Justice Department was prepared to argue that white citizens with only a third-grade education had been allowed to register, while black college graduates had been turned down. It had 270 witnesses, mostly black, sworn in to testify. (Thirty-six of them were employees of the county school system, who lost their jobs as a result. Dallas County had been exempted from the teacher tenure law, which Judge Hare regarded as Communist.)

By this time, a new board of registrars headed by businessman Victor B. Atkins, son of the former mayor, had been in office for almost a year. Judge Thomas agreed that discrimination had occurred in the past, since only fourteen black voters had succeeded in registering between 1954 and 1962. However, he felt sure that the new board was going by the book. This was evidenced by the fact that 71 of the 114 black applicants who had been tested by the new board had succeeded in registering. So in November 1962, Judge Thomas denied the Justice Department's request for an injunction to simplify the registration procedure. This verdict was appealed to and reversed by the federal Court of Appeals in October 1963.

The real issue, of course, was the registration law itself. Some provisions of the 1901 Constitution, like the property requirement, no longer applied. However, the would-be voter was still required to take a written examination on the US Constitution, to take an additional oral examination, and to bring two registered voters along as character references. Some of the questions that seemed quite fair to the white registrars, such as "what are the duties of a Vice President?," seemed irrelevant to many black applicants.

Different people had different ideas about the proper qualifications for voting. Amelia Boynton tells the story of an elderly farmer of limited education who tried to register. When the registrar explained that he had already flunked the exam by failing to fill out part of the application correctly, the old man was indignant. He owned a hundred acre farm, he said. He paid taxes and had raised four children to be respectable members of society, "and if that ain't enough to be able to vote, then God help America!" Boynton did not record the registrar's reaction but did note that the man was allowed to take the examination.

Samuel Boynton died on May 13, 1963—the day before Selma's black residents held their first mass meeting—but Mrs. Boynton did not slacken her efforts. She provided office space for the Student Non-Violent Coordinating Committee (SNCC) and sought to persuade other groups, such as the Southern Christian Leadership Conference (SCLC), to send workers to Selma.

Another leader began to emerge in the early 1960s, when Frederick Douglass (F. D.) Reese returned to his native Selma to teach science and math at R. B. Hudson High. Reese, also a graduate of Alabama State University, had previously taught for nine years in Wilcox County. After coming back to Selma, he became president of the Selma Teachers Association and led that organization in winning increased benefits from the school board. Reese was both teacher and preacher, serving as pastor of Ebenezer Baptist Church. The combination of his eloquence of speech and his organizational skills led to his 1962 election as president of the Dallas County Voters League.

In early 1963, two young activists from the Student Non-Violent Coordinating Committee (SNCC), Bernard and Colia Lafayette, arrived in Selma. At first, they were unable to persuade any black church to provide them with space for a voter registration class. Lafayette's "Freedom Rider" past made him a glamorous figure among Selma's black youth. Many of the city's older leaders who had struggled for black rights over the years —educators like P. L. Lindsey and W. H. Dinkins of Selma University and ministers like Claude Brown and C. C. Hunter—were appalled by the prospect that this "Pied Piper" might lead the young into launching "sit-ins" and other demonstrations in Selma. Maurice Ouellet, the white pastor of St. Elizabeth's Catholic Mission, finally agreed to allow the Lafayettes the use of his parish hall.

When minister L. L. Anderson made Tabernacle Baptist Church available to them in mid-May, the Lafayettes were able to hold their first mass meeting. Taber-

FIGURE 7.23 Rev. Frederick D. Reese, president of the Dallas County Voters League; courtesy of Selma–Dallas County Museum of History and Archives, Selma, Alabama.

nacle's deacons initially opposed Anderson's decision; Dinkins told his future son-in-law, "You are leaving your friends, and going with strangers." The minister's determination and zeal finally gained their support. About three hundred fifty persons attended the meeting. Sheriff Clark was also in attendance, along with a host of deputies. When the meeting closed, the participants were appalled to find a large crowd of whites, many of them teenagers "wielding freshly lathed table legs from a nearby furniture company" waiting for them outside the church. According to Taylor Branch, Sheriff Clark ordered the mob to disperse to no avail. But when the football coach from Selma High arrived and started "taking names and kicking butt," the teenagers scattered like fall leaves before a storm. When asked how a football coach succeeded when the sheriff failed, one black leader explained, "Well, they knew Coach meant it" (Taylor Branch, *Pillar of Fire*, New York, 1998, 84).

Later mass meetings were held at Clinton Chapel AME Zion, at Mt. Zion Primi-

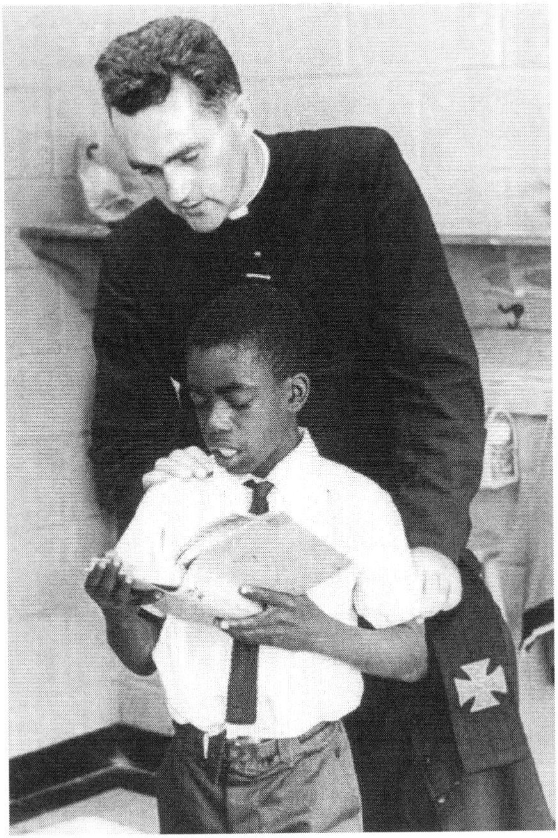

FIGURE 7.24 Edmundite Father Maurice Ouellet, pastor of St. Elizabeth's Mission from 1961–65; courtesy of the Edmundite Missions.

tive Baptist Church, at First Baptist, and at Brown Chapel AME on Sylvan Street, which is in the middle of a large housing project, George Washington Carver Homes.

Some of the more militant members of the Voters League welcomed the ideas proposed at the mass meetings—people like James Gildersleeve and Ulysses Blackmon, brothers-in-law who taught at Alabama Lutheran, barber Henry W. Shannon, and the old warhorses John D. Hunter and Ernest Doyle. Together with dental hygienist Marie Foster, schoolteacher F. D. Reese, and Amelia Boynton, they made up the group that later came to be known as "the Courageous Eight." In the course of the year, the militants took over the Voters League and allied themselves with SNCC.

Early that summer, Edwin Moss, Claude C. Brown, and other black moderates organized the Dallas County Improvement Association (DCIA) to seek concessions from Selma's white leadership. First, the group sent four pastors of black congregations—L. L. Anderson of Tabernacle, Claude C. Brown of Reformed Presbyterian, C. W. Cleveland of First Baptist, C. C. Hunter of Clinton Chapel—along with Maurice Ouellet of St. Elizabeth's and physician W. C. Dinkins to approach Mayor Chris Heinz with a petition. They explained that unrest was building in the black community, unrest that might lead to demonstrations in the fall. They tactfully urged the city to head off potential trouble by setting up a biracial committee to discuss black grievances and offered their assistance in promoting racial peace and harmony. Heinz, who had already refused to meet with SNCC, made it clear he would have nothing to do with DCIA either.

DCIA president Ed Moss hoped that the group would have better luck with the white business community. On August 29 he wrote the Selma Retail Merchants Association, urging its members to meet with him and other black leaders and asked them to respond by September 15. They did not respond. He also approached the *Selma Times-Journal* with equal lack of success.

Father Ouellet, the only white member of the DCIA, spent much of the summer trying to set up a meeting with the city's white ministers, in hopes of heading off trouble. Ouellet (1926–2010), a native of Vermont, wanted the ministers to issue a statement similar to appeals for racial harmony issued by ministers elsewhere. By the time he was finally allowed to address the Dallas County Christian Ministers' Union on September 16, however, the demonstrations had already begun. The rattled ministers decided not to vote on the proposed statement, for fear it would provoke dissension that would destroy their group. Ouellet left the meeting in despair and later sent a letter to the *Times-Journal* stating that "every avenue of approach to Selma's whites has been tried and failed" (September 22, 1963).

8

Selma, Birthplace of Equal Voting Rights

The Queen City in Crisis, 1963–1968

"Selma stands on the threshold of what is probably the most important era in its history since the Civil War," proclaimed the *Selma Times-Journal* on March 20, 1964. "This is not because Joe T. Smitherman has been duly elected mayor; nor, that Chris Heinz will no longer serve that office after his term expires. But, simply because the social, economic and industrial complexion of this community has suddenly and simultaneously arrived at a point from which there can be no turning back." The city faced the challenge "to take advantage of an expanding economy and to face the growing social changes which are imminent."

The *Times-Journal* was only too correct. Mayor Smitherman and the young businessmen who supported him were eager to take advantage of an expanding economy; but they were much less enthusiastic about facing "growing social changes." Most white Selmians still believed that Selma could maintain its segregated way of life for many years to come. The Queen City was less than a year away from Bloody Sunday and the Selma-to-Montgomery March, which was to fix its national image for decades to come.

In the years since *Brown v. Board of Education*, Selma and Dallas County had attracted the attention of the US Civil Rights Commission and the Justice Department. The Justice Department began bringing suits against the county in 1961. In 1963 the Student Non-Violent Coordinating Committee (SNCC) had arrived in Selma, to assist the Voters League in protesting racial discrimination. In late 1964 the Southern Christian Leadership Conference (SCLC) committed itself to launching a campaign in Selma. These groups concentrated their attention on Selma's racial injustice much as Wilson's Raiders had done when they set out to destroy the

FIGURE 8.1 New mayor Joseph T. Smitherman with Gov. George Wallace and Wallace's chief of staff Cecil Jackson; courtesy of Martha Jackson.

arsenal of the Confederacy. In fact, it was almost one hundred years to the month between the time Wilson and his soldiers sacked the city and the time Dr. Martin Luther King Jr. and his army of demonstrators began a march to Montgomery that drew the attention of the world. Dr. King chose to involve Selma in what was probably his greatest victory for civil rights, a successful effort to force the nation to deal with the need for a voting rights act.

After King and his immediate followers moved on to other areas, Selma's citizens were left to sort out the implications of what had taken place. They tried to establish workable order in a town scarred by the traumas of Bloody Sunday and the Selma-to-Montgomery March. In the course of that struggle, both racial communities split down the middle: white moderates openly broke with the hard line pushed by the Citizens' Council and black militants rebelled against the leadership of the Dallas County Voters League. These splits complicated the desegregation of Selma's public schools and the city's attempts to organize a federally approved antipoverty program.

Figure 8.2 Librarian Patricia Swift Blalock; courtesy of the Blalock family.

Round One: 1963

Remarkably, one institution in Selma quietly integrated in May 1963 without any outside pressure. Pat Blalock, the new director of the Carnegie Library, had long been unhappy that Selma's black residents had no access to the library (except by having the library maid give them books at the back door). Patricia Swift Blalock (1916–2011), a native of Gadsden, had trained as a social worker at the University of Chicago. She moved to Selma in 1937 to work with crippled children, but after her marriage wound up with a new career as a librarian. Blalock warned her board that other libraries around the state were facing demonstrations and urged them to spare Selma from such unpleasantness by opening the library's doors to black and white people alike. Selma's white community might be willing to give up their public swimming pools to avoid integration, but she felt sure they would never give up the Carnegie. One by one she won over the members of her board, till finally even Mayor Chris Heinz and Probate Judge Bernard Reynolds reluctantly gave way. Heinz did require her to remove chairs from the library (so that white patrons and black patrons would not be sitting next to each other), but that was the only concession she had to make. On May 20, 1963, the library integrated. One local segregationist was so outraged that he tore up his library card and threw it on the floor.

When he returned a few weeks later shame faced, Blalock presented him with his old card, which she had taped back together.

In sharp contrast, Selma officials cracked down hard on the demonstrations that began in September of that year. The demonstrations caught official Selma by surprise, and its response was overwhelmingly negative. The demonstrators (mostly students from R. B. Hudson High School) picketed some businesses, asked to be served at several downtown drug stores and cafes, and attempted to attend services at a number of white churches.

The "kneel-ins" particularly infuriated whites. Church Street Methodist and First Baptist set up "sidewalk committees" to keep black demonstrators from entering their doors. John Newton, the pastor at First Presbyterian, was subjected to a torrent of abuse after he allowed four black girls to attend services. An angry letter to the *Selma Times-Journal* denounced the Church of the Assumption of Our Lady as "Erroneous Assumption" for allowing black people to attend Mass there: by so doing they were committing sacrilege and "defiling the House of the Lord."

On September 19 Judge Hare summoned fifteen "representative blacks" and Father Ouellet, the pastor of St. Elizabeth's Mission, to his courtroom and lectured them on the wickedness of using children to fight their battles. "You are sowing the wind and will reap the whirlwind," he warned them (*Selma Times-Journal*, September 20, 1963). If necessary, he would issue an injunction to close down the mass meetings and the demonstrations. The downtown merchants joined with the chamber of commerce, the Cattlemen's Association, the bar association, and a host of other professional organizations to take out a full-page ad in the September 22 *Selma Times-Journal*, titled "A Declaration of Basic Rights and Principles," which asserted their freedom to run their businesses as they chose. "Responsible Negro leaders should take immediate steps to put down agitation among their people," they said earnestly.

Sheriff Clark had been harassing SNCC workers since the spring, arresting Bernard Lafayette for "vagrancy" after a mass meeting on June 17. Now he found excuses to arrest some 350 of them, and Solicitor McLeod came up with ingenious charges to bring against them. For example, he charged SNCC chairman John Lewis with "inciting violence" for giving a speech in favor of nonviolence. Judge Reynolds sentenced most of the teenage demonstrators to probation for their first offense, but repeat offenders were liable to be sentenced to the penitentiary. Barber Henry Shannon, the Voters League's man in charge of youth work, was sentenced to a year at hard labor for "corrupting the young."

In October, the judges of the US Third Circuit overruled Judge Thomas's decision that the Dallas County Board of Registrars was above reproach. They ordered Thomas to direct the board of registrars to speed up their procedures and to simplify their requirements. The black leaders responded by announcing a "moratorium" on demonstrations. Even if their demonstrations had failed to integrate Carter Drug or Church Street Methodist, they did have some effect. They had at least encouraged black citizens to attempt to register to vote; the number of applicants that month climbed to 215, the highest number ever.

The segregationist leaders were indignant when Sheriff Clark discovered that the car Dr. King used on a visit to Selma belonged to a Justice Department employee, Thelton Henderson. They protested and succeeded in forcing Henderson's resignation. On November 12 Judge Hare charged a grand jury to investigate the Justice Department, which he felt sure was behind the demonstrations; he smelled a conspiracy. The grand jury's chairman was Robert D. Wilkinson Jr., chairman of the Dallas County Republican Party and former chairman of the Citizens' Council. Wilkinson and his fellow jurors were preparing to fly to Washington, DC, (with Gov. George Wallace paying their expenses) when the assassination of President Kennedy on November 23, 1963, interrupted their plans.

The Justice Department in turn brought suit against Solicitor McLeod and Sheriff Clark, charging them with acting to intimidate and discourage black would-be voters. Judge Thomas heard the department's case on December 17. Rev. L. L. Anderson, Rev. W. T. Menifee of Brown Chapel, and Father Ouellet all testified. Thomas put off the decision once again. When he did rule in March 1964, he once more found in favor of the local authorities.

Intermission and Round Two: 1964

In 1964 Selma had been described by the African American *Birmingham World* as run by "an encrusted and entrenched political and business leadership." Discontent with Selma's civic leadership was not limited to the black community; it had also been brewing in the white community for some time. A number of the city's young businessmen were keenly aware that its economic future was at risk in spite of Craig Air Force Base, and they felt that the Selma–Dallas County Chamber of Commerce was not enthusiastic enough about recruiting new industry.

They were concerned because Selma had been a railroad town for over a century but US railroad traffic was declining. Union Station closed in 1959, leaving Selma without the passenger service it had enjoyed since the 1840s. Increasingly, the highways were replacing railroads as arteries of commerce, and I-85, the interstate highway that might logically have gone through Selma to Meridian halted in Montgomery and went no further west.

The city lost its professional baseball team in 1962 when the major leagues would no longer work with farm teams that did not accept black players. Although Selma's

Cloverleafs were willing to make the adjustment, the Montgomery team was not and, as a result, the whole Southeastern League went out of existence.

In 1962, a group of energetic young men organized a Committee of One Hundred to recruit new industry for the city. Their seriousness of purpose was demonstrated by the fact that each member was to donate one hundred dollars for the cause. Restaurant owner Otis "Red" Adams, grocer James F. Gaston, appliance salesman Joseph T. Smitherman, and drugstore owner George "Cap" Swift were among the young leaders who felt that the city was stagnating economically. In their eyes, the chamber of commerce, which was closely tied to both the City National Bank and the Heinz administration, was not that eager to recruit industry that might rock the boat. Gaston served as the first president of the group, and Harvard graduate Jerome Siegel became one of its most effective industry hunters. Both men were distressed that Selma's children were growing up, going off to college, and pursuing careers away from their hometown. Siegel's own Jewish community was dwindling: in the early twenties it had supported two rabbis, but by the late seventies it was unable to support even one.

By 1964 the group had become convinced that the Old Guard that was running Selma (i.e., the Burns-Heinz machine) was an obstacle to progress. The candidate they settled on to challenge the city's political establishment was in sharp contrast to incumbent mayor Chris Heinz. Heinz, an insurance agent whose grandfathers had both served on the city council, had been appointed to the council in 1934 and served continuously until his election as mayor in 1952.

Joseph Thomas Smitherman, a thirty-five-year-old appliance salesman, often described his having grown up "a poor white from East Selma," losing his father when he was two months old and his mother when he was eleven. Of course college had been out of the question for "Joe T.," as everyone called him. But his energy and ambition gained him a seat on the city council in 1962 and won him selection as one of Alabama's Outstanding Young Men of the Year in 1963.

Smitherman was not the Old Guard's only challenger. Tractor dealer Carl Morgan ran for president of the city council. Morgan (1920–2006), a native of Uniontown, graduate of Auburn University, and veteran of World War II, had moved to Selma in 1946 and established the Black Belt Tractor Company dealership. Other members of the Committee of One Hundred also ran for seats on the council. On top of that, three black candidates filed for seats on the city council for the first time since Reconstruction. Mayor Heinz actually made some concessions, allowing Pat Blalock to replace the chairs in the library and taking the "white" and "colored" signs off the water fountains at City Hall. But these concessions proved too little, too late.

Smitherman won the March election by 2,562 votes to 2,068. The three black

FIGURE 8.3 Mayor Chris Heinz served from 1952 to 1964; courtesy of Selma City Hall, Selma, Alabama.

candidates for the council lost by wide margins but took comfort in the fact that their 240 votes had helped provide roughly half of Smitherman's margin of victory. "Joe T." was not the only challenger to triumph; the city emerged from the election with a new mayor, a new council president, Carl Morgan, and five new councilmen, including "Cap" Swift and "Red" Adams.

The new leaders of city government wanted to acquire more industry, to build a second bridge across the Alabama River, and to establish the best possible junior college. These men were not necessarily moderates on racial issues; as Smitherman later observed, he had been supported by both diehards like Sheriff Clark and by Clark's nemesis, the moderate Wilson Baker. But their anxiety to acquire new industry made them more open to the pleas of the moderates that the city could not afford the negative image that continued racial confrontations might provide.

They had been promised a technical school in 1965 and had hopeful visions of what that year might bring to Selma. However, not even with their active imaginations could they have expected the things that did occur in that fateful year.

Smitherman did not take office until October 1964, and during the summer black discontent came to a boil once again. Ever since Judge Thomas had found the board of registrars to be a model for the nation, the board had reverted to form and begun rejecting the vast majority of black applicants. After the passage of the Civil Rights Act of 1964, which was concerned primarily with public accommodations, Selma's black residents became active once more. On July 3, the day after President Johnson signed the act into law, attempts were made to see if Selma drug stores and restaurants would now serve blacks. Hare had denounced the act as "unconstitutional," and the downtown businessmen insisted on waiting to see what the courts would decide. When black people tried to integrate the Wilby Theatre, Clark closed it down. Later, when Clark and his deputies were waiting outside a mass meeting at the AME Zion Hall, some stones were thrown at the officers (or so they said); Clark's men responded with tear gas and clubs.

Mayor Heinz heard that carloads of Ku Klux Klansmen from Georgia and National States Rights Party (NSRP) members from Tennessee were arriving to help local segregationists "deal" with any black person who tried to integrate local restaurants and theaters. Heinz and Sheriff Clark went to Judge Hare to ask for an injunction against the Klan, the NSRP, and some local black leaders. On July 9 Hare issued a sweeping injunction forbidding black leaders, including seventeen ministers of various congregations, fifteen black organizations, the Klan, and the NSRP from holding any meeting at which more than three people were present.

This injunction closed down the public meetings held each Monday night by the Dallas County Voters League; a meeting had been called for Tabernacle Baptist for July 13, but after word spread of Clark's threat to "surround the church and arrest everyone there" nobody showed up for the meeting. Private meetings were not necessarily safe either. When a group of black airmen from Craig Field met with a white minister at the black Elks' Lodge in July 1964 to discuss grievances, Sheriff Clark and his deputies entered the building, broke up the meeting, and removed the club's liquor license from the wall.

A number of white citizens thought Selma needed to accept change more gracefully. As early as 1963, Charles Hohenberg had been so appalled by the church bombing in Birmingham that he tried in vain to organize a group of "moderates" to meet with black leaders before something similar happened in Selma. By late 1964, a group of bankers, lawyers, and businessmen were meeting secretly at the People's Bank to discuss alternative approaches to the problem. Rex Morthland, the chairman of the board at People's Bank, was worried that his birth in California and his degree from the University of Chicago might make him seem like an outsider. But he took com-

FIGURE 8.4 Banker Rex Morthland, among Selma's leading moderates in 1965, later became director of consumer services for the Federal Deposit Insurance Corporation in Washington, DC; courtesy of the Alabama Department of Archives and History.

fort from the fact that his fellow moderates included members of Selma's old families like bank president William B. Craig, son of one Selma congressman and grandson of another; lawyer Edgar A. Stewart Jr., president of the school board and grandson of former mayors H. S. D. Mallory and H. H. Stewart; attorney Samuel Earle Hobbs, son of Selma's last congressman and great-grandson of a Civil War mayor; and banker Roger ap Catesby Jones, descendant of the commander of the Selma Arsenal. Other important members of the group included the editor and publisher of the *Selma Times-Journal*, Roswell Falkenberry, city council president Carl Morgan, and YMCA general secretary Paul Grist. They urged the mayor and probate judge to adopt a "moderate" approach to the situation.

When Smitherman finally took office in October, he followed Heinz's example by publicly refusing to even consider meeting with a biracial committee. He also appointed hard-line segregationist McLean Pitts as city attorney. At the same time, he took a major step toward defusing racial tensions by appointing Wilson Baker as public safety director.

8.5 Lawyer Sam Earle Hobbs, among Selma's leading moderates in 1965, was later named chancellor of the University of Alabama; courtesy of the Hobbs family.

Baker, a native of South Carolina and graduate of Newberry College, came to Selma and joined the police force in 1940. He had been teaching at the University of Alabama since his defeat by Clark in 1958, had some understanding of the feelings of black people, and was willing to talk with their leaders about complaints of police brutality and harassment.

People's Bank executives Rex Morthland and Frank Wilson, along with Paul Grist, established communications with Claude Brown, Ed Moss, and F. D. Reese. Mayor Smitherman initiated a meeting with Brown, Moss, and Reese to discuss paving streets in black neighborhoods and assisting black residents in finding jobs at Dan River Mills' new plant.

Probate Judge Bernard Reynolds also responded to the moderates' pleas. He quietly removed the "white" and "colored" signs from courthouse water fountains, though he could not bring himself to do the same for the ladies' washrooms. And he made no move to block the integration of NBF Homes.

The moderates had reasons to be optimistic. The Committee of One Hundred had achieved their first great success in 1964, when Dan River Mills decided to build

FIGURE 8.6 Selma's director of public safety, Wilson Baker; courtesy of the Selma–Dallas County Library.

a plant in Benton, just over the line in Lowndes County. "We chased a lot of wild geese," recalls "Cap" Swift, "but we caught that one." January 1965 brought even better news: Hammermill Paper Company of Erie, Pennsylvania, was persuaded to locate its new plant in Selma. (Today, as part of International Paper Company, it remains one of the city's largest employers.)

In the long run, the moderates felt certain that the arrival of new industry would solve all of Selma's problems, including its racial problems. They failed to realize that many of Selma's black residents were no longer willing to wait for the "long run." "We were ahead of our time," Rex Morthland told the author, "but I guess we weren't quite far enough ahead."

In December 1964, C. T. Vivian arrived from Atlanta to meet with the Dallas County Voters League. He brought the important news that Dr. Martin Luther King Jr. would come to Selma with all the resources of the Southern Christian Leadership Conference, if the Dallas County Voters League invited him. (Mrs. Boynton had been trying for over a year to persuade SCLC to come.)

It was a momentous decision. The attempts by Ed Moss and the Dallas County

FIGURE 8.7 Probate Judge Bernard Reynolds; courtesy of Nancy Reynolds Bennett.

Improvement Association to win concessions from Selma's businessmen had proved fruitless, the Justice Department's suing Dallas County had not made much impact in Selma (thanks to Judge Thomas's reluctance to rule against the county), and SNCC's sit-ins and demonstrations had failed to bring major changes. After consideration, a letter was written and signed by Reese to invite King and see what he and the SCLC could accomplish.

THE MAIN EVENT: MARTIN LUTHER KING JR. IN SELMA

In 1965, Dr. Martin Luther King Jr. was one of the most controversial men in America. King (1929–68), a native of Atlanta and the son and grandson of the city's most prominent black Baptist ministers, earned a PhD in philosophy from Boston University before becoming pastor of the Dexter Avenue Baptist Church in Montgomery. It was King whom civil rights activist E. D. Nixon chose to lead the Montgomery Improvement Association during the bus boycott that was begun in Montgomery in December 1955. King's philosophy of nonviolent resistance, combined with his

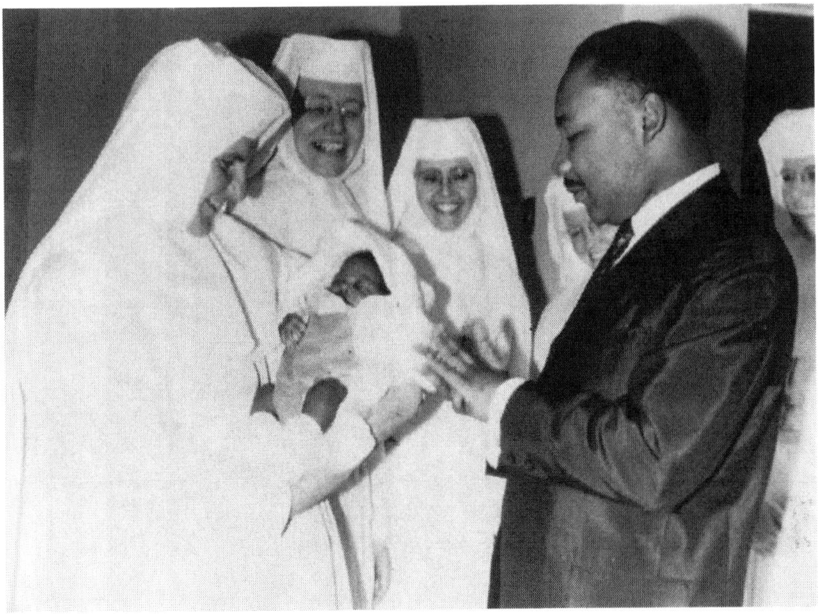

FIGURE 8.8 Dr. Martin Luther King Jr. with the Sisters of St. Joseph and newborn Synethia Perkins; courtesy of the Edmundite Missions.

persuasive oratory, kept the nation's attention on the bus boycott and its successful outcome.

King left Montgomery for Atlanta but returned to Alabama in 1963 to lead a series of demonstrations in Birmingham. The bombing of a black church and commissioner Bull Connor's use of police dogs helped to create the national groundswell needed to pass the Civil Rights Act of 1964. Now, at the invitation of the Dallas County Voters League, King agreed to come to Selma in hopes of generating the support needed to pass a federal voting rights bill.

King had critics, both black and white. Even though he had been awarded the Nobel Prize for Peace, many white Selmians thought King was a troublemaker, who stirred up communities that had previously been peaceful, at least on the surface. The October 16, 1964, *Times-Journal* referred to the prize as "The Absurdity of the Year." "If King is the current symbol of world peace," the paper observed, "then this old planet is due for some turbulent times." Many moderate white and some black people disapproved of King's willingness to use school children to fill the jails, as he had in Birmingham.

Locally, the legions in King's nonviolent army were divided among themselves. Some of Selma's black community, and especially the older ministers, regarded SNCC

FIGURE 8.9 Richie Jean and Dr. Sullivan Jackson, who sheltered Dr. King during his stay in Selma; courtesy of Jawana V. Jackson.

workers as "beatniks." Some SNCC people suspected SCLC of being more interested in national publicity than in local progress, and some SCLC aides feared that the local leaders were too trusting, too eager to reach an agreement with the white establishment.

Why did King choose Selma as the site for his campaign to dramatize the need for a voting rights law? He was no stranger to Selma, having attended Baptist meetings at Selma University for years. He and his chief aide, Ralph Abernathy, had stayed with Selma dentist Dr. Sullivan Jackson and his wife, Jean, who was an old friend of King's wife, Coretta, and of Abernathy's wife, Juanita.

One of Selma's attractions was the progress made by its black citizens. With two black colleges, two black hospitals, and a black credit union, the city had enough educated, middle-class black residents to offer King a strong base of support. However, the city's greatest attraction may have been its sheriff. King and his allies had learned that their campaigns went best when they could focus attention on an opponent who symbolized blatant southern racism. When they were up against someone like Bull Connor in Birmingham who used dogs and fire hoses, they could win, but when they faced someone like police chief Laurie Pritchett of Albany, Georgia, who "met nonviolence with nonviolence," they lost. In Jim Clark, they thought they had the perfect opponent.

However, when King and his aides arrived in Selma on January 18, 1965, it was public safety director Wilson Baker they faced at first. Baker had learned from Pritchett how to handle King's legions: be polite, use maximum self-restraint, and, at all costs, avoid creating "martyrs" by mistreating demonstrators in front of the national media, who were covering events in Selma with more than their usual attention and detail.

The *Selma Times-Journal* urged the white community not to get upset over the arrival of this "controversial darkie," and most readers took the paper's advice. They, like the rest of the country, saw what was going on downtown only on the evening news. The city's merchants fell in line behind Baker, serving black people at restaurants without complaint. When King arrived at the Hotel Albert, he was given a room as smoothly as though black guests had stayed there often before.

There was one unpleasant incident when National States Rights Party leader George Robinson of Bessemer attacked King in the hotel lobby. He was dragged away to jail, convicted of assault, and fined one hundred dollars. However, because Robinson was an "outside agitator," like American Nazi leader George Lincoln Rockwell, who was also in town for the occasion, Selma could not be blamed for their actions. (Baker found an excuse to arrest Rockwell as well, and both Robinson and the Nazi leader wisely chose to leave town the next day.)

Even the march to the Dallas County Courthouse was accomplished without incident. Baker's rules were that the people would march four or five abreast, ten feet apart, and King's people abided by them. The courthouse was Sheriff Clark's jurisdiction, and he had the marchers wait outside in the alley all day while the board of registrars processed some white applicants. This was highly irritating to the marchers but not dramatic enough to interest the nation's press. Indeed, the day went so quietly that SCLC's leaders feared they would lose the attention of the press and, perhaps, find it necessary to focus their voting rights campaign on some other Black Belt city whose citizens would provide more drama.

The next day, however, Sheriff Clark lost his temper and shoved Mrs. Boynton in full view of the press, before arresting her and sixty other marchers for minor offenses. The arrests made national headlines, and SCLC decided it had made the right choice: Selma was turning out nicely. On the following day, Clark arrested 156 hymn-singing applicants for insisting on using the front door of the courthouse rather than its side door. A bewildered Wilson Baker "didn't know of any law requiring the use of a specific door" (*Birmingham World*, January 27, 1965).

On January 22, one of the most unusual events of the civil rights movement took place: the black teachers of Selma gathered at Clark Elementary and marched to the courthouse en masse, led by F. D. Reese and veteran teacher A. J. Durgan. Nothing similar had happened in Montgomery, Birmingham, Albany, or Saint Augustine. If the teachers, usually regarded as the most conservative element of the black middle class, were willing to put their careers on the line, then the black community's determination went deeper than any white person had suspected. The teachers expected to be arrested and to probably spend the weekend in jail. School superintendent Joseph A. Pickard and school board president Edgar A. Stewart, knowing that Clark's posse was waiting inside the courthouse with their clubs ready, begged the teachers not to involve themselves in a confrontation with the sheriff. Clark threatened to arrest the teachers, but was persuaded by Solicitor McLeod not to do so. When it became clear that Clark would neither arrest them nor allow them into the courthouse, Reese and the teachers turned and marched to Brown Chapel, where they were greeted as heroes by their students and most of the black community.

What made more impact on the nation at large was the fight Sheriff Clark got into with Mrs. Annie Lee Cooper, one of the marchers, on the following Monday, January 25. When Clark shoved the fifty-three-year-old Mrs. Cooper for being out of line, she responded by punching him in the face. The stunned sheriff fell to his knees, whereupon she hit him again. Cooper actually got in a third blow before two deputies were able to wrestle her to the ground. "I wish you would hit me, you scum!" she yelled at Clark, and the infuriated sheriff brought his billy club down on her head (David S. Garrow, *Bearing the Cross*, New York, 1986, 381). The resulting photograph made the front page of the *New York Times* and page two of the *Washington Post*, and helped to seal Clark's reputation as a brutal racist. Mrs. Cooper's actions were a violation of nonviolent discipline, but they were deeply satisfying to many in the black community. Years later, a Selma street was renamed in her honor.

On February 1, King decided to raise the pressure on Selma by provoking his own arrest. Admitting "this is a deliberate attempt to dramatize conditions in this city, state, and community," he and his fellow marchers disregarded Baker's instructions for conducting marches and cheerfully accepted the arrests that followed (*Bearing the Cross*, 382). His "Letter from Selma Jail" appeared in the *New York Times* the following Friday.

> By jailing hundreds of Negroes, the city of Selma, Alabama, has revealed the persisting ugliness of segregation to the nation and the world. When the Civil Rights Act of 1964 was passed many decent Americans were lulled into complacency because they thought the day of difficult struggle was over.
>
> Why are we in jail? Have you ever been required to answer 100 questions on government, some abstruse even to a political science specialist, merely to

> vote? Have you ever stood in line with over a hundred others and after waiting an entire day seen less than ten given the qualifying test?
>
> THIS IS SELMA, ALABAMA. THERE ARE MORE NEGROES IN JAIL WITH ME THAN THERE ARE ON THE VOTING ROLLS. . . .

Even with this drama, King found, on his release from jail, that President Johnson was still reluctant to push a new bill after having one passed the year before.

Meanwhile, local moderates offered concessions that were very tempting to Reese and other local leaders. Judge Thomas had ordered Clark to stop harassing the demonstrators and the board to speed up its registration process. On February 8 the board agreed to put out an "appearance book" that could be signed by potential registrants at any time, so that they would not have to wait in line all day. The Voters League was delighted by this concession, which SCLC staffers bitterly denounced as a trick. The movement's unity was beginning to unravel, and King told aides that Selma reminded him of Albany, where black cooperation had collapsed at a crucial point in the campaign.

On February 10, however, Sheriff Clark temporarily restored black unity by force-marching a group of young protesters out into the country. When Clark checked into the hospital the following Friday complaining of chest pains, demonstrators marched to the courthouse and knelt to offer public prayer for Clark's recovery "in body and in mind." Even though there may have been Christian charity in those prayers, SCLC was still counting on the sheriff to provide the dramatic opposition they needed to achieve their goal.

When massive violence did break out in mid-February it was not in Selma but in Marion, the seat of neighboring Perry County. On February 18 Col. Al Lingo's state troopers broke up a night march to the courthouse there. (According to James Bonard Fowler, he and the other troopers had been told that the marchers planned to burn down the town.) The local white community saw to it that the national press was not allowed to take pictures of the troopers' brutality; one reporter (Richard Valeriani of NBC) wound up in the hospital as a result. During the melee, twenty-six-year-old Jimmie Lee Jackson was shot in the stomach by Officer Fowler. Since the Marion hospital lacked facilities for blood transfusions, Jackson was rushed to Good Samaritan Hospital in Selma for treatment. He died from infection a week later, on February 26.

During Jackson's funeral on March 2 SCLC leader James Bevel cited the Old Testament's account of Queen Esther's going to the king to plead for her people. Using that idea, he said, "We must go to Montgomery and see the king [Governor Wallace]!" The people echoed his cry, "We must go to Montgomery and see the king!"

FIGURE 8.10 Brown Chapel AME Church, after the death of Jimmy Lee Jackson; courtesy of Selma–Dallas County Museum of History and Archives, Selma, Alabama.

The projected fifty-mile march along Highway 80 from Selma to Montgomery touched off a conflict within the Wallace administration. Some of Wallace's aides urged him to permit the march because they felt that King's forces were not ready for a hike of that length, and the attempt would be a flop. Lowndes County representatives, however, told the governor that marchers would need heavy police protection to get through their county without being attacked. After some hesitation, Wallace ruled that state troopers should be present at the Edmund Pettus Bridge on Sunday, March 7, to prevent the marchers from leaving Selma. The governor's legal advisor, Selma native Cecil Jackson, assured Selma city officials that state troopers would use as little force as possible.

Members of the Concerned White Citizens of Alabama (CWCA) arrived in Selma on Saturday, March 6, to demonstrate on behalf of blacks. This group of teachers, preachers, and other professional people from Birmingham and Tuscaloosa was led

FIGURE 8.11 Rev. Joseph Ellwanger, leader of the Concerned White Citizens of Alabama; courtesy of Ellwanger.

by a former Selmian, Joseph Ellwanger, whose father had served as president of Alabama Lutheran Academy and who was himself pastor of a Lutheran church in Birmingham. Seventy members of CWCA gathered at Claude Brown's Reformed Presbyterian Church and marched to the courthouse. The CWCA demonstration began to get out of control with white bystanders singing "Dixie" to drown out Ellwanger's speech, the CWCA countering with "America," and the handful of black bystanders beginning a chorus of "We Shall Overcome." Wilson Baker arrived barely in time to avoid the situation's becoming a riot and, thereby, averted major trouble. Ellwanger and his fellow concerned citizens returned to Reformed Presbyterian, where James Bevel assured them he had been so stunned to learn of their coming that he thought the Second Coming of Christ might be imminent.

On the following day, however, Baker's luck, and Selma's, ran out. The public safety director begged Smitherman to let him arrest the marchers before they reached the bridge because he was convinced that there would be a "bloodbath" once the participants passed into the hands of state troopers and a Dallas County posse. The

FIGURE 8.12 The marchers, led by Hosea Williams and John Lewis, crossed the Edmund Pettus Bridge to find state troopers waiting for them; courtesy of Selma–Dallas County Museum of History and Archives, Selma, Alabama.

mayor felt that everything was already arranged and that any confrontation would take place while Lingo was meeting Clark at the Montgomery airport on his return from appearing on ABC'S *Issues and Answers* television show.

If the march had left on time, events might possibly have gone as the mayor expected. However, there was a great deal of confusion at Brown Chapel that Sunday. Dr. King was not yet back from Atlanta, and local leaders were not sure they should march without him. Finally, they called King and secured his reluctant permission for the march to begin. Because of the hesitation, the 525 to 600 marchers who left Brown Chapel were several hours late, and many were not dressed for a long walk. A number of women were wearing high-heeled shoes.

SNCC opposed the march, feeling "the objectives of the march do not justify the dangers and the resources involved" (John Lewis, *Walking with the Wind*, New York, 1998, 318). However, their leader, John Lewis, participated as an individual, and he and SCLC leader Hosea Williams headed the march. The group walked down Sylvan Street to Selma Avenue, down Selma to Broad Street, and on Broad across the Edmund Pettus Bridge. By then, the troopers had been waiting for hours, and Jim Clark and Al Lingo arrived to take charge just as the marchers crossed the bridge.

Maj. John Cloud told the marchers that theirs was an "unlawful assembly" and ordered them to disperse and go back to Brown Chapel or to their homes (*Bearing the Cross*, 398). When Hosea Williams asked for "a word," Cloud replied, "There is no word to be had. You have two minutes to turn around and go back to your church." Cloud began counting off the seconds. The marchers stood their ground. Shortly the order came: "Troopers, advance!"

The troopers, already wearing gas masks, advanced with billy clubs held chest high, parallel to the ground and plowed into the marchers. There was the sound of a shot, and then the first tear gas canister landed among the marchers. (Cloud testified later that Sheriff Clark had discharged the first canister of tear gas and that Director Lingo had then ordered the troopers to use theirs as well.) The demonstrators found themselves the targets not only of savage blows from the troopers' billy clubs but also of forty canisters of tear gas, twelve canisters of smoke, and eight canisters of nausea gas. They broke and ran, with the troopers and the posse (fifteen of them on horseback) behind them.

Sheyann Webb, one of the children on the march, recorded her terror in *Selma, Lord Selma*:

> I just knew then that I was going to die, that those horses were going to trample me. So I kind of knelt down and held my hands and arms up over my head, and I must have been screaming—I don't really remember.
>
> All of a sudden somebody was grabbing me under the arms and lifting me up and running. The horses went by and I kept waiting to get trampled on or hit, but they went on by and I guess they were hitting at somebody else. And I looked up and saw that it was Hosea Williams who had me and he was running but we didn't seem to be moving, and I kept kicking my legs in the air, trying to speed up, and I shouted at him, "Put me down! You can't run fast enough with me!"
>
> But he held on until we were off the bridge and down on Broad Street and he let me go. I didn't stop running until I got home. All along the way there were people running in small groups; I saw people jumping over cars and being chased by the horsemen who kept hitting them. When I got to the apartments there were horsemen in the yards, galloping up and down, and one of them reared his horse up in the air as I went by, and he had his mask off and was shouting something at me.
>
> When I got into the house my momma and daddy were there and they had this shocked look on their faces and I ran in and tried to tell them what had happened. I was maybe a little hysterical because I kept repeating over and over, "I can't stop shaking, Momma, I can't stop shaking," and finally she

> grabbed me and sat down with me on her lap. But my daddy was like I'd never seen him before. He had a shotgun and he yelled, "By God, if they want it this way, I'll give it to them!" And he started out the door. Momma jumped up and got in front of him shouting at him.
>
> And he said, "I'm ready to die; I mean it! I'm ready to die!" I was crying there on the couch, I was so scared. But finally he put the gun down and sat down. I remember just lying there on the couch, crying and feeling so disgusted. They had beaten us like we were slaves. (*Selma, Lord, Selma*, 97–98)

Sheyann's father was not the only one ready to respond to violence with violence, and it was with great difficulty that Andrew Young and other SCLC staffers were able to maintain nonviolent discipline. It took some while before Wilson Baker was able to get Clark's "cowboys" to withdraw so that the wounded could be transported to Good Samaritan and to Burwell Infirmary. At least sixty-five people sought medical treatment that afternoon; seventeen of them had to be hospitalized, John Lewis with a fractured skull.

The *Selma Times-Journal* reported two days later, "We are still confounded by the action resorted to by law enforcement officers on the scene. There appears to be no logical reasoning behind the display of force employed by state troopers and mounted units who participated in dispersing the demonstrators." Other Alabama papers expressed their feelings more bluntly, and the *Anniston Star* was angry because of a group of "mounted posse men that portrayed Alabama as the home of Cossacks and head-crackers unable to cope with a situation without losing control."

Until "Bloody Sunday," the Johnson administration had been too tied up with Vietnam and the war on poverty to devote itself to another civil rights bill. After that day, however, the passage of the Voting Rights Act of 1965 became one of its major goals.

Hundreds of concerned white citizens arrived in Selma from across the country. King appealed to America's clergy to come to Selma and help in this hour of crisis. Ministers, priests, and nuns were soon arriving from all directions. One of the nation's leading rabbis, Abraham Joshua Heschel, came to stand behind King, along with Archbishop Iakovos, Greek Orthodox primate for North and South America. When the white-bearded Iakovos arrived at the Jackson house where Dr. King was staying, four-year-old Jawana Jackson told her mother, "It's Santa Claus! Mama, it's Santa Claus!" (Jackson, *House by the Side of the Road*, 126).

On March 9, King personally led a second march, this time over the protests of the Justice Department and an injunction by Judge Frank Johnson. The state troopers stopped the march once more, this time without violence; and King led the marchers back across the Edmund Pettus Bridge to Brown Chapel. Some mili-

FIGURE 8.13 Selma martyr, Rev. James J. Reeb; courtesy of Selma–Dallas County Museum of History and Archives, Selma, Alabama.

tants never forgave King for what they called "Turnaround Tuesday." But King was reluctant to violate a federal court order, especially since he thought Judge Johnson would ultimately rule in favor of the march (as he did).

That evening James Reeb, a thirty-six-year-old Unitarian minister from Boston, was struck down by men outside the Silver Moon Cafe on Washington Street. Reeb was rushed to Burwell Infirmary where Dr. Dinkins diagnosed his head injury as serious, too serious to be treated by any Selma surgeon. Dinkins ordered an ambulance to carry Reeb to the University of Alabama Hospital in Birmingham. The ambulance broke down en route, and by the time Reeb reached Birmingham, complications had set in. Two days later he became the second person to die in the local movement, and the only one struck down in Selma. The Selma Ministers' Union sent their condolences to Mrs. Reeb, and Baker arrested four men for the crime, three of whom had previous criminal records.

The national wave of indignation over Reeb's death brought more demonstrators to Selma, and also brought the voting rights bill closer to reality. Everett Dirksen, the Republican leader in the Senate, began meeting with President Johnson's aides to work out the details of legislation that both parties could support. Johnson himself went on national television March 15 to endorse the voting rights movement in Selma, comparing the city to such historic sites as Concord, Lexington, and Appomattox Court House. "We shall overcome," he said, adopting the marchers' anthem as his own.

On Sunday, March 21, the march to Montgomery "to see the king" finally took place. President Johnson federalized the Alabama National Guard to provide protection for the marchers, and Selma guardsmen, like city council president Carl Morgan, were called back to duty.

The march took four days. On March 24, it climaxed in a rally near the state capitol. The "king" they had come to see refused to meet with the marchers or hear their petitions. However, the crowd listened as Dr. King unleashed the full powers of his eloquence.

> How long will it take? I came to say to you this afternoon, however difficult the moment, however frustrating the hour, it will not be long, because truth pressed to earth will rise again. How long? Not long, because no lie can live forever.
>
> How long? Not long, because you reap what you sow.
>
> How long? Not long, because the arc of the moral universe is long, but it leans toward justice.
>
> How long? Not long, because "Mine eyes have seen the glory of the coming of the Lord, trampling out the vintage where the grapes of wrath are stored. He has loosed the fateful lightning of his terrible swift sword. His truth is marching on!"

Some of the "grapes of wrath" were still left. One of the white volunteers who had been helping to drive organizers back and forth between Selma and Montgomery, Mrs. Viola Liuzzo of Detroit, was shot and instantly killed in Lowndes County. Viola Gregg Liuzzo (1925–65) was the wife of a Teamsters Union official and the mother of five children. Later, three Klansmen from Jefferson County were tried for the murder.

The Voting Rights Bill passed on August 6, 1965, removing all the barriers set up by Alabama's 1901 Constitution and placing elections in six southern states under the surveillance of the federal government. Citizens of Selma were given credit for helping to change the face of the South and the nation. Mrs. Boynton was on hand to witness President Johnson's signing of the bill.

The last of the "Selma martyrs" to lose his life, a twenty-six-year-old Episcopal seminarian from New Hampshire named Jonathan Daniels, was shot down in Lowndes County on August 20. Daniels (1939–65) had lived in George Washington Carver Homes and attended services at St. Paul's Episcopal Church for several

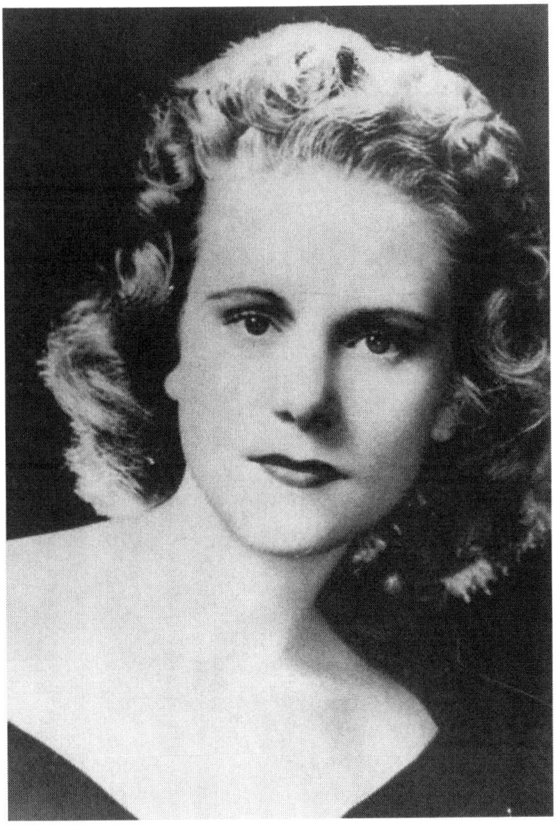

FIGURE 8.14 Mrs. Viola Gregg Liuzzo; courtesy of Selma–Dallas County Museum of History and Archives, Selma, Alabama.

months the previous spring, so he left friends to mourn him in both of Selma's racial communities. In the summer he had begun working with SNCC in Lowndes. Along with a Catholic priest from Chicago (Father Richard Morrisroe) and a group of students from Tuskegee Institute, Daniels was arrested for demonstrating in Fort Deposit. When the group was released from the county jail in Hayneville a week later, Daniels, Morrisroe, and two of their fellow demonstrators tried to buy a soft drink from an all-white store. They were met by a state employee with a shotgun. Daniels's last action was to shove Ruby Sales, a Tuskegee Institute student, out of the way of the shotgun blast that was to take his life. He was later canonized as a martyr by the Episcopal Church in the United States. (Sales's brother Joseph was later to play a significant role in Selma history as Yussuf Salaam.)

The Selma-to-Montgomery March was the high point of the civil rights movement and King's last great triumph. It was the moment when "black and white together" seemed to be coming true. Within a year, the cry of "Black Power" was shat-

FIGURE 8.15 Jonathan Daniels with Bunnie West, whose family provided him with shelter during his stay in Selma; courtesy of the West family.

tering what little interracial unity the movement had engendered. King's increasing involvement in opposition to the Vietnam War created even more enemies for him. He was attacked from the right as a traitor and from the left as an "Uncle Tom." King's death in Memphis in 1968 was influential in the passing of an open housing bill—a posthumous triumph. It could not, however, restore the accord the civil rights movement had known for one brief, shining moment in Selma.

Of course, stories of the atrocities associated with the civil rights movement live on, and even one of King's key aides, Stanley Levinson, expressed puzzlement over the national response to the violence in Selma. "Few were seriously hurt in the 'bloody events of Sunday.' The murders of Jackson and Reeb were not the direct work of the authorities but of the extremist fringes. . . . The bombings in Birmingham and the deliberate and continuous violence of Connor there were far worse. Yet Selma provoked a far greater indignation and resolution to halt the injustice. How is this explained?" (Garrow, *Bearing the Cross*, 419).

Noted journalist Gay Talese makes a similar assessment: "Memphis was where Dr. King was murdered in 1968 by a white man, and yet that city had not been demonized as Selma had been after Bloody Sunday, even though on the latter occasion not a single demonstrator had been killed" (*A Writer's Life* 224). Talese suggests that the media coverage of the state troopers' brutality was "so riveting and revolting that Selma thereafter represented the national nadir in narrow-mindedness, the last lingering remnant of the Civil War South and of white-columned bigotry and enslavement."

Whatever the explanation, Selma's name has been etched indelibly into the nation's memory. Visitors to the city often ask to be shown the place where Bull Connor unleashed his dogs, which is in Birmingham; or where George Wallace stood in the schoolhouse door, an event in Tuscaloosa; or even where Martin Luther King Jr. was assassinated, a Memphis tragedy. It is hard, sometimes, to convince them that every significant event in the history of the civil rights movement did not take place in this one small southern town.

After the Shouting Had Died

During the marches, each race felt compelled to maintain a united front against the other. Beneath the surface, however, both communities were deeply divided. When the vestry at St. Paul's Episcopal voted to open the church's doors to black churchgoers, members of the Citizens' Council warned the vestrymen and their wives that they would "regret" such a betrayal of the white race.

The Council also deeply resented the *Times-Journal*'s coverage of the marches and was about to call on local merchants to withdraw their advertising from the paper until Mayor Smitherman and Councilman Swift intervened. They warned the council that such an open attack on the paper would make it impossible to maintain "white unity." This did not keep individual white people from cancelling their subscriptions and complaining that the paper's objectivity "furnished aid and comfort to this kinky-haired, thick-lipped, mulatto, race-baiter Martin Luther King" (as Sol Tepper charged in the August 24 issue of the *Selma Times-Journal*). The diehard segregationists were further outraged when the Alabama Press Association named Roswell Falkenberry 1965's Journalist of the Year because of the paper's impartial coverage.

Some moderates also found it hard to restrain their feelings. Art Lewis (1911–67), a native of New Jersey who moved to Selma in 1941 to set up a cigar factory, had always striven to fit in with southern ways; but Clark's brutal tactics were too much for him to take. A private letter written by Lewis and his wife, Muriel, a letter that expressed their dismay at Clark's tactics, fell into Citizens' Council hands and was widely circulated as evidence of the Lewises' betrayal of their race. Lewis's attempt to get other moderates to join him in an open statement failed, and he found himself ostracized by most of his fellow white citizens.

Some black people also disagreed about the tactics employed by Dr. King and

FIGURE 8.16 Publisher Roswell Falkenberry's coverage of the Selma movement was too objective to suit the Citizens' Council; courtesy of Anne Falkenberry Knight.

the leaders of SCLC. The use of students as demonstrators upset many older blacks, and the attempt to hold night marches in Selma struck even SNCC as "suicidal." On March 22, a month after the movement had announced a boycott of all Selma's white merchants, Rev. C. C. Hunter publicly broke ranks. In a letter to the *Selma Times-Journal*, he insisted that any boycott that hurt the black community's friends as well as its enemies was unfair and counterproductive. The divisions in the white community came to the surface in mid-April when the Alabama Chamber of Commerce released a statement entitled "What We Believe and Where We Stand," which pledged obedience to the civil rights laws passed by Congress. The local chambers of every major town in Alabama, except Selma, signed the statement. Moderates promptly began attempting to obtain a reversal of the chamber's decision not to sign and get the city and county on record as endorsing obedience to the law.

FIGURE 8.17 City attorney McLean Pitts was in favor of signing the Alabama Chamber of Commerce's "What We Believe and Where We Stand"; courtesy of the *Selma Times-Journal.*

Bank official Frank Wilson and businessman Charles Hohenberg called a meeting of concerned moderates at the Hotel Albert. As a direct result of this meeting, the Selma City Council met in special session on Friday, April 16, to hear the moderates' request that it endorse the statement. On the other side, the White Citizens' Council demanded that the chamber's refusal be allowed to stand. According to the *Times-Journal* account, "names were called, tempers flared, and voices became impassioned" during the two-hour debate.

City attorney McLean Pitts said that, as much as he disliked the new civil rights law, it was the law; and if Selma were unwilling to pledge obedience, it would become extremely difficult to attract industry. Jerome Siegel, of the Committee of One Hundred, agreed with Pitts, noting that Hammermill and Dan River Mills were both unhappy with the city's current stance on the issue.

Attorney Joe Pilcher, who had been Smitherman's campaign manager, attacked

FIGURE 8.18 Joe Pilcher opposed signing the Alabama Chamber of Commerce's "What We Believe and Where We Stand"; courtesy of the *Selma Times-Journal.*

the mayor for the secret meetings he had begun holding with Reese and other black leaders on April 7 (a month to the day after Bloody Sunday). He also denounced by name the bankers and lawyers who had been misleading the mayor with their counsels of moderation. Sol Tepper and other diehards insisted that if only whites maintained their unity behind Sheriff Clark, they could somehow defeat integration. Banker W. B. Craig replied bluntly that he and other community leaders were not willing to "lower [themselves] to achieve this unity."

Paul Grist, chairman of the ministers' organization, lent moral authority to the position of the moderates, and, after hours of debate, the city council endorsed the moderate position by a unanimous vote. The following day, the chamber of commerce reversed its previous position and, by nightfall, the Dallas County Commission had concurred with the other two bodies. On Easter Sunday, the *Selma Times-Journal* proclaimed the triumph of moderate Selmians and published a list of eleven hundred local citizens who endorsed their stand.

While the White Citizens' Council was losing its grip on the white community, the Dallas County Voters League (DCVL) was facing challenges to its leadership in the black community. The challenges came on the heels of a series of setbacks for local leaders of the civil rights movement. Archbishop T. J. Toolen of the Mobile diocese expelled Edmundite priest Maurice Ouellet from Alabama, explaining, "I don't want a dead priest on my hands." The Selma School Board refused to renew F. D. Reese's contract at Hudson High School, citing excessive absences as its reason. After that came the real dividing factor: in July Reese was arrested on charges of misusing Voters League funds for personal expenses. Resentment of Reese and other middle-class leaders had been building for some time, and the arrest precipitated the organization of a new group called the Dallas County Independent Free Voters Association in opposition to the Dallas County Voters League. Charges against Reese were dropped within a year, but, by that time, black unity had been shattered beyond repair. The SCLC workers assigned to Selma, Harold Middlebrooks and Shirley Mesher, were more interested in working with the poor, especially the rural poor, than in working with middle-class leaders like Reese.

Selma schools began the process of desegregation in 1965, a few grades at a time. When Governor Wallace learned that the Selma City School Board had voted on March 1 to comply with the court order to integrate, he was quite displeased. He summoned board members Edgar Stewart and Kathryn Windham to Montgomery for a semi-private meeting and warned them that the state would not help Selma maintain law and order if the city defied him by allowing black students to attend previously all-white schools.

"I cannot be responsible for what might happen in Selma," he told them, implying that the Klan, the National States Rights Party, and other radical groups might commit some atrocity (Kathryn Windham, *Odd Egg Editor*, Athens, GA, 162). The board voted 7–1 to go ahead in spite of the governor's opposition and adopted a "freedom of choice" plan that would desegregate Selma schools four grades at a time, starting with grades one through four.

On June 28, Citizens' Council president R. D. Wilkinson called a meeting at the courthouse on behalf of the Dallas County Private School Association (DCPSA). Judge Hare spoke at the meeting, warning white Selmians of the "unprecedented trouble come September" and the opening of school. Since the schools of Louisville, Kentucky, had integrated, he assured the crowd, "all decent teachers have fled the knives, ice picks and derringers of the Louisville classrooms" (*Selma Times-Journal*, June 29, 1965). In short, their children would not be safe in integrated schools. Some 133 parents responded by signing up for spaces in the private school to be set up by the DCPSA. (Mayor Smitherman and Judge Reynolds were conspicuous by their absence and let it be known that their kids would stay in the public schools.)

On September 3, 1965, the city schools opened, with thirty-one black students

FIGURE 8.19 School Board Chairman Edgar A. Stewart oversaw the desegregation of Selma's public schools; courtesy of Allen S. Reeves, Reeves & Stewart, PC, Selma, Alabama.

registering at Frances Thomas, Edgewood, Baker, and Byrd schools without any difficulty. Only one out-of-state newsman showed up to cover the event. That same day, Morgan Academy opened in Sen. John Tyler Morgan's old home with 116 students in grades one through six, with Mary Faye Hodges Ellis (former principal of Orrville High and the wife of county commissioner Furniss Ellis) as headmistress. The following year, when the public schools integrated grades five through eight, Morgan added grades seven and eight, offering them in the education rooms of the Houston Park Church of Christ. By 1967, when Selma had integrated its high schools, Morgan had added the ninth grade and had opened a brand-new campus on West Dallas Avenue.

On November 5, 1965, Mayor Smitherman called for the establishment of a "broad-based" biracial committee to fight poverty in Selma. (The city had earlier set up an all-white committee under Councilman Martin Coon, but it had been rejected by the federal government.) The Dallas County Committee for the Anti-Poverty Program, headed by black Presbyterian Rev. Ernest Bradford, had been meeting since September but had been unable to attract significant white support. Black leaders were suspicious of Smitherman's intentions.

Rob Hereford's MA thesis suggests why the antipoverty programs were so important: "After almost three years of protest, black Selmians could eat where they wanted, send their children to integrated schools, and vote for candidates of their choice. These victories were important, but they made it no easier to feed, shelter, and clothe a family" ("A Study of Dallas County, Alabama, 1930–1970," University of Georgia, Athens, 1992, 109). Antipoverty programs like food stamps might provide more concrete help than the voting rights act.

Rev. Joseph Knight, native of Dallas County, ex-marine, and Baptist minister, played a key role in persuading some black leaders to take a chance by joining forces with the mayor. "I was naive," he told the author. "I quit my job in Florida and came back to Selma, thinking I could save my home town by bridging the gap between the races. But the gap was deeper and more bitter than I realized." His task was complicated by the black community's division along class lines, with the "masses" suspicious of the "classes." SCLC's Shirley Mesher insisted that the war on poverty should be directed by the poor themselves; the Voters League felt that middle-class expertise was more important. J. D. Hunter expressed the league's views: "When I go to court, I want a lawyer, and when I go to church, I want a preacher."

On March 25, 1966, the Dallas County and City of Selma Economic Opportunity Board (EOB) was formally incorporated with a biracial group of officers: a white president (banker B. Frank Wilson), a black vice president (extension agent Charles D. Scott II), a white secretary (county school superintendent Frank Earnest Jr.), and a black treasurer (Edwin L. Moss). The EOB chose Knight as executive director and a black man, Ed Johnson, as deputy director.

While some white people were adapting to a new era, the sheriff was not. Jim Clark's antics had made him a hero to hard-line segregationists across the state; his autobiography, *I Saw Selma Raped*, assured readers that the Communists had deliberately plotted to ruin his reputation because county sheriffs represent the main barrier to a Communist takeover of the United States, and he was the best sheriff in the country. He planned to run for governor until George Wallace announced that his wife, Lurleen, would be a candidate for the position. Clark then decided to run for reelection as sheriff. Wilson Baker's campaign for that office was already organized and running, and the bitter clash between the two men reflected the divisions in the white community and in the black. Smitherman and the moderates backed Baker and so did his old adversary F. D. Reese and the Dallas County Voters League. But not all black voters were that fond of Baker; the Independent Free Voters Association rather liked the idea of electing a black sheriff but decided to wait for the general election in November rather than enter a candidate in the Democratic primary in May.

Baker led the voting in the May primary, but the Democratic county executive

Figure 8.20 Rev. Joseph Knight tried to bring the black and white communities together in support of an antipoverty program; courtesy of Anne Falkenberry Knight.

committee, headed by Alston Keith, decided to throw out six boxes from black precincts that would have given Baker the victory without a runoff. (There were two minor white candidates.) However, what had worked during Reconstruction worked no longer, and the federal courts ordered that the boxes be counted. Though Baker was now the official Democratic nominee, Clark ran against him in the general election as an independent, hoping that Stokely Carmichael's third party would drain away enough black votes from Baker to insure the public safety director's defeat. The Independent Free Voters nominated Samson Crum Sr., a black postal employee, for sheriff, and things looked bad for Baker. In the end, Crum withdrew and Baker was able to defeat Clark a second time, although by a much smaller margin. Wilson Baker's victory was almost the only "moderate" triumph that year, but it bore permanent fruit. Baker hired black deputies, showed himself an excellent sheriff, and held the position until his death in 1975.

The "antipoverty wars" continued after Baker's election. Shirley Mesher succeeded in organizing the Southwest Alabama Farmers Co-Operative Association (SWAFCA) and winning a $500,000 grant from the federal government. Mayor Smitherman, Judge Reynolds, and other white leaders from the ten-county area bitterly opposed SWAFCA, seeing it as a "Black Power" movement. In turn, some black activists strongly opposed Smitherman's efforts to get government money for urban renewal.

Selma's local "wars" took place at a time when the *Times-Journal* was reporting the city's first casualty in Vietnam, PFC James Mooney. Mooney, a member of the Reformed Presbyterian Church, had played trombone for the Hudson High band for four years. Another Hudson graduate, Lt. Freddie L. Johnson, died in December, drowning "while attempting to assist another individual on a training mission." Johnson left a widow and three children to mourn his passing. Other deaths were to follow.

The city's most notable loss in combat was Maj. Joseph Edgar Wilkinson III (1929–67). A student at the University of Alabama when the Korean War broke out, Wilkinson had enlisted in the US Air Corps. He then made the air force his career, serving at various bases in the United States and Canada and graduating from the Command Staff School at Maxwell AFB in 1964. While serving in the Pacific, Wilkinson earned an Air Medal and a Distinguished Service Cross. His plane, *Puff the Magic Dragon*, was shot down over the Mekong Delta in January of 1967.

When Dr. King returned to Selma for the last time on February 16, 1968, to speak at Tabernacle Baptist, he announced that Selma had probably made more progress than any other city in the South. He was particularly pleased to have been met at the airport by one of Baker's black deputies rather than Jim Clark's posse. He went on to appeal for support for his Poor People's Campaign and to endorse L. L. Anderson's candidacy for mayor of Selma.

King might well have been pleased that Selma's white clergy were finally adjusting to a new era. In March the Dallas County Christian Ministers' Union welcomed its first black members—Charles Lett of Green Street Baptist, P. H. Lewis of Brown Chapel, and F. D. Reese of Ebenezer Baptist. (The group had only admitted Catholics as members in the previous month.) The Ministers' Union also called on Mayor Smitherman to set up a biracial committee.

King's candidate for mayor, L. L. Anderson, went down to defeat on March 5, amassing 2,852 votes against Smitherman's 5,932. The Voters League had refused to endorse Anderson, feeling that Smitherman had done more for the black community than any previous mayor and deserved support. Some white Selmians felt that Smitherman had done too much for the black community, but they could hardly fail to support him over a black opponent. The *Times-Journal* noted that while voting had mostly followed racial lines, about 250 black voters had crossed over to sup-

FIGURE 8.21 Maj. Joseph Edgar Wilkinson III; courtesy of the Wilkinson family.

port Smitherman and about 125 white voters had voted for Ed Moss for city council. This "apparent tiny defection of white voters to a Negro candidate" offered some hope for the future.

In April King's assassination in Memphis touched off turmoil across the nation. The *Times-Journal* responded by expressing once more its disapproval of King's "nonviolent lawlessness" but quickly added that "murder is not the answer." The students at R. B. Hudson responded by erupting. A week of demonstrations followed, with repeated marches to City Hall by outraged students. The city police showed maximum restraint, and while some windows were broken, Selma did not suffer the violence that took place in some 210 cities across the United States.

When the Ministers' Union met in May, it chose Lett as first vice president and Father Edward Leary, of the Society of St. Edmund, as secretary-treasurer. The meeting closed with anxious discussion of "the split occurring among the local ministers and the concern we should have . . . for the future of our Union." The concern proved well justified; the Union dissolved over the summer. One of the groups to emerge from the split was the Dallas County Evangelical Ministers Association, which welcomed Lett when he ventured to attend a previously all-white meeting at Central Baptist. The split was not about race, they assured him, but about theology; Catholics like Leary just weren't "evangelical" enough.

As the divided city struggled toward a solution to its problems, it seemed caught up in a dance of "two steps forward, one step back," with progress coming bit by bit. The year 1970 brought fresh hope. Dallas County had voted for George or Lurleen Wallace for governor in 1958, 1962, and 1966, and for president in 1968. But 1970 was a different story: the county went solidly for moderate candidate Albert Brewer over Wallace both in the May 2 primary and the June 2 runoff. In part this was because Governor Brewer had delivered something the county's leaders had wanted for decades: a community college. "Alabama needs a full time governor," the *Times-Journal* proclaimed. "Too long has Alabama been crippled by those who would pit race against race, class against class, section against section. Too long have prejudice and hatred separated us, clouding our thinking and sapping our strength. Too long have we squandered our talents and wasted our time by clinging to a dim and faded past rather than joining other states in the mainstream of national progress by facing the reality of change." The rest of Alabama did not follow Dallas's lead, choosing to reelect Wallace after one of the dirtiest campaigns in Alabama history. The city fathers felt constrained to name the college that Brewer had set up for them the George C. Wallace Community College, hoping that the tribute would avert Wallace's wrath.

9

The Queen City Recovers Its Poise

Selma, 1968–1988

On August 11, 1979, the National Funeral Directors and Morticians met in Selma to dedicate a monument to Martin Luther King Jr. outside Brown Chapel. One of the main speakers at the ceremony turned out to be Selma's former mayor, Joseph T. Smitherman, who was not on the original program.

"You remember me?" Smitherman began cheerfully, "I'm the fellow who was on the other side!" There was a second of startled gasps, then a burst of applause. Smitherman went on to admit how young, inexperienced, and afraid he had been in 1965, when he and Wilson Baker had tried to outmaneuver Dr. King and the SCLC.

"Dr. King freed us all, white and black," he said earnestly. Smitherman confessed that he knew now that segregation had been harmful to both races. Then, he had been afraid to greet his black friends when he met them on the street—afraid of what his white friends would think. Acknowledging that those days were gone forever, he was encouraged that all people could join together in fighting their true enemies—the poverty and ignorance that continued to plague Alabama.

A year later, Smitherman ran for mayor once again—and was elected over two white opponents with the overwhelming support of Selma's black community. This represented a dramatic change since 1968, when he had polled roughly 5 percent of the black vote. His former opponent L. L. Anderson had promised to run again in 1972 and vowed that "the Negro community will never support a white segregationist for mayor of Selma." But neither Anderson nor any other black opponent ran against Smitherman in 1972, 1976, or 1980. Nobody ran against "Joe T." in 1972. He had just secured millions of federal dollars to build public housing in Selma and persuaded the Selma City Council to switch to election by district (thereby guaranteeing black candidates places on the council). It was no wonder that Ed Moss was

FIGURE 9.1 Monument to Dr. Martin Luther King Jr. in front of Brown Chapel AME, Selma, Alabama; courtesy of Janet Gresham.

endorsing Smitherman as "the best mayor we ever had." In 1976, he faced a challenge from a white opponent, Roy McLaughlin, the highly respected director of the Methodist Children's Home. McLaughlin claimed it was "Time for a Change," but Selma voters must not have agreed since he did not carry a single precinct.

In 1979 Smitherman decided that he needed a change and resigned as mayor. He was succeeded by Carl Morgan, who had served as president of the council since 1964. Apparently private life did not suit Joe T., because by 1980 he was preparing to run again. He was opposed by both Morgan and Jean Sullivan, a Republican national committeewoman. These were formidable candidates, each of whom had some claim to black support. Morgan had cast the deciding vote both to rename Sylvan Street after Dr. King and to reopen the city's pools on an integrated basis.

Sullivan's liberal reputation was such that many of Selma's black Democrats had crossed over to the Republican primary to vote for her for national committeewoman in 1972. Morgan and Sullivan divided the majority of the white vote between them; but they were no match for the old master, who won 80 percent of the black vote and was triumphantly returned to office.

Smitherman's ability to dominate the city's political scene was one of the most striking features of the 1970s and 1980s; he held the office of mayor longer than

FIGURE 9.2 Republican leader Jean Sullivan; courtesy of the *Selma Times-Journal.*

any previous mayor in the city's history. He managed to hold on to most of his white supporters while reaching out to make concessions to the black community.

Other leading figures from the 1960s passed from the scene. Judge Hare died in 1969, to be replaced by Edgar Russell, who was far more open to change. Judge Thomas stepped down in 1971, to be replaced by W. Brevard Hand as federal district judge. Hand was to prove far less patient with the Selma City Council than Thomas had been with the Dallas County Board of Registrars. Wilson Baker died in 1975 and was replaced by his deputy "Cotton" Nichols (1919–2009). Senator Givhan died in early 1976, bringing to a close the longest career of any member of the Alabama Senate. Judge Bernard Reynolds retired that same year and was replaced by Johnny Jones. Mrs. Boynton remarried and moved to Tuskegee, leaving her son Bruce to carry on her work. City attorney McLean Pitts died in 1982 and was succeeded by his son Henry. Joseph Pilcher Jr. died in 1987 and was succeeded as attorney for the Craig Airport Authority by his son. But Joe T., like Old Man River, just kept rolling along.

The early 1970s were challenging times for many Selmians. Desegregation had been frightening enough for many white conservatives; full-scale integration was terrifying. Whites who had adjusted to their children having a handful of black classmates were rattled at the prospect of their kids attending majority-black schools. Smitherman managed to both express white anger over the changes and to make sure they took place peacefully.

In fact, integration proved traumatic for both white and black communities. It forced the closing of a number of institutions (like St. Elizabeth's Mission and Good Samaritan Hospital) that had served the black community for years, and it put others (like Alabama Lutheran and Selma University) at serious risk.

But the 1970s also brought a reconciliation of sorts to the city. In January 1972 the Selma City Council voted to accept election by wards, opening the door for black candidates to be elected from wards four and five. In the following month, the "antipoverty wars" between the mayor and some black activists were finally resolved by the Selma Accords of 1972. The accords, drawn up between the city and the federal government, outraged some conservative white people, but they also made it possible for the city to garner some $6 million in federal funds.

The closing of Craig Air Force Base in 1977 proved a major blow to Selma. Selmians sought new ways to build up their city and replace the jobs lost. City and county joined to set up the Craig Airport Authority and to launch a renewed effort to recruit new industry. Many Selmians felt that the city could become a major tourist attraction by drawing on its long and colorful history; as director of tourism Elise Blackwell told the author, "Our history *is* our future!"

The 1980s saw historic progress for black politicians. For the first time since Reconstruction, black Selmians were elected to the Alabama legislature and to the Dallas County Commission. State senator Hank Sanders became the most prominent black politician from Dallas County since Jeremiah Haralson and, like Haralson, played a significant role in state and national politics.

The Travails of Integration

During the early 1970s, Selmians had to grapple with the problems posed by integrating previously all-white and all-black institutions. The public schools, the black colleges, the churches, and the recreational facilities all had to make adjustments.

Year by year the federal government raised its standards for what constituted "integration" of public schools. On August 14, 1969, for example, Kathryn Windham reported to the school board that the government would require five hundred black students and twenty-one black teachers in formerly all-white schools, in addition to twenty-one white teachers in predominantly black schools, for the 1969–70 school year. As it turned out, this was not enough for the courts, which decreed in

September that Selma must erase all traces of its former "dual system" by the opening of the 1970–71 school year. Parrish High and Hudson High must both cease to exist, to be replaced by a single, integrated secondary school. The city's elementary schools and junior high schools must reflect their neighborhoods more accurately, so that the old Hudson High (now Westside Middle School, later to become CHAT Academy and still later Hudson Middle School) should have a significant white enrollment, and Baker Elementary (now Eastside Junior High, later to become the School of Discovery) and Frances Thomas should have a black majority.

As the board prepared to face this challenge, it came under fire from several directions at once. The working-class whites of east Selma were particularly upset over having to send their children to majority-black schools. They were well aware that most school board members lived in west Selma, which was less affected by integration. In November, a group of white ministers led by Warren Cooper of Central Baptist met with the board to express their displeasure with its actions and declare "their intention to bring about legislation . . . to change present means of selecting City School Board members to elective vote of the people." The following month board chairman, Dr. Sam Moseley, laid down the law for his fellow board members; they could not ask the community to accept full integration unless they were keeping their own children in the public schools (School Board minutes, December 13, 1969, stored at Baker School). Two board members resigned at once, and a third followed several months later. The remaining eight—J. Miller Childers, Peter Diffley, R. R. McKenzie, Dr. Philip B. Moss Jr., Ralph O'Gwynn, John M. Porter, Kathryn Windham, and Moseley himself—pressed forward as the board came under fire from all sides.

In February a black delegation led by the Revs. P. H. Lewis of Brown Chapel and Charles A. Lett of Green Street Baptist urged the board to add black members. On July 22 the board responded by adding its first black members—Rev. Lewis and Mrs. Mary L. Coleman. Lewis was transferred to Mobile in December, but Mrs. Coleman (a kindergarten teacher with six children in Selma schools) stayed on the board through the critical years that followed.

Meanwhile, a group led by the parishioners of Meadowview Christian Church started organizing to create a new private school for Dallas County. On March 24, 1970, the Meadowview Christian School was incorporated with J. Marshall Williams as president and Ralph T. Walker as vice president. The school's constitution, recorded at the courthouse on November 19, 1970, stressed its religious purpose: "The first section [of this constitution] shall consist of twelve articles which are irrevocable until the second coming of Christ."

FIGURE 9.3 School board chairman Dr. Sam Moseley led the school board during the merger of the two school systems; courtesy of the Moseley family.

Among the board members was Rev. Cecil Williamson, a Presbyterian minister who was rapidly emerging as a spokesman for conservative whites. A native of Montgomery, Williamson became pastor of the Alabama Avenue Presbyterian Church in 1965 and moved the congregation to Crescent Hill in west Selma. He was also instrumental in the organization of the Presbyterian Church of America (PCA), which broke off from the Presbyterian Church in the United States (PCUSA) in 1973. Williamson was later to serve on the Selma City Council and the Dallas County Board of Education.

As the opening of classes drew near, a group of white parents calling themselves the "Concerned Parents of Dallas County" sponsored an August 5 rally at the courthouse to vent their frustration. During the rally attorney Henry Pitts called for "massive defiance" of the federal mandate, Rev. Cecil Williamson denounced the "liberal" *Selma Times-Journal*, and Mayor Smitherman lashed out at both the school board and the *Times-Journal*, describing Kathryn Windham, who served on both the board and the newspaper, as a "corn field intellectual."

FIGURE 9.4 Conservative leader Rev. Cecil Williamson, later president of the Selma City Council; courtesy of the author.

Kathryn Tucker Windham (1919–2011), a native of Selma who grew up in Thomasville, was a graduate of Huntingdon who had worked as a journalist for newspapers in Montgomery and Birmingham. She moved to Selma with her husband in 1948; after his death in 1956 she went to work for the *Times-Journal*. Windham was yet to win national recognition for her ghost story collections; but she was already someone to reckon with. She treasured Smitherman's insult, claiming that the mayor was the first person who had ever called her an intellectual and presenting him with several ears of corn in gratitude. Windham also noted that in spite of their angry rhetoric, both Pitts and Smitherman kept their children in the public schools.

Not all black people were pleased by the board's actions. Quite a few were upset that the Selma School Board chose the former principal of Parrish High, James Street, to head Selma High, rather than the former principal of Hudson, Joe Yelder, who had more years of service. Yelder himself did not contest the appointment, thinking that it would be easier to keep white students in the system with a white principal, contenting himself with serving as principal of the new Eastside Junior High.

The *Times-Journal* insisted in a September 6 editorial that the transition had gone as smoothly as could be expected, stating that the first home football game between Selma High and Demopolis has shown "a new school spirit being born, the emergence of a new sense of pride and confidence, as the Selma Saints swept

FIGURE 9.5 Kathryn Tucker Windham, later a nationally revered author; courtesy of Dilcy Windham Hilley.

to victory over their Demopolis gridiron opponents." In most of the counties surrounding Dallas, massive white flight to private academies left the public schools as segregated as ever. Some six hundred of Selma's white students did withdraw from the system. But 80 percent of the white students enrolled in the public schools in the spring of 1970—2,644 out of 3,303—were still enrolled in the fall.

The May 2, 1971, *Times-Journal* expressed pride that "the schools have operated almost an entire academic year without major disruption or incident" and predicted that "more white students will return to the public school system . . . each year that the public school system operates as successfully as it has this year." While the white enrollment in the public schools did increase slightly in the years that followed, Morgan Academy and Meadowview Christian continued to hold their own and to compete vigorously with the public schools for white students.

The Dallas County system went through a similar experience, losing most of its white students from west Dallas (who were assigned to majority-black Keith High School) and many of those in south Dallas (assigned to majority-black Southside

High) but holding on to most of those in north Dallas (who were assigned to majority-white Dallas County High).

Selma's Catholic schools also merged in 1970, with Assumption Academy and St. Elizabeth's joining to become Selma Catholic School. Within a year the new bishop of Mobile announced that Selma was too small a town to have two Catholic parishes. It was time for the Church of the Assumption and St. Elizabeth's Mission to merge into one integrated parish to serve as "a sign of reconciliation" to their fellow Selmians. The bishop entrusted the new parish to the Edmundites, who called Rev. Nelson Ziter back to Selma to make the merger work. Black and white Catholics alike protested the loss of their parish traditions and identities; but their protests were in vain. Ziter, who had a host of friends in both communities, chose Our Lady Queen of Peace as the name for the new parish and worked feverishly to make it a success. The parish survived and seemed to flourish, but the new Queen of Peace School did not last long. By 1976 its enrollment declined so much that it had to close its doors. Catholic education in Selma, which had begun in 1884, thus came to an end.

Selma's Protestant churches had problems of their own. Many white Selmians objected to what they felt was the excessive liberalism of their denominational leaders. In 1968, after Church Street Methodist opened its doors to people of all races, a group of parishioners left to form the Independent Protestant Church. In 1973, Crescent Hills Presbyterian seceded from the Presbyterian Church in the United States (PCUSA) to become one of the charter members of the new Presbyterian Church in America (PCA), a markedly more conservative group. Woodland Heights Presbyterian later followed its lead. On the other hand the members of Selma's upper-middle-class parish, First Presbyterian, and of its black parish, Northern Heights Presbyterian, both chose to stay with the PCUSA.

The YMCA was building a new branch for the black community on Minter Avenue in the late 1960s, but still faced the dilemma that its "main branch" on Broad Street only opened its doors to white people. "One of my board members, Rev. Frank Matthews, told me it was time to integrate the Y," Pat Knight told the author. Claude Kirkpatrick ("Pat") Knight (1931–2012), an Auburn graduate and Korean War vet, took over as executive director of the Y in 1970. "And the national Y said the same thing. So I took it to my Board, and they voted 16 to 8 to integrate. I talked with Rev. Reese, and we managed to integrate very quietly." The YMCA was going through other changes as well, making the transition to being a "family center" rather than one serving primarily males; by the end of the decade, male swimmers were being required to wear bathing suits.

Selma's municipal swimming pool had been closed to prevent integration in the

1960s and was only reopened in 1976 after the city built a new swimming pool in east Selma, one that would be far more convenient for most black families. (The city named the pool after William H. Dinkins, the former president of Selma University.) The handful of black people that came to the old pool on Dallas Avenue were not enough to disturb most white people. The west Selma pool later closed due to maintenance problems and declining use. It was demolished and tennis courts were built on the site.

If Selma's historically white institutions found integration traumatic, some of its black ones found themselves struggling for survival. At a time when integration was seen as the answer to everything, what role was there left for a black Lutheran college, a black Catholic hospital, or a black branch of the YMCA?

Some Lutherans wanted to close the schools they had set up to serve African Americans. They succeeded in closing the college in North Carolina and the day schools in Wilcox County, but ran into stiff resistance from the Selma school's alumni. The black Lutheran clergy fought back, demanding that Alabama Lutheran be allowed to continue and that it do so under black leadership. In 1970, the school acquired its first black president on a permanent basis, Dr. Willis Wright.

Wright, a native of Louisiana (d. 1990) who had previously worked at Southern University in Baton Rouge, launched the school on a new course, transforming it from a training school for Lutheran church workers into a general liberal arts college open to all. He aggressively recruited students, going into "the highways and hedges . . . wherever he could find a warm body," according to Richard C. Dickinson's *The Miracle on Green Street* (91). Wright also pushed the faculty to work toward advanced degrees, looking forward to the day when Alabama Lutheran could win college accreditation from the Southern Association of Colleges and Schools (SACS).

In 1980 Wright passed the torch to Dr. Julius Jenkins, a native of Pine Apple who became the first graduate of Alabama Lutheran to serve as president. School chaplain David DeRamus later told the author that "Dr. Wright was our Moses, who gave us the vision of where we were to go. And Dr. Jenkins was our Joshua, who led us into the Promised Land."

In 1981 Alabama Lutheran changed its name to Concordia College Selma; within two years it had won accreditation from SACS as a two-year institution entitled to award the associate of arts degree. In 2014 it changed its name again, this time to Concordia College Alabama.

In the same year that Alabama Lutheran won accreditation, Good Samaritan Hospital closed its doors. The integration of Selma's white hospitals, Selma Baptist and Vaughan Memorial, meant that Selma's white doctors would now find it more convenient to place all their patients, black and white, at the same hospital. This

FIGURE 9.6 Dr. Willis Wright, president of Concordia College, Selma, 1970–80; courtesy of Concordia College, Selma, Alabama.

was especially true after the doctors at Selma Baptist moved out to the new Selma Medical Center on the edge of town in 1971.

In 1976 the Dallas County Medical Society accepted its first black member, surgeon Chudy Okoye. Okoye, a native of Nigeria, had earned his medical degree at Emory University in Atlanta. Okoye was one of the first doctors recruited by John Crear when he took over as the first black administrator of "Good Sam" in 1974. Crear fought valiantly to keep the hospital going by recruiting a new medical staff and expanding the hospital's services. The hospital helped launch the Rural Medical Health Program in 1978, setting up rural clinics in Uniontown and Pine Apple. But in the end the changing finances of medicine were too much for the hospital, and by 1983 the Edmundites could no longer sustain it. Smitherman offered the pithy epitaph, "It was integration that killed Good Sam." And in a sense it was.

FIGURE 9.7 Dr. Julius Jenkins, president of Concordia College, Selma, 1980–2007; courtesy of the *Selma Times-Journal.*

FIGURE 9.8 Civic leader John Crear; courtesy of the Edmundite Missions.

Concerns about integration also hampered Claude Brown's crusade to build a new recreational building for the black YMCA. He won support from such white leaders as Paul Grist, Harry Gamble, and Dr. Philip "Buddy" Moss but ran into opposition from attorney J. L. Chestnut Jr., who thought this would help to preserve segregation. When Selma University's leaders went to Claude Brown for help in getting the school out of debt, the Presbyterian minister explained sadly that dealing with Chestnut's threatened lawsuit was keeping him too busy to help. As Chestnut recalls the result, "Three Baptist preachers came to my office and advised me in very certain language to shut up or they would lose the school" (*Black in Selma*, 157). Chestnut did as he was told, and Brown was able to see the completed George W. Carver YMCA opened on Minter Avenue before his death.

Selma University survived but faced one difficulty after another. According to Wilson Fallin's *Uplifting the People*, "In the late 1970's mishandling of federal funds, a debt of $2 million to the Department of Education, and a fire that destroyed Foster Hall put the university in jeopardy" (253). Fallin became president in 1982, launched a major fund-raising drive, and pulled the school out of debt. Under his successor, B. W. Dawson, Selma University finally achieved its long-sought goal of accreditation by SACS in 1986. Within a few years, however, the school was in financial difficulties once more, and lost its accreditation in 1994.

Reconciliation and Progress: 1970–1980

In the early 1970s, the black community began working together more effectively. Reese regained his teaching job. Ed Moss gained a useful ally when Catholic priest James P. Robinson returned to Selma as assistant director of the Edmundite Missions. Robinson was able to pull the black community's major factions together and to establish a relationship with such key white leaders as Dick Morthland, the president of People's Bank, Republican state committeewoman Jean Sullivan, and Joe T. Smitherman.

Robinson's classmate J. L. Chestnut Jr. (1931–2008), a Selma native with a law degree from Howard University, emerged as one of the foremost advocates of the black movement in west central Alabama. As noted in his autobiography *Black in Selma*, in 1972 Chestnut both overcame his drinking problem and gained two valuable new associates—Harvard graduates Hank and Rose Sanders, who joined with him to form the law firm Chestnut, Sanders and Sanders, which became for a time the largest black law firm in the state of Alabama.

In 1971, Ed Moss approached the all-white Selma City Council with a request that the city change its method of electing its ten council members. As long as elections were at large and a majority of voters were white, east Selma's majority-black

FIGURE 9.9 Attorney J. L. Chesnut; courtesy of the author.

wards four and five would always be represented by whites. Moss wanted his fellow black citizens to be able to share in the government of their city. When city attorney McLean Pitts checked the laws, he was astonished to discover that Selma's elections were illegal. By state law, towns with a population of twenty thousand or more were required to elect their council by district instead of at large, unless the council had no more than five members. Selma had ten, two from each ward. On top of that, elections had to be held in August instead of March, as the custom had been in Selma. The city had the choice of switching to election by wards or cutting the number of council members in half.

The white residents of east Selma had already lost "their" school (Frances Thomas, which now had a black majority) and did not want to lose "their" four council members as well. Naturally they wanted to keep the at-large system; but the six council seats from west Selma were not enthusiastic about cutting the council in half. Councilman George "Cap" Swift even suggested that it might be a good thing to have black representatives on the council. On January 24, 1972, the council voted 5 to 3 to elect by wards. A second vote was held on February 7, with one east Selma representative (Luther Pepper) leaving his hospital bed to cast his vote to keep at-large elections; his presence gave his side a 6–5 majority but not the two-thirds majority required by law. Herman Blagg, Martin Coon, Irby Moore, and Cap Swift all voted with Carl Morgan to open the door for black residents to win seats on the city council.

Moss expressed "deep and profound gratitude" for the vote, and the *Times-Journal* confessed that the conscience of the white community had been troubled by "setups which deprived half of Selma's citizens of direct representation on the Council." J. L. Chestnut was "stunned" by this development and dismayed to realize that the mayor "was locking up the black vote" (*Black in Selma*, 260).

On the same day, February 7, 1972, the Selma Accords were drawn up between representatives of both races. The city's plans to expand its public housing had been hobbled by a series of lawsuits filed by the NAACP and other organizations representing black citizens, wanting them withdrawn.

Father Robinson served as the "go-between" between Mayor Smitherman, the militants, and the US Department of Housing and Urban Development (HUD). Cecil Jackson was present, and a lawyer from HUD was the spokesman for the federal government. The accords promised black neighborhoods full city services and black people a fair share of city jobs. Funeral director Randall Miller was appointed director of urban renewal and soon became one of Smitherman's strongest supporters in the black community.

The *Selma Times-Journal* had to defend Mayor Smitherman against charges by segregationists that he had "sold out." In a February 13 editorial, the newspaper reminded critics that "there are other people, hundreds of them, who need the decent housing this federal grant will provide. For their sakes and for the sake of a city that needs to unify for desirable progress, no feuds or bickering among groups of Selmians should be permitted to put this housing project in jeopardy." The mayor himself scoffed at charges that federal money was "tainted"; "the real problem is there tain't enough of it."

During the years that followed, federal money poured into Selma. The streets in Selma's black neighborhoods were paved at last, and the sewer lines extended throughout the city. Public housing was erected. A new city hall, convention center, and library were erected on the block bounded by Broad Street, Dallas Avenue, Washington Street, and Selma Avenue. Part of the block was already empty, due to the earlier demolition of the Hotel Albert, but many Selmians were sorry to lose the historic Gill house in order to make room for the library.

It was no surprise that Smitherman was reelected in August 1972 with no opposition from either black or white. Shortly before the election, one incumbent councilman in ward three (Martin Coon) died and his black opponent (Ernest Doyle) ran unopposed. Thus, the city council elected in 1972 had five white members and five black ones with Carl Morgan as council president. Doyle, Lorenzo Harrison,

Figure 9.10 Edmundite Father James P. Robinson presents Mayor Smitherman and council president Morgan with a papal blessing for the City of Selma; courtesy of the Edmundite Missions.

William Kemp, J. C. Kimbrough, and F. D. Reese became the first black members of the city council since the days of Reconstruction. The official picture of this council shows all five black members standing stiffly in back while the five white members sit in front; nobody looks comfortable.

One factor that may have helped reconciliation was the winding down of the Vietnam War. Ronald Sharpe was the last Selmian to die in Vietnam in 1971; the twenty-year-old Sharpe, a graduate of R. B. Hudson who worked in construction before volunteering for the service, died from "friendly fire" on November 20. When the city erected a park in east Selma, it named it after Sharpe, the first black soldier to be honored by the council in this fashion.

During the 1970s, Selma reasserted its position as the medical center for west central Alabama. The Hospital Corporation of America (HCA) took charge of Selma Baptist in 1968 and began planning a new facility. Soon HCA was constructing a 150-bed hospital at the edge of town, and on July 20, 1971, Selma Medical Center Hospital accepted its first patient. In that same year, Minnie Anderson closed down the Burwell Infirmary and opened the new W. J. Anderson Memorial Nursing Home on Range Line Road.

In 1973 a group of citizens from Dallas, Perry, and Wilcox met to form the board of directors for the Cahaba Center for Mental Health and Mental Retardation. Its

FIGURE 9.11 The first integrated Selma City Council since Reconstruction, 1972. Seated, left to right: Irby Moore, Percy Zeigler, Bill Driggers, Otis "Red" Adams, and Herman Blagg Sr. Standing, left to right: council president Carl Morgan, Lorenzo Harrison, Ernest L. Doyle, William Kemp, J. C. Kimbrough, F. D. Reese, and Mayor Joe Smitherman; courtesy of Selma–Dallas County Museum of History and Archives, Selma, Alabama.

first office was in the courthouse annex with Dr. Clyde Walker as its director. Six years later, it was able to move to a new facility, the Bernard Reynolds Building, out on Medical Center Parkway. In 1976 Dr. Donald Overstreet and other Selma physicians, concerned about the scarcity of doctors in rural Alabama, persuaded the University of Alabama in Birmingham (UAB) to begin a family practice residency program here. In addition to assisting with the heavy caseloads of established local doctors, the residents are encouraged to plan for future small town practices of their own. Yet another local initiative was launched in 1977, when the Rural Health Medical Program was organized, with John Crear as its first president. This federally funded organization organized clinics in neighboring Perry and Wilcox Counties.

The addition of George C. Wallace State Community College, previously known as the William Rufus King Trade School, to the already firmly established Selma University and Concordia College increased the opportunity for local young people to extend their education beyond the high school level. Its current enrollment of over 1,800 in regular college programs means that Wallace provides for more students (black, white, and Asian) than the city's other two colleges combined.

FIGURE 9.12 After 1975, reenactments of the Selma-to-Montgomery March became an annual thing, with prominent figures like Jesse Jackson taking part; courtesy of the *Selma Times-Journal.*

Some Selmians feared that the city was losing many of its most attractive and historic buildings. Anxiety to preserve what was left of the city's architectural heritage prompted state representative Val Hain, district judge Miller Childers, attorney Sam Summers, homemaker Chris Vaughan, and others to organize the Selma–Dallas County Historic Preservation Society in 1971. Smitherman joked about the "Hysterical Society" but came to realize the preservationists had a point.

The year 1975 saw both the first reenactment of the Selma-to-Montgomery March (with Mrs. Coretta King joining Father Robinson, F. D. Reese, and other leaders in marching across the bridge) and a revival of protest. When Street resigned as principal of Selma High and another white principal was appointed in his place, Yelder filed a lawsuit. There were other issues bubbling to the surface by then. On August 21, the school board met to hear complaints from black parents and teachers about a wide range of issues. The Selma–Dallas County Legal Defense League complained that Selma High did not have enough black cheerleaders, enough black students on the debate squad, or any black coaches. The league also complained that too many black students had been "herded" into vocational education, that the school was not sponsoring integrated proms, and that white churches were being allowed to hold graduation ceremonies for their parishioners. The group's chief grievance seemed to be the board's failure to appoint black principals at Westside and Selma High. The board appointed a black principal (Evans Rutledge) to Westside but left the question of Selma High's principal to the courts.

In 1976 Judge Brevard Hand ordered the Selma board to make Joe Yelder, former principal of Hudson, principal of Selma High. It was while Yelder was principal that the Rochester, New York, *Courier-Journal* asserted that Selma's schools were still "all black" or "all white." Yelder's office responded indignantly that "we're completely integrated; we even have white boys on our basketball team!" Yelder stepped down after a year and was replaced by a white principal, but the black community was gratified by the selection of Andrew Sewell, the former head coach at Hudson High, as Selma High's first black head coach. Sewell filled the vacancy created when his predecessor, James Booth, resigned to become head basketball coach at Wallace Community College.

Judge Hand also found the self-perpetuating school board unconstitutional but left it to the legislature to come up with a better way to select the board's members. In 1977 the legislature passed a law directing that the Selma City Council would elect the eleven members of the school board, with two members being selected for five-year terms each year (except for the fifth year, when three have to be selected). Within a few years, the board consisted of six white members and five black members.

In 1980 Jean (Bunny) Gamble became the first woman to serve as chair, and in the following year Reverend Lett became the first black chair and the first Baptist minister to serve in that role. Charles A. Lett (1915–2014), a native of Pensacola, had served as a principal in Baldwin County before being called to Selma as pastor of Green Street Baptist Church in 1958. He was widely respected in both white and black communities. In 1982 Dana Waters became the first Presbyterian minister to serve as chair, and in 1983 Mary Ellen Williams became the first black female chair. For some time, the board continued to alternate its chairs between the races in this way.

To some people, however, these political changes were less impressive than the growing acceptance of black members of the chamber of commerce. In 1976, businessman Edwin Moss became the first black member elected to the chamber's board of directors, followed by hospital administrator John Crear in 1979. Crear, a Xavier University graduate with a wry sense of humor, served as the first black person on so many boards and committees that he finally announced: "This token is just about spent!" Unlike some "tokens," Crear tended to wind up serving as chair of many of the boards he served on.

In 1982, Smitherman succeeded in getting the voters to approve a $4 million bond issue in spite of the bitter opposition of Councilman Cecil Williamson and other conservatives. Once again, it was black support that made the difference. Smith-

FIGURE 9.13 Rev. Charles A. Lett, the first black chair for the Selma School Board; courtesy of Yvonne Hatcher.

FIGURE 9.14 1979 Judge Johnny Jones and Mayor Carl Morgan join in honoring Ed Moss; courtesy of the *Selma Times-Journal.*

FIGURE 9.15 Even Mayor Smitherman's longtime critic J. L. Chesnut ended up allying himself with the mayor on some issues; courtesy of the *Selma Times-Journal*.

erman and J. L. Chestnut toured the black churches the Sunday before the vote, urging the worshippers to support a measure that would benefit their schools and their community. Williamson estimated that 95 percent of Selma's black voters had done as the mayor asked.

The Closing of Craig and the Development of Tourism

One factor that might have prompted Smitherman's resignation in 1979 was the economic crisis prompted by the 1976 announcement that Craig Air Force Base was going to be closed. The city had succeeded in blocking a previous move to close the base in 1971. However, in 1976 the closure would happen, and after forty years of having the base as a major source of jobs and income for Selma residents, the prospects of losing it were frightening.

A reporter for the *Los Angeles Times* noted in an article, "Craig's annual $32 million payroll was larger than that of all the 54 Dallas County manufacturers combined. Craig personnel rented more than 250 homes and sent their children to city schools. They enjoyed such harmonious relations with the civilian population that any man in uniform can usually cash a check downtown without showing identification and any homesick student pilot never had to look far for a home cooked meal" (*Selma Times-Journal*, May 2, 1976).

White and black leaders joined together, first to attempt to reverse the decision to close the base and then to find industry to replace the air force. After the base closed, the city and county set up a five-person board, the Craig Field Airport and Industrial Authority, to administer the base. The first board consisted of county commissioner James S. Wilkinson, president; William H. Bruce, vice chair; attorney Joe Pilcher, secretary and treasurer; credit union president Edwin L. Moss; and Wallace Community College administrator Stanhope E. Frazier.

In the years that followed, the group was successful in bringing Beechcraft, a major manufacturer of private planes, to Selma, even though they lost it in the late 1980s, when the market for private planes diminished sharply. Local industries moved into the vacuum, and for some years the largest employer at Craig was the American Candy Company, a manufacturer of hard candies that dated back to 1899.

Even before the closing of Craig, some Selmians saw the possibility that tourism might become a major source of income for the town. As early as 1973, the Historic Society was responsible for two significant events: the restoration of the old Vaughan Hospital on Alabama and Union, and the launching of Riverfront Market Day. The city and county joined in returning the Vaughan to its former glory. This building, which, since 1847, had been a Masonic hall, a school, a Confederate hospital, the county courthouse, a Presbyterian academy, and a private hospital, is now known as the Vaughan-Smitherman Building and serves as a museum and tourist attraction.

Riverfront Market Day was inaugurated to draw attention to one of the oldest surviving authentic riverfront areas in the nation. On the second Saturday of each October, hundreds of vendors set out their wares in the five blocks of Water Avenue between the Old Depot Museum and the Edmund Pettus Bridge. For over forty years crowds came for the arts, crafts, refreshments, and Selma hospitality.

The Selma Pilgrimage was instituted during the bicentennial year of 1976 to exhibit the city's fine old homes. Held each year during the third week of March, it is another of Selma's major enticements. The most impressive of these was the old Gillman house on Mabry Street, which was built by architect Thomas Helm Lee in 1853. In 1957 the Sturdivant family purchased the house and donated it to the city. Restored to its antebellum splendor and renamed Sturdivant Hall, it became a "house museum," which interests visitors from across the nation, and is one of the city's leading tourist attractions.

In 1978, Elise Blackwell became the chamber of commerce's first director of tourism, and began touting Selma's history and beauty anywhere she had opportunity. In that same year Selma held its first Tale-Tellin' Festival, bringing in storytellers from across the country. The city's "corn field intellectual" Kathryn Windham had become famous as the author of a series of books about southern ghosts. It was her energy and her contacts that made the festival a reality.

A major effort was begun to rescue what was left of Cahawba, Alabama's first permanent capital. To publicize it, Cahawba Day was begun in 1979 as an annual celebration on the last Saturday of May. The groundbreaking for the development of Cahawba as an interpretive history park took place in 1989.

Later Jamie Wallace, longtime journalist who assumed executive leadership of the chamber of commerce in 1986, launched an effort to emphasize the city's black heritage. The effort won wide acclaim and a few critics. The city's marketing slogan became "Civil War to Civil Rights and Beyond." In coordination with the city, tourism directors Edie Morthland Jones and Lauri Cothran developed an aggressive marketing program, bringing thousands to the city and providing an enormous boom to the lodging industry.

After the Selma Mall was opened in 1974, downtown business seemed to founder for a while, but enterprising business owners and property owners began restoring their original storefronts, giving the city a distinctive appearance. The Walton Theatre, an old movie house built in 1914, was converted into a "miniature jewel box" at the heart of the Larry Striplin Jr. Performing Arts Center.

Larry D. Striplin Jr. (1929–2012), a Selma native, was an outstanding student-athlete at Spring Hill College in Mobile and Birmingham Southern. He earned a master's degree in education from George Peabody College for Teachers (now part of Vanderbilt University) and became a coach. In 1956 he gave up coaching and channeled his enormous energy into business, rapidly becoming a success. In 1971 he returned to his home town, bringing with him a new industry, DISCO Aluminum, which was to provide a host of jobs to the area. He founded other businesses as well (American Fine Wire and Circle S) and proved a generous benefactor to Selma, Birmingham, and other cities as well. Former president Gerald Ford visited the city in 1986 to dedicate the Striplin Performing Arts Center, a well-planned complex which contains not only the theater but also exhibit space that is used for a number of community functions.

Striplin was also responsible for the restoration of the Welch house on Mabry Street, which he renamed Henderson House in honor of his mother and used for a hospitality center for Circle S Industries. In addition, Circle S restored the Victorian houses surrounding Henderson House, which now make up the Fairoaks Square area of Old Town, one of Selma's original residential areas. This restoration

FIGURE 9.16 Businessman and philanthropist Larry D. Striplin Jr.; courtesy of the City of Selma, Alabama.

sparked a desire in many residents to restore some of the lovely homes built during the nineteenth century.

Black Power Comes to the Black Belt: 1980–1988

Yet another impact of Craig's closing was a marked change in the city's racial makeup. Selma's black population was no longer declining, but its white population was; the 1980 census showed 14,000 black residents and 12,500 white ones living within the city limits. The Selma City Council had admitted its first black members in 1972, after switching from at-large elections to elections by district. After 1980, every election provoked a fresh attempt by one race or the other to redraw the boundary lines of ward three, the "swing ward." In 1980, Judge Hand simply divided all five wards in half, giving ward three a northern district with a white majority and a southern one with a black majority.

The Dallas County Commission stayed all white until 1988, when the Eleventh Circuit Court of Appeals finally forced it to adopt election by district. By that time,

Dallas County's black residents had already won one political position after another for the first time since Reconstruction: a member of the county school board, a state senator, a county tax collector, and a district judge. Some white residents began referring to the rapid rise of local black people to positions of power as "a second Reconstruction."

In 1981 the county board of education, which was also elected at large, decided to show its good faith by choosing a veteran black educator, Dr. Catherine Bozeman, to fill a vacancy on the board. Bozeman, a Dallas County native with a master's degree from Columbia University, had previously served as supervisor of instruction for the county school system and as longtime president of district eight of the Alabama State Teachers Association (ASTA). While her appointment and subsequent election to a full term in 1984 gratified the black community of Dallas County, it did not satisfy their leaders, who continued to demand elections by district.

In addition, the white community showed increasing signs of coming to terms with the city's black heritage. In April 1981, an interested group agreed to create a museum that would pull together all of Selma's history "from William Rufus King to Martin Luther King." The group included black leaders like Willis Wright and Richie Jean Jackson as well as members of the old, established white families like Jean Martin and Shirley Quarles. Richard S. Bean served as the first president. Bean (1923–2007), a native of Sioux City, Iowa, had moved to Selma in 1966 to work for Wallace Community College and became intensely involved in community affairs. The Selma–Dallas County Museum of History and Archives was established in the old L & N railroad station and is popularly known as the Old Depot Museum. Its first big exhibit, put together by Charles Mauldin (who had been a leader of the student demonstrators back in 1965) depicted the history of Dallas County's black population. The museum's first major coup was persuading the US Navy to return one of the Brooke cannons to Selma. "Some people had a hard time grasping that we were trying to create an inclusive museum," noted tourism director Elise Blackwell. "When we had the black history exhibit, whites decided we must be a black museum; and when we got the Brooke cannon, blacks decided we were an Old South museum!" Suzanne Cansler served as the Old Depot's first curator. In 1984 former county agent Sam O'Hara (1910–89) became curator and worked hard to pull together exhibits representing every aspect of Selma and Dallas County history.

Racial progress could also be noted in the twin memorials erected outside Memorial Stadium in 1983 by the Veterans of Foreign Wars and the Disabled American Veterans to the men of Dallas County who had lost their lives in the Korean War and the Vietnam War. The veterans chose to list the names of black and white casualties alike, without the racial designations shown on the World War II memorial.

Selma had made so much progress by 1984 that some black residents thought the city might be ready for a black mayor. This prompted Councilman F. D. Reese to challenge Smitherman's reelection as mayor. Many white voters, who had voted against Smitherman four years earlier and opposed his bond issue in 1982, now rallied behind the man they feared would be "the last white mayor of Selma." Joe T. won handily, buoyed up by a massive white turnout and drawing approximately 20 percent of the black vote. It was also in this year that Judge Hand, vexed by the council's repeated failure to redistrict itself, decided to teach the city a lesson. He cut the Selma City Council in half, reducing it from ten members to five and creating a new ward three with a 55 percent black majority. The ward's white incumbent, George Swift, won reelection easily over black challenger Ed Moss, and black leaders adopted the rule of thumb that it took a 65 percent black majority to ensure a black triumph.

The Alabama legislature was forced to reapportion itself in 1982, and in the process Dallas County was split into two different house districts. District sixty-seven elected W. F. "Noopie" Cosby, a white businessman who had already served one term in the legislature; district sixty-nine chose James L. Thomas, a black school principal. Thus Selma gained its first black state legislator since Reconstruction. It nearly gained a black state senator as well, with Hank Sanders being narrowly edged out by incumbent Earl Goodwin in the Democratic primary.

Also in 1982 Selma became "the butterfly capital of Alabama" with some help from Senator Goodwin. The drive had been launched by Mrs. Mallieve Breeding, whose concern for preserving Alabama's native wildlife led to her being christened "Madam Butterfly." Mallieve Wicker Breeding (b. 1921) attended Huntingdon College, where she met and married a bomber pilot from Oklahoma. When Lt. Col. Charles Breeding retired from the service in 1952, the family moved to Selma, where she dedicated herself to beautifying her hometown. It was largely through her efforts that the butterfly became the symbol of Selma's positive side, of a city not entirely taken up with racial conflict.

The federal courts were less interested in butterflies than in black representation in government. Thus in 1983, the Alabama legislature redrew its district lines, splitting Dallas County into two senatorial districts. East Selma became part of district twenty-three, which consisted of five predominantly black counties and was the largest district in the state. It quickly chose Sanders as its new senator. West Selma, where Goodwin lived, became part of district twenty-four, comprised of three counties whose populations were primarily white. The local joke was that the city now enjoyed "separate but equal state senators."

In some ways, Goodwin and Sanders offered a striking contrast, one symboliz-

FIGURE 9.17 "How Selma Became Butterfly Capital of Alabama," the *Montgomery Advertiser*'s cartoon depicts "Madame Butterfly" and the gardeners of Selma descending on the Alabama legislature; courtesy of the *Montgomery Advertiser*, Montgomery, Alabama.

FIGURE 9.18 Earl Goodwin, one of Dallas County's "separate but equal" state senators; courtesy of the Selma–Dallas County Library.

FIGURE 9.19 Hank Sanders, one of Dallas County's "separate but equal" state senators; courtesy of the Selma–Dallas County Library.

ing the strengths of conservatism and experience, the other the dynamism and expectation of youth. Interestingly, neither was a Selma native.

Goodwin (1910–2003) was born in Jefferson County and graduated from Howard College, now Samford University. He first came to Selma in 1945 as an air force veteran and played a major role in founding and developing Bush Hog, a manufacturer of farm equipment, into one of central Alabama's major industries. While most white Selmians were going Republican, he remained a "yellow dog Democrat," that is, so loyal to the party he would support it even if it nominated "an old yellow dog." Goodwin represented the state at every national Democratic convention but one between 1964 and 1988. He was elected to the Alabama senate in 1976 and served as one of Governor Wallace's chief lieutenants in the legislature. Goodwin was chair of the senate's Democratic Caucus in 1987.

Sanders was born in Baldwin County, one of thirteen children in a sharecrop-

FIGURE 9.20 Rose Gaines Sanders, who later changed her name to Faya Rose Toure; courtesy of the National Voting Rights Museum, Selma, Alabama.

per's family. Like so many ambitious black Alabamians, he went to the North to earn money and get an education. Unlike most, after his graduation from Harvard Law School, he came back to the South. He and his wife, Rose, also a graduate of Harvard Law School, came to Selma in 1972 and joined with J. L. Chestnut to form the law firm of Chestnut, Sanders and Sanders. Within a year of his election, Sanders helped lead a rebellion against the Alabama Democratic Conference (ADC), which had long dominated Alabama's black politics. When the ADC endorsed Walter Mondale for president over Jesse Jackson, Sanders joined with black leaders in Birmingham and Mobile to set up a rival organization to ADC—the New South Coalition. "New South" continues to be powerful to this day, carrying the state primary for Barack Obama over Hillary Clinton, who was supported by the ADC, in 2008.

In 1985, Senator Sanders pushed through a series of local bills requiring most of the counties in his district to elect their commissions by district rather than at large. One result was that Wilcox and Greene Counties, which previously had all-black commissions, both elected their first white commissioner in a number of years.

The senator's wife, Rose Gaines Sanders, has had a great impact on Selma in her own right. (She ultimately rejected the "slave name" of Sanders to become Faya Rose Toure.) A native of Salisbury, North Carolina (b. 1945), she became Alabama's first black female judge, serving as municipal judge in Uniontown from 1973 to 1977. But her real gift was as a community organizer, founding a series of groups to tackle a variety of problems. Most of them had catchy acronyms: MOMs (Mothers of Many), SMART (Students Marching against Racial Tracking), BEST (Better Education Support Team), and so forth. Her flair for dramatics led to the creation of the African Extravaganza, an annual event in Selma to this day.

While many black people came to regard "Miss Rose" as Joan of Arc reborn, most white people tended to see her as the Wicked Witch of the South. Chestnut explains in his autobiography that the law firm had assigned her to play "the abrasive role—raise the issue of racism, file the lawsuits, attack this and that, make speeches denouncing the mayor and county commission" (*Black in Selma*, 257). This was a role that she played to the hilt.

The Sanders' extended family was to play a major role in Selma politics in the years that followed. Hank Sanders's brother-in-law, Raymond Major, served on the city council; Sanders's sister, Dr. Fannie Major McKenzie, ultimately became superintendent of the county schools. His mother-in-law, Ora Lee Gaines, established the McRae Learning Center. His wife Rose's brother-in-law, Perry Varner, served as manager of the Chestnut Sanders law firm and was elected to the Dallas County Commission. Varner (1946–2000), a native of Gadsden, graduated from Tuskegee, served in Vietnam, and earned a law degree from Boston College before moving to Selma in 1976. He played a major role in Dallas County politics until his death and had a boot camp named in his honor.

In 1984, Jackie Burns Walker was elected as Dallas County's tax collector. Tragically, Mrs. Walker died in an automobile accident before she could take office and become the first black courthouse official since 1876. Black leaders asked the county commission to appoint her husband, Nathaniel Walker, in her place; but the commission voted 4 to 1 (Judge Jones dissenting) to appoint her defeated rival, Tommy Powell, instead. Two years later, Walker was to win election in his own right as district judge of Dallas County. Walker, a Selma native and graduate of Fordham Law School, succeeded Miller Childers, scion of one of the oldest families in Dallas County, who chose not to run again.

In 1985 Selma showed a willingness to come to terms with its Reconstruction history. Two black fraternal organizations, the Benevolent and Protective Order of Elks and the Worthy Matrons of the Eastern Star, began a campaign to erect a monument on the unmarked grave of Reconstruction congressman Benjamin S. Turner. They sought assistance from white liberals like Mallieve Breeding and from the members

Figure 9.21 Dallas County Commissioner Perry Varner Jr.; courtesy of the *Selma Times-Journal.*

of the Old Depot's Board of Directors, and a biracial committee was formed with Mayor Smitherman as honorary chair.

The *Times-Journal* reminded Selma's white citizens of Turner's role in winning amnesty for their grandfathers, and the money for an impressive marker was quickly raised. US Senator Jeremiah Denton, Alabama's first Republican senator since Reconstruction, attended the dedication ceremonies and paid fervent tribute to Turner's patriotism. Senator Sanders also spoke, taking the occasion to urge the appointment of a black tax collector.

In 1988, the federal courts ruled that Dallas County had to replace its four-member county commission elected at large with a five-person commission elected by district. The probate judge would no longer serve as chair. The county board of education was also transformed into a five-person board, also elected by district. The Justice Department regarded the changes as necessary to create a black majority

FIGURE 9.22 Nathaniel Walker served as district judge of Dallas County from 1986 to 2004; courtesy of the *Selma Times-Journal.*

on the commission, and it worked. Perry Varner, D. L. Pope, and Erskine Minor were elected to the Dallas County Commission, once again the first black members to serve on this body since Reconstruction. They replaced the commission's longtime white attorney, Cartledge Blackwell, with Bruce Boynton. The county board of education was a different story; while it acquired its first black members in 1988, Karl Lewis and Bill Minor, it retained its white majority, with Elton Ralston winning reelection from a majority black district.

In many ways the city seemed to have overcome much of its racial division and animosity. When a vacancy occurred on the Selma City Council in 1987, Councilman Charles Morris announced that since ward three now had a black majority, he would be open to voting for an "outstanding black candidate" like Edwin Moss to replace the white incumbent. Moss was chosen by four votes to one, thereby giving the council a black majority for the first time in its history.

That same year saw the council manage to reapportion itself without judicial help for the first time, creating an eight-member council evenly divided between the races. The council president would still be elected at large so that the council would still most likely have a white majority.

Yet another sign of progress took place in 1987 when the Selma City School Board selected an educator from New Orleans, Dr. Norward Roussell, as its first black superintendent of schools. When longtime superintendent Joe Pickard had stepped down in 1982 and been replaced by Dr. Martha Barton, the interim superintendent at Auburn, there had been black protests that a black person had not been chosen. In 1985 the federal courts ruled that Selma's schools were fully integrated and no longer needed federal supervision.

Roussell's selection had the incidental effect of integrating Selma's civic clubs. Carl Barker, the president of the school board, was a staunch Rotarian and took pains to see that the new superintendent was welcomed into Rotary. The other civic clubs followed suit by recruiting black members of their own. There was some feeling that the Selma Country Club should do the same, but Roussell assured his supporters that he had no interest in paying $2,500 a year to play golf.

In 1988 local publisher Clare Ralston convinced the city council that the city needed a new history that would cover the city's history down to the present. This would be the first authorized history of Selma since Jackson's *Story of Selma* in 1954. This decision took for granted the possibility that a noncontroversial history of the city could be written, one that would be fair to black and white alike. *Selma, Queen City of the Black Belt* appeared a year later.

When Charles L. Byrd stepped down as president of George C. Wallace Community College in 1988, Noopie Cosby complained that the local committee set up to help search for a new president was stacked in favor of hiring a black president (*Selma Times-Journal*, January 13). The committee consisted of two black activists, Ed Moss and F. D. Reese, and two liberal white members, Edmundite priest Roger J. La charite and Bobbie Morthland. The committee did in fact choose a black man, Dr. Julius Brown, for the post. Brown, a native of Bessemer who earned his doctorate from the University of Michigan, had previously been serving as vice president of the Community College of Allegheny County in Pittsburgh. Even before the new president took charge, the Confederate flag that had previously flown at the college was quietly taken down. The *Times-Journal* approved heartily: "That's how a flag issue is supposed to be handled—quietly" (February 26, 1989).

As 1990—which would commemorate the 125th anniversary of the Battle of Selma and the 25th of the Selma-to-Montgomery March— approached, the city's future looked bright in spite of its economic problems and its periodic racial squabbles. Selma had come a long, long way since "Bloody Sunday."

10

More Bridges to Cross

Selma, 1989–2008

In January 1990 the Alabama River reached its highest level since 1961, overflowing its banks and flooding portions of east Selma. Elmwood, the city's second oldest cemetery, presented a striking and grisly spectacle; a number of recently buried coffins emerged from the mud and were seen bobbing about on top of the waves.

This seemed almost symbolic of what was happening to the city, which found itself haunted by racial conflicts that the city fathers thought had been left behind in the 1960s. Ironically enough, it was plans to stage a biracial celebration of the progress Selma had made since 1965 that set the stage for the town's bitterest confrontation in twenty-five years. And it was a campaign against supposed remnants of segregation in the city's public schools that led to a virtual resegregation of those very schools.

On September 18, 1989, Mayor Smitherman and the chamber of commerce announced plans for a symposium on the significance of Selma's role in the movement, inviting back the newsmen who had covered Bloody Sunday and the events of the Selma-to-Montgomery March. The committee in charge would be chaired by retired banker Rex Morthland and Selma High principal F. D. Reese. Morthland had been a leading white moderate in 1965 and Reese the leader of the Dallas County Voters League. To the *Times-Journal*, they were obviously "the right men for the job."

The mayor's announcement provoked immediate outrage from the activists associated with the Chestnut Sanders law firm. While Smitherman saw the anniversary as providing millions of dollars worth of free publicity for Selma, they saw things differently. "That march belongs to black people all over the country," thundered Chestnut at a September 21 press conference. "It's the most important event in black history since the Emancipation, and we are not going to let it become a

FIGURE 10.1 Sen. Henry and Mrs. Rose Sanders led the opposition to the mayor's plans for a biracial celebration of the twenty-fifth anniversary of the Selma Movement; courtesy of the *Selma Times-Journal.*

Chamber of Commerce event" (*Selma Times-Journal*). They had been working toward their own vision of a twenty-fifth anniversary celebration for some time and had recruited Atlanta congressman John Lewis to serve as national chairman of the National Right to Vote Celebration. Mrs. Sanders spoke of a voting rights museum to be erected at the foot of the Edmund Pettus Bridge, as well as a reenactment of the Selma-to-Montgomery March.

Sanders and her associates were indignant at what they saw as Smitherman's attempt to steal "their" celebration and to paint an idealized portrait of the city's race relations. Chestnut pointed to the white-majority school board as evidence that "the cancer of racism" still infected the city. They denounced the mayor as racist and his black appointees as "dupes" and threatened to bring in demonstrators from around the country to disrupt the symposium.

Efforts were made to work out a compromise between the two groups, allowing both the symposium and the reenactment of Bloody Sunday. Reese resigned from the mayor's committee and was replaced by Rev. Joseph Rembert, the pastor of Brown Chapel. In the end, however, the mayor's group threw up its hands in despair and withdrew from the field altogether. The Sanders group then appointed several young white people to serve on various committees, but the dispute left a bad taste in many mouths. "They don't want me as mayor," Smitherman observed, "let alone involved in their party" (*Birmingham Post-Herald*, October 25, 1989). Several white leaders became convinced that the Sanders group was determined to stage a confrontation of some sort in 1990 and that no white concessions could head it off.

Perhaps the most obvious target was the Selma School Board, which was considering whether or not to reappoint black superintendent Norward Roussell. The schools had been a flashpoint ever since integration, with periodic clashes over the appointment of a new principal or the dismissal of a controversial teacher. The board itself had split along racial lines in 1979 when it voted to dismiss a controversial black teacher (Bennie Ruth Crenshaw) for "insubordination." Three of the four black members of the board had resigned in protest; only one (Rev. C. A. Lett) had stayed at his post. The Chestnut Sanders group periodically denounced the board as "elitist" and demanded that it be made elective rather than appointive.

Selma's white population declined sharply during the 1980s; white students had made up 40 percent of public school enrollment in the 1970s but had fallen to 30 percent in the 1980s. Enrollment at the private academies also declined, with some white families returning to the public schools. This led to some speculation that Morgan and Meadowview Christian might have to merge to survive and made the competition between the public schools and the private academies more intense. The decline also helped to convince some black parents, whose children now made up 70 percent of enrollment, that they should also constitute a majority of the school board. There was also some resentment that Selma High had produced only one black valedictorian (Terri Sewell in 1982) and one black salutatorian (Kwambi Dover in 1989) since integration, that a white girl had been chosen homecoming queen in 1989, and that white students made up a majority of the debate squad.

When the board voted along racial lines not to renew Roussell's contract, it provided the occasion for Selma's worst racial confrontation since 1965. While the clash brought national attention, it failed to generate enough national support for the protesters to secure their triumph. When the conflict was finally brought to a close in August 1990, it was a peace of exhaustion that left long-lasting scars.

The struggle between Smitherman and Chestnut Sanders that occupied the following decade was framed largely in terms of the quest for "unity." Given the steadily increasing black majority, the mayor's best chance for reelection was the creation and maintenance of a biracial coalition. To Joe T., unity meant "black and white together." But J. L. Chestnut saw things differently. To him unity meant the black community uniting against its white oppressors. Since most of the white voters would automatically oppose any candidate identified with Chestnut Sanders, the law firm's only path to power was to mount a polarizing campaign that would bring about a massive turnout of black voters.

In 2000, an unprecedented black turnout swept James Perkins Jr. into office as Selma's first black mayor. Perkins soon found that unity of either kind would be hard to achieve. He was never able to win much support from the white community, and he ran into resistance from a number of his fellow black residents. A majority of the council, black and white alike, had reservations about his budget and was reluctant to give up the powers of appointment they had wrested from Smitherman.

In the decade after Perkins's election, two Selma politicians who had been racially polarizing figures in 1990 (white councilman Kimbrough L. Ballard and black attorney Yussuf Salaam) were able to moderate their images enough to muster sufficient biracial support to be elected to major offices (Ballard as probate judge, Salaam as state legislator).

Perkins himself was less successful. After his reelection in 2004, Perkins had more supporters on the council but failed to get his proposed bond issue accepted by voters. In 2008 George Evans defeated Perkins for reelection with support from a biracial coalition.

The School Blowup, 1989–1990

"Dr. Norward Roussell has charged into his first year as chief administrator of the Selma city schools with all the charm and delicacy of a gored bull," the *Times-Journal* observed on May 29, 1988. Within a year of taking office, Selma's new superintendent had alienated many of his initial supporters. A survey by the Selma Educational Association (SEA) revealed that a majority of the teachers responding felt "intimidated" and under stress. The *Times-Journal* had brought the difficulties to the surface with a May 20, 1988, editorial urging the board to either "back him . . . or boot him," support Roussell or fire him. The paper referred to rumors about "the manner in which [Roussell] was dealing with certain teachers, coaches and school personnel." If these rumors were true, then he should be fired, although "we don't relish the thought of the city's first black superintendent being fired."

Selma's black community liked the thought even less. A number of leading black moderates, including Ed Moss and Sullivan Jackson, began rallying support for the superintendent. White councilman Charlie Morris joined with Moss and J. L. Chestnut in setting up a biracial committee to head off a possible confrontation. The board affirmed its support for the superintendent and went on to approve some of his pro-

FIGURE 10.2 Dr. Norward Roussell, superintendent of Selma City Schools, 1987–1990; courtesy of Mrs. Joan Roussell.

posals for reforming the school system. But it was clear that Roussell's job might well be in peril when his three-year contract came up for renewal in December 1989.

Roussell was able to win over his critics in the black community in the months that followed. He won the indignant support of black parents by pointing out the out-of-date materials in use at some predominantly black schools (e.g., maps of the United States that did not show Alaska and Hawaii). He also picked up the fervent support of the Better Education Support Team (BEST), which was convinced that black students were being deliberately oppressed by what it called "tracking." Alice Boynton, wife of county attorney Bruce Boynton, served as president and Ronald Peoples, a dean at Selma University, as vice president of BEST, but the group's most visible member was Rose Sanders. Mrs. Sanders charged that 90 percent of Selma High's white students were in the top level (advanced studies) and 90 percent of its black students in the lowest level (basic studies). (In point of fact, there were an equal number of black and white students enrolled in advanced studies; but Sanders was right that the percentage of white students [35 percent] was greater than the

FIGURE 10.3 Mrs. Alice Boynton and Dean Ron Peoples served as president and vice president of the Better Education Support Team (BEST); courtesy of the *Selma Times-Journal.*

percentage of black students [15 percent]. The majority of both races were in general studies.) Roussell had modified the three-tier system, making it more objective; BEST wanted to get rid of it altogether.

However, the white members of the school board continued to regard Roussell as a poor manager, who was "insensitive to employee needs and feelings." One board member also commented on the school system: "'The system has deteriorated considerably during the last year,' asserted one board member. 'The fact that several board members and their relatives have removed their children from our system attests to that fact'" (*Selma Times-Journal*, December 31, 1989). They resolved not to renew Roussell's contract, even if they were unable to persuade their fellow board members of his faults.

Ed Moss saw the blowup coming and sought to head it off, just as he had tried in 1963. He and his fellow black council members wrote school board chairman Carl Barker, urging him to resign, so that the board would be evenly divided between the races.

Barker had expressed a strong desire to resign. After serving on the board for eight years and as chair for four years, he was tired. Moreover, he felt that his effectiveness as chair had been undermined by his ex-wife's withdrawing their children from the public schools. But Smitherman persuaded Barker, a banker, to stay on for another year to help resolve matters related to a $3 million bond issue for the schools.

Moss himself believed that Roussell's problems with the board probably came from personality conflicts but knew that most black Selmians were convinced they were racial in origin. If any decisions about Roussell's future were made by a board evenly divided between the races, then this step "will save heated arguments and loss of friendship. It will prevent a terrible split on the council, it will save the city the possibility of boycotts and demonstrations" (*Selma Times-Journal*, December 1, 1989).

Smitherman responded angrily to Moss's letter, saying that "it is disgusting, after all the progress we've made . . . in the past 25 years for a black councilman to use this old worn out threat of boycott and demonstrations to get things that other people are pushing him to get" (*Selma Times-Journal*). He saw Chestnut Sanders as the source of the suggestion and was not inclined to grant any request coming from them.

Unfortunately, Moss's warning was less threat than prophecy of the bitter dispute that was to erupt on December 21. On that day, the school board met to vote on Roussell's contract. For an hour it listened to one of the superintendent's critics (white councilman Kim Ballard) and eight of Roussell's passionate supporters (all black people). "We will picket, we will boycott until Selma is drained of every nickel it has," said Selma High guidance counselor Otelia Moss. "Do right or we will close Selma down. It's not just Rose Sanders and the law firm behind this, it's the people" (*Selma Times-Journal*, December 21, 1990). Finally the board voted along racial lines, six to five, not to extend Roussell's contract. Edie Morthland Jones defended the decision, pointing out that the board had chosen a black principal (F. D. Reese) for Selma High and a black assistant superintendent (James Carter) as well as choosing Roussell to begin with. Surely nobody could think she and the other white board members were racist. But they could and they did.

The sad fact was that the white board members had failed to convince a single one of the five black members serving on the board—Rev. Charles A. Lett, Sheila Okoye, Jim Spicer, Dr. Julius Jenkins, and Freeman Waller—that Roussell's flaws were enough to justify his dismissal. In addition, the black members thought that the white members of the board had been meeting secretly to decide policy and had offered to buy out Roussell's contract without bothering to inform them. Lett, who had stood by the board majority back in 1975, now led the walkout. He and the other black members of the board vowed not to return until and unless Roussell's contract was extended and black members were given control of the board.

There were mass meetings night after night as there had been in 1965—but at

First Baptist (Chestnut's church) this time instead of Brown Chapel and the students usually chanted "fired up! Not going to take it no more!" instead of "black and white together." Roussell himself claimed that Selma was at the Pettus Bridge once more, and Rose Sanders denounced Edie Jones and the other white members on the board as "the Jim Clarks of their day" (*Selma Times-Journal*, December 28, 1989). The issue as BEST saw it was not the right to vote but the right to an equal education, and they hoped to launch a national crusade against "tracking."

"Our only power is the power to disrupt," Senator Sanders told the author; and the protesters made good use of their power. "Until the six white members are removed from the board, there will be no peace in Selma," Mrs. Sanders said. "This is really war" (*Selma Times-Journal*, February 4, 1990).They launched boycotts of First Alabama (Barker's bank), People's Bank (where Jones served on the board), and various local gas stations (all owned by white people with relatives on the school board). They picketed the *Selma Times-Journal*, pitched tents on the lawn outside city hall, and disrupted the meetings of such majority-white groups as the American Cancer Society. Roussell himself was appalled by their periodic calls for a boycott of the schools, a boycott that kept a fourth of the students out of class on January 3 and over a third out on January 17.

While the protesters failed to close Selma down, they did succeed in closing its schools for a week. It was an explosive confrontation at city hall that did the trick. The school board had suspended Roussell on February 2 and appointed F. D. Reese, the principal of Selma High, as acting superintendent in his place. Mrs. Sanders announced that it was "time to go back to the civil disobedience practiced by Dr. King. It may mean going to jail" (*Montgomery Advertiser*, February 3, 1990). On February 5, Mrs. Sanders, Commissioner Perry Varner, attorney Carlos Williams, and other activists became impatient and tried to force their way into the mayor's office at city hall. During the resulting melee, "fists flew, throats were choked, people got pushed against walls or knocked down, were grabbed in headlocks or thrown to the carpeted floor" (*Montgomery Advertiser*, February 6, 1990). This resulted in the arrest of Mrs. Sanders and three other activists.

Word flashed through the black community that Mrs. Sanders had been brutalized by the arresting officer—had been sexually molested on the way to the jail—and was now in dire straits in the hospital. A wave of rage swept through black Selma, as activists announced that the day would henceforth be remembered as "Bloody Monday." (The Alabama Bureau of Investigation found no evidence for the charges.)

On the following day, February 6, racial tension was high at Selma High, where several fights broke out between black and white students and a large crowd of demonstrators gathered in front of the school. Roussell and board member Jenkins tried in vain to persuade the crowd to leave; at nine thirty in the morning, Reese closed the school. A group of demonstrators led by adult members of BEST promptly marched over to Westside Middle School, where they trooped through the building announcing: "School's out!" This touched off a panic in the white community, which was already rattled by the news that a white carpenter working on a house on Union Street, not too far from Westside, had been shot by a black man for no apparent reason. It seemed as though Judge Hare had been right after all back in 1965: their children were not safe in the public schools any more.

Reese resigned, virtually forcing the board to reappoint Roussell for the remainder of the school year. The schools remained closed from February 7 through February 12 as Selma moderates desperately tried to work out a compromise. Councilman Edwin Moss and contractor Tom Bolton organized a biracial group of businessmen and professionals, One Selma, to try and mediate between the two sides. (Moss later resigned, leaving Yvonne Hatcher, a black nurse, as cochair.) The occupation of Selma High on February 9 by student demonstrators further angered the white community, which tended to blame Roussell for all actions committed on his behalf. The compromise proposed by Moss and Charlie Morris—that Roussell be given a one-year extension and the board evenly divided between the races—was rejected by both sides. The black members insisted on complete control of the board, while the white ones insisted on getting rid of Roussell at all costs. According to council member Ballard, the mayor had initially wanted to accept the compromise but had changed his mind after seeing how bitterly opposed his white constituents were.

In a bizarre reversal of the school integration crises of the 1960s, it was white parents who begged for federal troops to protect their children's right to attend the public schools. "If the federal government could send troops so that eleven black kids could attend high school in Little Rock," manufacturer Otey Crisman asked repeatedly, "can't it also send help so that four hundred white kids can attend Selma High?" Crisman's leadership of the Public Education Support Team (PEST) was ironic in a way, since his grandfather had been one of the founders of Meadowview Christian. But Otey Crisman III (b. 1941) was himself a graduate of Dallas County's public schools who had gone into his family's business (making golf clubs) after graduating from the University of Montevallo. His public appeals for integration, which back in 1965 might have brought denunciations by and economic reprisals from white supremacists, evoked a very different response in 1990. A number of his

FIGURE 10.4 Otey Crisman III led the Public Education Support Team (PEST), which opposed the boycott of the schools; courtesy of the Crisman family.

black employees walked out, charging him with "hating black people," and Mrs. Sanders with her characteristic flair branded him "a real Communist" (*Selma Times-Journal*, April 19, 1990).

In contrast, the lawyer who had filed suit after suit to integrate the public schools in the 1960s and 1970s responded with indifference to Henry Pitts's charges that BEST was deliberately provoking "white flight" in order to create an all-black system. "I attended a segregated school system," said Chestnut, "and so did Mayor Smitherman, and we both survived." Some black residents said openly that white students were fleeing not out of fear, but out of racism, and that the schools would be better off without such racists.

The National Guard was, in fact, sent to reopen the schools, giving "Rose's Raiders" the opportunity to relive 1965 by filling the TV screens with shots of demonstrators confronting Alabama troopers. The troopers, many of whom were black, disappointed their taunters by responding with smiles rather than tear gas.

But the city's national image suffered nonetheless. "Selma Is Still Selma," ran

FIGURE 10.5 The picture the *New York Times* refused to run of Randall and Betty Miller on their wedding day; courtesy of the Miller family.

the headline in the *Nation*. The *Birmingham World* was reminded of Bull Connor's brutal ways. Some reporters who had been in Selma in 1965 pointed out some differences. *Dallas Times* reporter Brian Woolley, who had taken part in the original march, observed, "The voting rights movement was led by ministers, this is led by lawyers. That movement had a clear goal, this one has half a dozen and seems to be striking out in all directions."

One noted writer felt that Selma was getting a raw deal. Gay Talese felt that "the city that had been identified with prejudice was presently on the receiving end of prejudice from the press" (*A Writer's Life*, 224). What interested him the most was "not the exodus of white children from the city's school system, or the estrangement being experienced by black and white adults; it was rather, that in the midst of this tumultuous mingling and discord there was in progress a private love affair between an attractive white woman . . . and a black man who was employed in City Hall as Mayor Smitherman's director of personnel" (211). The *New York Times* ran Talese's article but chose not to run the picture he had taken of the happy couple (Randall and Betty Miller), running an old picture of the 1965 violence instead.

Repeated efforts to work out a compromise failed. Selma's clergy tried, One Selma tried, and state judge Leslie Johnson tried. Johnson finally gave up in disgust, saying that agreements had been reached three times, but that "elements on both sides who did not really want a settlement kept interfering to prevent the implementation of the terms" (Thornton, *Dividing Lines*, 550).

After Roussell's resignation in late April, the board named Assistant Superintendent James Carter to serve as acting superintendent. This did not pacify the protesters; Mrs. Sanders had vowed that she would never accept anyone named by white members, "even if they brought Martin Luther King back from the grave." BEST continued its daily picketing of the mayor's office and announced plans to bring in five thousand protesters from around the country to protest the start of a new school year. Only fifty demonstrators showed up to protest on August 20. Carter noted that while the number of white students had dropped significantly over the summer, some 1,066 (20 percent of total enrollment) did show up for class.

At this point two black civic organizations, Twelve High and the Chesterfield Club, approached Mayor Smitherman about bringing the crisis to a close. Fred Williams, George Evans, Johnny Moss Sr., Thomas Cater, and Dr. I. B. Hopson served as the negotiating team. The five were all moderates who were widely respected by the white community; Williams had been the first black man to join the Alabama State Florist Association and had gone on to serve as its president.

At roughly the same time, Larry Striplin approached the mayor of Birmingham, Richard Arrington, to ask him to use his influence with Hank Sanders to bring about a settlement.

After a week of feverish negotiations, black and white leaders agreed to set up a "rotating majority" on the school board, with the board's first black majority taking power as soon as all school board litigation was resolved. Chestnut Sanders grimly agreed to see about having lawsuits against the city and the school board withdrawn, and the city in turn dropped over 130 criminal charges pending against "Rose's Raiders."

So Selma's racial conflicts of 1990 ended not in violence and federal intervention, as those of 1965 had, but in a negotiated settlement worked out by local leaders. Dr. Julius Brown, president of Wallace Community College Selma, proclaimed August 27 "a day for dancing!"

The settlement did not erase all the hard feelings left over from the months of confrontation. Many black students at Selma High felt they had been wronged and that their white classmates were somehow to blame. Many of the white students who had remained at Selma High felt themselves unwelcome even if not unsafe; and by and large they did not encourage their younger brothers and sisters to stay in the system. Repeated efforts by the school board to find a way to hold on to white students did not succeed; by 1995 both Westside (now Selma Middle School, and later to become CHAT Academy and finally R. B. Hudson Middle School)

FIGURE 10.6 Florist Fred Williams helped negotiate an end to the school crisis of 1990; courtesy of the *Selma Times-Journal.*

and Selma High had black enrollments over 95 percent. It was not till May 1991 that the school board, now with a black majority, named Carter superintendent, over protests from BEST.

Carter, a native of north Alabama, had "a different personality" from his predecessor, and Chestnut predicted that he would last longer than Roussell. Carter would go on to serve for seventeen years. He maintained the three-tier system as reformed by Roussell. Sanders continued to protest "tracking," but once the white students had fled, the issue lost most of its popularity.

Dallas County selected its first African American superintendent of schools a few years later. On February 28, 1994, the majority-white board (Elton Ralston, chair) selected Assistant Superintendent George Evans to succeed Marvin Warren, who resigned after five years as superintendent.

FIGURE 10.7 James Carter, superintendent of Selma city schools, 1991–2007; courtesy of the *Selma Times-Journal.*

Evans, a Selma native, belonged to Claude Brown's Reformed Presbyterian church and had attended St. Mary's College in Kansas. He had been one of the negotiators who helped settle the city school crisis in 1990 and was able to maintain good relations with the county's white population during his six years in office. Indeed, some of Selma's white residents moved to north Dallas so that they could send their children to Dallas County High, which had a white majority.

Curiously enough, one of Selma's private schools went through a crisis that echoed that of the public schools but produced a very different outcome. In 1998 Meadowview Christian's board voted to oust Dr. John Niblett, who had been headmaster since 1995. Niblett's supporters responded by setting up a new private school on Bell Road, Central Christian, and sending their children there. According to the August 21, 1998, *Times-Journal*, "all of Meadowview's junior and high school teachers left Meadowview with Niblett, as did the coaching staff, 25 football players and many other students." Central Christian announced its willingness to accept students of every race, and so many black parents responded by enrolling their children that within a few years the school had a black majority. It was finally sold to a black church and is now Ellwood Christian Academy.

FIGURE 10.8 George Evans, superintendent of Dallas County Schools and, later, mayor of Selma, Alabama; courtesy of the *Selma Times-Journal.*

Meadowview brought back its legendary headmaster, Bobby Wasden, and held on to most of its student body. When it integrated some years later, the admission of its first black students was handled so quietly that most Selmians had no idea what was taking place.

AFTERMATH: SELMA 1990–2000

Three of Selma's state legislators—Earl Goodwin, Hank Sanders, and Noopie Cosby—suffered from the fallout. Earl Goodwin, who had gone along with the black request for an elected school board, was endorsed by New South for reelection to the Alabama Senate in 1990. But enough white voters turned against Goodwin that he faced opposition from fellow Selmian Charlie Morris as well as from Walter Owens from Bibb County. After Morris failed to make the runoff, he threw his support to Owens. This brought an effective end both to Goodwin's service in the state senate and to Morris's career in county politics.

Noopie Cosby, who had killed the house bill to make the Selma school board elective, was reelected over an opponent backed by New South (David Hodo) in 1990. By 1994, however, this district had been redrawn to create a black majority, and Cosby decided it would be futile to run again; he was replaced by Edward Maull, a retired air force sergeant and a former teacher. A bitter critic of the Sanderses, Maull won with heavy support from the white community.

And Hank Sanders's run for a seat in the US House in 1992 failed because white Selmians voted for Birmingham's Earl Hilliard over their fellow Selmian. Sanders had been endorsed as the superior candidate by the *Birmingham Post-Herald* and the *Montgomery Advertiser* as well as the *Times-Journal*. But for most white voters, as noted journalist Al Benn observed, it was "payback time."

Sanders later came to see his defeat as providential. Within a few years, he became chairman of a key committee in the Alabama Senate and able "to do much more practical good for this area than I could in Congress."

Chestnut lost his column in the *Times-Journal* in 1992 after the *Montgomery Advertiser* printed a threatening letter that had been sent to Alvin Benn under his name. The letter denounced Sanders's critics in obscene terms. However, he continued to write a weekly column, "The Cold Hard Truth," for various black newspapers. And his autobiography *Black in Selma*, published in 1990, made him famous nationally.

Mrs. Sanders's vision of a voting rights museum became a reality in 1991, after the purchase of a Water Avenue building that had once served as the headquarters of the White Citizens' Council. The Alabama Highway Department contributed some of the pictures taken by state forces of the 1965 march. Additional rooms were dedicated to portraits of all the black congressmen elected during Reconstruction, "the Golden Age of Black Politics," and the campaign for women's suffrage. Anniversaries of Bloody Sunday were now celebrated as a "Bridge Crossing Jubilee" and attracted national political candidates who were eager to win the support of black voters.

The year 1992 saw the Selma City Council wrangling once more. The 1990 Census showed that Selma's black population had grown to 58 percent. Perry Varner and other African American leaders demanded that ward four, which still had a white majority, be converted into a "swing" ward with a 70 percent black majority. The white council members rejected the Varner plan, which they felt would give incumbent John Ingram no chance at all; the black council members in turn rejected Ingram's plan, a ward only 60 percent black, which they felt gave Ingram too good a chance. The city council election, originally scheduled for August 25, was postponed for a full year while the squabbling continued and Judge Hand warned the city that he would draw up his own redistricting plan if the city failed to do so.

Hand allowed the election of mayor and council president to go on as originally scheduled. Three black opponents ran against Smitherman: Lorenzo Harrison

Jr., former councilman Cleophus Mann, and Selma businessman James Perkins Jr. Perkins emerged as the mayor's most effective foe; his call for more effort to recruit industry sounded very much like Smitherman's call in 1964. When the August 25 election showed Smitherman winning without a runoff, Perkins thought the mayor's margin in the absentee box suspicious and charged voter fraud. The case limped on for years and was resolved by setting up an electoral commission (composed of two Perkins supporters and two Smitherman supporters) to oversee the next election.

A compromise "Citizens' Plan" that would give Ingram a 65 percent black district was drawn up by a handful of white and black council members. The plan was approved by a 6–3 vote on April 5, 1993, only to be denounced by J. L. Chestnut and vetoed by Mayor Smitherman. Once the two whites who had supported the plan (Carl Morgan and Ingram himself) had fallen into line behind the mayor, the council's white majority changed the rules to give the mayor the right to appoint positions previously appointed by the council. Judge Hand then adopted the Citizens' Plan as his own and imposed it on the city, effectively passing it over the mayor's veto.

When the council election was finally held on August 24, 1993, Nancy Sewell defeated Ingram for the "swing" seat. Nancy Gardner Sewell, longtime librarian at Selma High, thus became the first black woman in history to serve on the Selma City Council. She was joined by Yussuf Abdus Salaam (born Joe Sales), the first Muslim elected to the council. The five black council members then chose Vietnam veteran Bill King (1947–2005) as the first African American president pro tem.

The tug-of-war between mayor and council lasted for months before a compromise was worked out in June 1994 that allowed the council to appoint all the department heads but three: the police chief (Randy Lewellen), the city attorney (Henry Pitts), and the cemetery director (Sam Smitherman).

Despite the prolonged squabbling among their leaders, Selmians were able to accomplish two major goals during the mid-1990s: the erection of an addition to the public library in 1995 and the restoration of the St. James Hotel in 1997. The city council appropriated $1.2 million to erect a ten-thousand-square-foot addition to the library, and Kathryn Windham led the drive to raise $200,000 to furnish the new building. Healthsouth founder Richard M. Scrushy, a Selma native (b. 1952), gave the largest contribution, and the new addition was named in honor of his father, Gerald M. Scrushy (1923–2005). The Gerald M. Scrushy Library Learning Center opened in February 1995, and the renovated public library of Selma and Dallas County had its grand reopening on April 18.

The restoration of the St. James took longer, cost more, and generated some controversy. Bringing the forty-two-room hotel into decent shape took some $5 million in public money and private contributions. The city purchased the old St. James

FIGURE 10.9 The restored St. James Hotel opened for business in 1997; courtesy of Janet Gresham.

in 1993 and launched a campaign to restore the hotel as a major tourist attraction. Ground was broken on April 18, 1996. Byrd Looper, former executive at American Candy, headed the Downtown Development Committee, which led the drive that brought the St. James back—a public-private partnership that included a major donation by Larry Striplin. The hotel opened to the public on December 12, 1997.

By 1995, mayor and council were united in supporting the thirtieth anniversary of the March, contributing $15,000 toward the celebration. Council members Martin and Sewell began working together to design a new medallion for the council chambers, since the old one (which included a design similar to that of the Confederate flag) was regarded as "racist" by some black residents. The new design juxtaposed Sturdivant Hall and the Edmund Pettus Bridge, along with a butterfly. (Selma had been named "the butterfly capital of Alabama" by the state legislature, and the butterfly had become a symbol of all that was positive about the city.) The city council announced on June 30, 1996, that it was running for reelection as a unit—as a "dream team."

Smitherman won reelection in 1996, but this time his margin over Perkins was much narrower: he won with 4,673 votes to 4,322 for Perkins and 39 for perennial candidate John Jowers. Once again the campaign was bitter and ended with Perkins leveling charges of voter fraud. Carl Morgan also won reelection, defeating Rev. Alvin Cleveland 4,893 to 4,104. Not all of the "dream team" did as well; two black incumbents were defeated by old-line activists, Bill King by B. L. Tucker and MacArthur Williams by Bennie Ruth Crenshaw.

To some Selmians, the "dream" of biracial cooperation was a snare and a delusion. When Virginia Military Institute erected a monument to Jonathan Daniels in Lowndes County in 1997, Mrs. Sanders was on hand distributing literature warning against white-black coalitions as the greatest threat to the black race. To her mind what the race needed most was "black unity," and the Nation of Islam's minister Louis Farrakhan was the man to bring this message to Selma. Ironically enough, it was the Southern Christian Leadership Conference's local chapter (Clarence Williams, chair) that invited Farrakhan to Selma, and it was Muslim council member Yussuf Salaam who opposed Farrakhan's coming most stridently. Councilwoman Nancy Sewell introduced a resolution declaring the coming unwelcome, which the council passed 7 to 1.

Farrakhan spoke at Tabernacle Baptist on November 12, 1997, where he was hailed as "the leader of our black nation." He severely criticized the city's black judge as well as most of the black members of the city council, county commission, and city and county school boards, saying that they were no better than the white people they had replaced.

When the city honored a hundred-odd Selmians with "Keeping the Dream" awards in January 1998, SCLC's Williams and other protesters picketed city hall, handing out leaflets, "Don't Let Them Kill Dr. King's Dream, Our Dream." Some of the white recipients of the awards, while active in interracial affairs, had been critical of Chestnut Sanders. The clash over telling the story of Selma's past was to recur again and again in the decade that followed.

The dedication of a monument to another white man, Selma martyr Rev. James Reeb, also drew criticism from black activists. In 1997 an anonymous white liberal had approached the city about erecting a memorial to James Reeb in Selma. He was referred to the Old Depot Museum, which was happy to assist both with research and a site. The monument, an eight-foot stone with a bronze plaque describing Reeb's life and impact, was unveiled on November 15, 1998, in a ceremony that included prayers from a Catholic priest, a Jewish elder, and a Muslim imam as well

FIGURE 10.10 Associate curator Earl Hopkins, Edmundite Father Roger La charite, and curator Jean Martin join in admiring the monument to Selma martyr Rev. James Reeb outside the Selma–Dallas County Museum of History and Archives; courtesy of the author.

as the white pastor of First Baptist and the black pastor of Brown Chapel. A delegation of Unitarians, including Reeb's mentor Duncan Howlett, came down from New England for the occasion.

The ceremony evoked sharp criticism from the December 12 *Black Belt Journal*, with the headline "Civil Rights Community Not Invited to Unveiling." In 2005 a second memorial was erected to Reeb by SCLC Women, in the form of a historic marker at the site of the attack on Washington Avenue. So Selma wound up with two separate (if not equal) memorials to the same man.

The Voting Rights Museum unveiled an impressive new monument, "International Voting Rights Memorial (How We Got over Memorial)" in 2000, to celebrate the thirty-fifth anniversary of Bloody Sunday. The monument, which it had erected in a new Voting Rights Park on the southern side of the Alabama River, consisted of twelve large stones representing the twelve tribes of Israel. One Selma issued a public appeal for the white community to join in the march across the bridge on March 7, 2000. As it turned out, the white turnout was increased dramatically by the news that Pres. Bill Clinton would attend the jubilee and himself join in the symbolic march across the Edmund Pettus Bridge.

A huge crowd of white and black alike turned out to hear Clinton's message, "There are still more bridges to cross." Alabama governor Donald Siegelman sent the Alabama State Troopers to the bridge once more—but this time to salute the marchers as they passed by.

To the activists associated with Chestnut Sanders, the next major bridge to be crossed was the election of a black mayor. Governor Siegelman did his part for this crusade, appointing Synethia Pettaway, Perkins's sister, to head the Dallas County Board of Registrars.

Smitherman's ninth term had gone badly. In November 1997 Police Chief Randy Lewellen and Chief Clerk Mary Ramsey were charged with embezzling hundreds of thousands from the city. A shaken mayor fired both of them, replacing them with "first blacks" Ernest L. Tate as police chief and Jackie Smith as chief clerk. In May 1998 the Alabama Ethics Commission found Smitherman guilty of using a city car for personal use and fined him $4,000.

But he did succeed in getting Selma voters to approve a $4.5 million bond issue over strong opposition from Mrs. Crenshaw and New South. On August 10, 1999, Selmians voted 1,829 to 817 for a bond issue to pave streets, repair historic buildings, and buy municipal equipment.

There was some speculation that Smitherman would step aside in 2000, leaving the white community free to support a black candidate not associated with Chestnut Sanders, somebody like George Evans or Yussuf Salaam. Carl Morgan chose not to run again, and George Evans was elected in his place on August 23, beating out one white and two black opponents to become Selma's first black city council president.

Perhaps the mayor was encouraged by Johnny Jones's success in winning his fifth term as probate judge: Jones easily defeated his black opponent, Kobi Little, on June 6, amassing 7,787 votes to Little's 5,131. At any rate, Smitherman did not follow Morgan's example, determining to defeat his old adversaries—James Perkins Jr. and "the law firm"—one more time. He relied on scare tactics, warning that the election of a black mayor would scare off white-owned businesses; the city would wither away like Uniontown, which had declined markedly since coming under black control. Yussuf Salaam also ran, trying to put together a coalition of biracial moderates. But most white voters stuck with Smitherman, and the national black support from the NAACP, SCLC, and New South was all massed behind Perkins. "JOE GOTTA GO!" the demonstrators chanted day after day. Salaam finished third in the primary, and in the runoff his support went to Perkins, who won 6,326 to 4,854. Smitherman amassed more votes than he had in either 1992 or 1996, but some 11,180

FIGURE 10.11 Mayor James Perkins Jr.; courtesy of Selma City Hall, Selma, Alabama.

people went to the polls September 12, 2000, as opposed to 9,033 in 1996. "JOE GOES" ran the *Times-Journal* headline.

The jubilant black community held the city's first inaugural parade in recent memory; one float evoked a Biblical theme, proclaiming: "For Unto Us a Mayor Is Given." One supporter hailed the new mayor as "another Moses" sent by God to lead Selma into the promised land (*Dallas Morning News*, September 25, 2000).

The Perkins Years: 2000–2008

After Perkins became mayor, the heavens did not open (as some black people hoped) nor did the skies fall (as some in the white community feared). The city did lose some industries—American Candy filed for bankruptcy in 2001 and Pilliod closed its doors in 2002. The city's white population continued to decline, as it had under Smitherman. But there was no general exodus, and soon the new mayor was using his celebrity status as Selma's first black mayor to campaign for more investment. By 2010, the city had actually gained population for the first time in decades.

Once Hyundai set up shop near Montgomery in 2004, "Team Selma" (which included Perkins, probate judge Jones, state senator Sanders, EDA executive director M. Wayne Vardaman, and Craig Airport and Industrial Authority executive director Menzo Driskell) was able to pick up several of Hyundai's suppliers. In March 2004 Renosol Seating located at Craig Industrial Park, followed by Lear/Kyungshin Sales & Engineering in August. Hanil E-Hwa Interior Systems, an even larger supplier, came on board in 2005. And the mayor took great pride in pointing out the new hotels and motels springing up along Highland Avenue, clear evidence that the city was continuing to attract tourists.

Efforts were made to reassure Selma's white community that it still had an important place in the body politic. The majority-black council elected Rita Franklin as its president pro tem as a gesture to the white community, and Mayor Perkins went out of his way to support the yearly reenactment of the Battle of Selma in spite of criticism from Mrs. Sanders and the Voting Rights Museum.

These gestures were overshadowed by a dispute over the new monument to Gen. Nathan Bedford Forrest, which was erected on the grounds of the Vaughan-Smitherman Historic Building the week after Perkins's inauguration. While many white people revered Forrest as the general who had defended Selma in 1865, most black people regarded him as the onetime leader of the Ku Klux Klan during Reconstruction. The Friends of Forrest (Benny Austin, president) insisted that they had received permission from the city to erect the monument and that the new mayor had been informed in advance. This did not pacify Mrs. Sanders and her followers, who made several attempts to deface or pull down the monument.

After months of squabbling, white councilwoman Jean Martin came up with a compromise proposal, to move the monument to Live Oak Cemetery. Her motion passed the council by 5–4 on February 26, 2001. This did not end the controversy; the Friends of Forrest went to court to compel the city to return the monument to its original place, and the lawsuit dragged on for two years before it was dismissed.

The struggle with the Friends of Forrest was not Perkins's only conflict. He also clashed with the Selma Water Works, the Dallas County Commission, and the Selma Police Department. The city council was in no hurry to give up the appointment powers it had wrested from Smitherman, and it was not till the 2004 election had provided Perkins with two additional supporters on the council (Johnnie Leshore and Jennie Venter) that he was able to select the police chief he wanted.

Selma leaders had been anxious for the city to expand for some time but had felt that the Justice Department would never allow any annexation that might "dilute the black vote." Now that the city had a black mayor and a solid black majority, they felt the government might allow the city to annex some of the majority-white

Figure 10.12 The bust of Gen. Nathan Bedford Forrest in its new setting in Live Oak Cemetery; courtesy of the author.

areas north of the city. However, many of the homeowners wanted to avoid Selma taxes or Selma schools, and they quickly launched a move to incorporate as "the city of Valley Grande." On January 9, 2003, they did so, providing Selma with a new neighbor to the north with 2,500 residents.

Selma continued to serve as a medical and educational center for the area. The year 2001 saw the close of the long competition between Selma's hospitals. Province Health of Tennessee purchased Selma Baptist (formerly Four Rivers) and the new Vaughan and announced plans to merge the two. The new owner tore down the facility on Dallas Avenue but took the name "Vaughan Regional Medical Center" in its honor. The Dunn Rest Home moved out to the Medical Center Parkway and was reborn as Park Place Nursing Home, a "state-of-the-art facility," in 2003.

Selma made history again in 2002, when Yussuf Salaam became the first Muslim elected to the Alabama legislature. Salaam edged out Latosha Brown, the candidate supported by both New South and Mayor Perkins, in the Democratic primary.

FIGURE 10.13 Rep. Yussuf Salaam, the first Muslim elected to the Alabama legislature; courtesy of the author.

Brown ran as a write-in candidate in the general election, in which Salaam faced a Republican opponent, Mark Story of Valley Grande. At the victory celebration held at Concordia, Salaam paid tribute to his supporters of various faiths and colors, including a black Catholic campaign manager (Penny Williams) and a white Methodist lawyer (John Wesley Kelley). When the US Civil Rights Commission wrote to ask if there had been any hate crimes committed against Selma's Muslim minority in the days after the attack on the World Trade Center, the answer went back that "we sentenced a Muslim man to four years in the Alabama Legislature; does that count?"

In 2004 Salaam ran for mayor again, only to discover that Selma was not ready to retire its first black mayor. Perkins won reelection without a runoff, amassing 4,519 votes to Salaam's 2,032, businessman Gene Hisel's 1317 and Rev. Glenn King's 171. He also gained two strong new adherents on the city council, making it easier for him to put his programs into action.

(Senator Sanders marveled that most of Selma's white Christians had voted for a black Muslim for mayor over their fellow white Christian Hisel; "What in the world is Selma coming to?" he asked in a September 22 column in the *Selma Times-Journal.* He also marveled that in ward three, he and the mayor had supported the white candidate [Jean Martin] over the black candidate supported by white neo-Confederates. His conclusion was "that Selma is coming to a better place in this world.")

The 2004 county elections offered further evidence that race was becoming less of a factor in county politics. The majority-white Selma bar endorsed Marvin Wiggins for reelection as circuit judge, and Wiggins swept to victory over his white opponent, Farrell McKinley Wright, in the June 1 Democratic primary. In sharp contrast, Judge Nathaniel Walker's three terms as district judge had left many of his black supporters feeling it was "time for a change," and he was defeated by native white Selmian Bob Armstrong in the June 29 runoff. Ten of Dallas County's thirty precincts voted for both Wiggins and Armstrong. Five of the ten also voted for Ed Greene as district attorney, but Greene's majority vote in Dallas County was overwhelmed by the strong support for his opponent, Selma lawyer Michael Jackson, from the other counties in the Fourth Judicial Circuit. Jackson thus became the first black district attorney for the Fourth Circuit. He was to win national attention by successfully prosecuting the state trooper who had shot Jimmie Lee Jackson back in 1965.

In October 2004 ground was broken on a new YMCA building to be erected off the Medical Center Parkway, a forty-two-thousand square feet facility that would cost an estimated $5 million. Eunice Walker Johnson of Chicago, the largest contributor, had strong Selma roots: she was the daughter of longtime physician Dr. Nathaniel Walker (1887–1971) and the granddaughter of Rev. W. H. McAlpine, the founder of Selma University. When the new facility was formally dedicated on October 11, 2006, it took the name of the Walker-Johnson Family Health Center in honor of her family.

It was also in 2006 that Kim Ballard succeeded Johnny Jones as probate Judge of Dallas County. Kimbrough (Kim) L. Ballard (b. 1943), a native of Marengo County, had been regarded as a leader of the anti-Roussell forces while serving on the city council from 1984 to 1993, but after his election to the county commission in 1996 he began reaching out to his new black constituents. "Back in 1990 I never dreamed I would work closely with Perry Varner and wind up serving as a pallbearer at his funeral," Ballard confided to the author. "When Johnny [Jones] asked me to run, I wasn't sure any white could be elected in a county that was 70% black, but as it turned out I won easily." Kobi Little and William Minor both ran against him for the Democratic nomination, but Ballard won without a runoff.

Selma continued to attract illustrious visitors—both of the leading candidates for the Democratic nomination, Hillary Clinton and Barack Obama, came for Jubilee in 2007, and John McCain, the Republican candidate for president, showed up in 2008. Under the circumstances it is no surprise that the city continued to attract new hotels—a Hampton Inn opened in 2004 and a Holiday Inn Express in 2008.

By 2008 Perkins had fallen out with some of his most prominent supporters, including Hank and Rose Sanders; the senator complained publicly that the Jubilee had received more support from the old white mayor than it had from the new

FIGURE 10.14 Probate Judge Kim Ballard; courtesy of the author.

black one. When Perkins submitted a bond issue to the voters on February 26, 2008, it was rejected 2,010 to 1,620. The mayor's defeat was widely seen as a bad omen as far as his chances of a third term were concerned. City council president Evans filed to run for mayor under the slogan "New Bridges to Build" with strong support from both white and black voters. Some Perkins supporters charged that Evans's election would put diehard conservatives like Cecil Williamson in charge of the city, but the charges fell on deaf ears. On August 26 Selma elected its second black mayor as George Evans outpolled Perkins by 4,303 to 3,267.

Interestingly enough, the October 7 runoff for city council president featured a white man (Gene Hisel) supported by the *Selma Post-Herald* (a black newspaper) against a black woman (Dr. Geraldine Allen). Dr. Allen won 2245–1993, becoming Selma's first female council president.

A native of Selma, Allen earned her doctorate in nursing from UAB and served as director of the Master's in Nursing program at Troy. She had previously served on the Selma School Board and as councilwoman from ward four. She died in 2010 and was succeeded by the council's president pro tem, Cecil Williamson.

Epilogue: What Bridges Lie Ahead?

Selma's history did not come to a close with the mayoral election of 2000 or with that of 2008. An era seemed to be ending as the decade went on. Earl Goodwin died in 2003, and Rev. J. D. Hunter passed the same year. Ed Moss died in early 2005 and Joe Smitherman later that same year. Smitherman's death prompted one final controversy: Mrs. Sanders outraged the mayor's friends by offering one last denunciation of her old foe before conceding that Joe T. had been a human being after all. Indeed, he had helped her get life-saving medical treatment after she was diagnosed with cancer. Carl Morgan passed quietly in 2006. J. L. Chestnut joined his friends and former adversaries in death in 2008.

Jamie Wallace retired as leader of the chamber of commerce in 2002, after serving since 1986. Dick Morthland stepped down as CEO of People's Bank in 2002, bringing a close to the Plant-Morthland banking dynasty, which had begun in 1933. People's, which had boasted for years that it was "Selma's only home-owned bank," merged with Mobile-based BancTrust a few years later. On September 10, 2007, the city acquired a new "home-owned bank," First Cahawba, with the scion of another Selma banking dynasty, Roger ap Catesby Jones, as its president.

Julius Jenkins stepped down in 2007 after twenty-seven years as president of Concordia College Selma, which under his leadership had undergone a dramatic physical expansion, more than doubled its enrollment, and became Selma's only accredited four-year college. James H. Carter also resigned in 2007 after seventeen years as superintendent of the city schools, to be succeeded a year later by Nigerian American Austin Obasohan. Selma's eleven-member appointed school board, the only one in the nation, was discarded by the voters in 2009 in favor of an elected five-member board.

Private schools continued to spring up in Selma, most of them sponsored by new churches like the Tabernacle of Praise and the Cathedral of Christ the King Charismatic Episcopal Church. They were no longer "seg" (segregated) academies, though;

FIGURE 10.15 Rep. Terri Sewell with her parents, Coach Andrew Sewell and Councilwoman Nancy Sewell; courtesy of the Sewell family.

Morgan Academy admitted its first black student in 2008, and Meadowview Christian had quietly integrated several years earlier.

Wallace Community College Selma dedicated a new technology building, named after Sen. Hank Sanders, in 2008. In the following year Selma University won accreditation as a Bible College. This represented a remarkable comeback on the part of the Baptist school, since it had been on the brink of bankruptcy ten years earlier. Rev. Alvin Cleveland, former pastor of First Baptist on Martin Luther King, had provided the leadership. Thus the school that had first won Selma the title of "Athens of Black Alabama" was able to continue into a new century.

Some people continue to see the city as frozen in time; the Southern Poverty Law Center's winter 2008 issue of *Intelligence Report* ran an article saying as much. To its author, "crossing the Edmund Pettus Bridge into Selma feels like entering a time warp in which the past maintains such a stranglehold on the present that a breeze off the Alabama River seems to carry a whiff of tear gas or the distant crack of a slave master's whip."

Others see the Queen City as having come a long way. The election of native Selmian Terri Sewell to the US House of Representatives in 2010 recalled more positive moments in Selma's past. Sewell was the first black woman elected to Congress from Alabama; she was following in the footsteps of her mother, Nancy Sewell, who in 1993 had become the first black woman elected to the Selma City Council; and also in the footsteps of Harriet Hooker Wilkins, who in 1922 became the first woman elected to the Alabama legislature. And she was also carrying on the legacy of Ben Turner, who in 1870 became the first black Alabamian elected to Congress. While Hank Sanders had lost his congressional bid in 1992 because of the massive white vote against him in the Democratic primary, Sewell, in contrast, carried every white precinct in Dallas in the July 14 runoff, amassing 80 percent of the vote. (In the general election, when she was opposed by a fellow Selmian, Republican businessman Don Chamberlain, Sewell won easily but lost some of the white precincts.)

Years ago the US State Department began sending delegations from other countries to visit Selma to learn about "tolerance, diversity and ethnic conflict resolution." Some are anxious to meet Selma's black mayor and see for themselves the success of the voting rights movement. Delegations from Muslim countries have been particularly interested in meeting with Alabama's only Muslim legislator, Yussuf Salaam, and learning how people of different faiths get along in Selma. Still others are curious about the role of women in Selma, which produced both Alabama's first female legislator and its first black woman elected to Congress, and at one point boasted a city council whose makeup was half men and half women. The Queen City has played many different parts in the past, and what role it will play in the future is yet to be seen.

Selected Bibliography

Anyone tackling the history of Selma has to draw on three major works: John Hardy's *Selma: Her Institutions and Her Men* (Selma, 1879; reprint, Spartanburg, SC, 1978), Walter Jackson's *The Story of Selma* (Birmingham, 1954), and J. Mills Thornton's *Dividing Lines: Municipal Politics and the Struggle for Civil Rights in Montgomery, Birmingham and Selma* (Tuscaloosa, 2002). Jackson corrects some of Hardy's accounts and carries the city's history down to the 1950s. He is especially valuable on the men he regards as Selma's heroes: William Rufus King, John Tyler Morgan, Edmund W. Pettus, and N. H. R. Dawson. Thornton brings the history down to 2000 and focuses on the city's racial progress and problems.

Religion

Hardy's *Selma* sketches the beginning of most of Selma's early churches, including a few founded by African Americans. F. Wilbur Hembold's *Selma: The Gospel at Work* (Birmingham, 1983), catalogues the city's white Baptist congregations. Octavius Boothe's *Cyclopedia of the Colored Baptists of Alabama and Their Work* (Birmingham, 1895), W. H. Mixon's *African Methodism in Alabama* (Nashville, 1902), and *Glimpses of the Missionary Operation of the Reformed Presbyterian Church to the Freedmen in Selma, Alabama And Vicinity* (Selma, 1911) all provide information on Selma's early black churches and schools. Boothe and Mixon were both Selma pastors. Rosa Young's *Light in the Dark Belt* (St. Louis, MO, 1929) describes the founding of Alabama Lutheran (now Concordia College Alabama) and the early years of Lutheranism in Alabama.

Wilson Fallin Jr.'s *Uplifting the People: Three Centuries of Baptists* (Tuscaloosa, 2007) brings the history of the state's black Baptists down to the current day, with particular attention to Selma University, which Fallin served as president from 1982 to 1986. Wayne Flynt's *Alabama Baptists: Southern Baptists in the Heart of Dixie* (Tuscaloosa, 1998) does the same with the white members of Alabama's largest denomination. Emir and Ergun Caner's *The Sacred Trust: Sketches of the Southern Baptist Convention Presidents* (Nashville, 2003) offers a flattering portrait of Judge Jonathan Haralson.

Chapter 1

Thomas P. Abernathy's *The Formative Period in Alabama, 1815–1830* (Tuscaloosa, 1965) is the standard authority on the state's pioneer days. William H. Brantley's *Three Capitals: A Book about the First Three Capitals of Alabama: St. Stephens, Huntsville and Cahaba* (Tuscaloosa, 1947) provides a wealth of details about Cahawba's brief reign as state capital. Theodore Jack's *Sectionalism and Party Politics in Alabama, 1819–1842* (Spartanburg, SC, 1975) illuminates the early emergence of a two-party system in Alabama and the role played by William

Rufus King as the "leading Union Democrat" in the state. Anna Gayle Fry's *Memories of Old Cahaba* (Nashville, 1908) offers an idealized portrait of the old South.

James Benson Sellers's *Slavery in Alabama* (Tuscaloosa, 1950) is still the classic study of the subject. The portrait of Redoshi ("Aunt Sally") is based on Quarles family tradition and on Amelia Platts Boynton Robinson's *Bridge across Jordan* (Washington, DC, 1991). Sylviane A. Diouf's *Dreams of Africa in Alabama* (New York, 2007) provides a wealth of background material on the slave ship *Clotilda* and its human cargo. Ben Turner's story is based largely on his testimony before the Southern Claims Commission on April 21, 1871 (case 285), and Frances W. Harper's article in the 1872 *Selma Press*. The saga of "Free Tom" Smith was pieced together from the mortgage records in the Dallas County Courthouse.

Chapter 2

Daniel Fate Brooks's biography of William Rufus King in the *Encyclopedia of Alabama* is top drawer; it can be accessed at www.encyclopediaofalabama.org/article/h-1886. King's career is depicted in two of John M. Martin's articles for *Alabama Review*, "WRK: Jacksonian Senator" (October 1965) and "WRK and the Vice Presidency" (January 1963). Sam Will John's article on Selma in *Northern Alabama: Historical and Biographical* (Birmingham, 1888) provides useful information about Selma's go-getters and corrects Hardy on several points. William Garrett's *Reminiscences of Public Men in Alabama, for Thirty Years* (Atlanta, 1872) offers sketches of most Selma legislators during the twenty years leading up to the Civil War, as does Willis Brewer's *Alabama: Her History, Resources, War Record and Public Men* (Montgomery, 1872). Thomas B. Owen's four-volume *Alabama* (Birmingham, 1930) has short biographies of most of Selma's nineteenth-century leaders.

J. Mills Thornton's *Politics and Power in a Slave Society: Alabama, 1800–1860* (Baton Rouge, 1977) explains why slaveowners sincerely believed they were fighting for freedom and equality and provides insights into almost every area of antebellum politics in Alabama. Eric Walther's *William Lowndes Yancey and the Coming of the Civil War* (Chapel Hill, 2006) depicts the career of Alabama's leading secessionist.

Chapter 3

I relied heavily on the *Official Records of the War of the Rebellion* (Washington, DC, 1881–1901) for the details of Edmund Pettus's military career and of the development of Selma's Confederate arsenal. His letters to N. H. R. Dawson are from Jackson's *Story of Selma*. His letters to his wife are in the Pettus Family Papers in the Alabama Archives.

The cornerstone address is found in Henry Cleveland's *Alexander H. Stephens in Public and Private, with Letters and Speeches* (Philadelphia, 1866).

John Tyler Morgan's speech is found in William R. Smith's *The History of the Convention of the People of Alabama Begun and Held in the City of Montgomery, on the Second Day of January, 1861* (Montgomery, 1861).

The Confederate debate over emancipation is treated in Robert F. Durden's *The Gray and the Black: The Confederate Debate on Emancipation* (Baton Rouge, 1972). Wiley Sword's *Southern Invincibility: A History of the Confederate Heart* (New York, 1999) devotes two chapters to N. H. R. Dawson's correspondence with Elodie Todd, and Elodie's experiences in Selma are described in Stephen Berry's *House of Abraham: Lincoln & the Todds, a Family Divided by War* (New York, 2007). Alice V. D. Pierrepont's *Reuben Vaughan Kidd: Soldier of the Confederacy* (Petersburg, VA, 1947) traces one Selma soldier's career and also tells of the city's fall.

When it comes to Selma's role as a major Southern arsenal, Ernest B. Johnson Jr.'s 1962 Harvard thesis, "Selma, Alabama, as a Center of Confederate War Production" is worth consulting, along with Sol Tepper's *"Torpedoes? Damn!" Ordeal at Selma Gun Foundry and Battle of Mobile Bay* (Selma, 1979) and William N. Still's "Selma and the Confederate States Navy" (*Alabama Review*, January 1982).

The battle of Selma itself is depicted in Capt. Lewis Hosea's *Campaign for Selma* (Cincinnati, 1888) and the looting afterward in Frances Ellen Phillips's "Reminiscences Concerning Wilson's Raid in Alabama" (typescript in Alabama Department of Archives and History). James Pickett Jones's *Yankee Blitzkreig: Wilson's Raid though Alabama and Georgia* (Athens, GA, 1976) seems to have consulted everything written by anyone on either side and to be as close to an impartial account as we are going to get.

Chapter 4

Burke Davis's *The Southern Railway: Road of the Innovators* (Chapel Hill, NC, 1985) describes the postwar difficulties of the Selma-based railroads and is the source for General Johnston's being "bored" with his job. Jack Hurst's *Nathan Bedford Forrest: A Biography* (New York, 1993) depicts Forrest's transformation as a railroad president. Wayne Cline's *Alabama Railroads* (Tuscaloosa, 1997) is outstanding.

The Freedmen's Bureau papers for Alabama were a major source, along with the Silsby correspondence in the American Missionary Association papers.

Walter Fleming's *Civil War and Reconstruction in Alabama* (New York, 1905) is still regarded as the classic study in spite of its pronounced racial bias. It is particularly prone to error whenever it touches Selma. John Witherspoon DuBose's *Alabama's Tragic Decade* (Birmingham, 1940) offers an exciting and colorful account of Radical Reconstruction from a Democratic perspective; he provides interesting details about a number of Selma politicians and incidents. Sarah Woolfolk Wiggins's *The Scalawag in Alabama Politics, 1865–1881* (Tuscaloosa, 1977) offers a far more balanced view of the party struggle. Loren Schweninger's *James Rapier and Reconstruction* (Chicago, 1978) sympathetically portrays the struggle of one of the state's leading black officials. Richard Bailey's *Neither Carpetbaggers nor Scalawags: Black Officeholders during the Reconstruction of Alabama, 1867–1878* (Montgomery, 1991) provides a wealth of information about a number of Selma's black leaders during this period.

Pettus's tribute to Ben Turner appears in *Testimony Taken by the Joint Select Committee to*

Inquire into the Condition of Affairs in the Late Insurrectionary States, Alabama, vol. 1 (Washington, DC, 1872).

Chapter 5

Jackson's *Story of Selma* has extensive portraits of John Tyler Morgan, Edmund W. Pettus, and N. H. R. Dawson. Morgan has attracted the most scholarly attention. Joseph A. Fry's *John Tyler Morgan and the Search for Southern Autonomy* (Knoxville, 1992) is an interpretive biography. David McCullough's *The Path between the Seas: The Creation of the Panama Canal, 1870–1914* (New York, 1977) illuminates Morgan's role as "Father of the Isthmian Canal." Thomas Adams Upchurch's *Legislating Racism: The Billion-Dollar Congress and the Birth of Jim Crow* (Lexington, KY, 2004) stresses Morgan's effectiveness in promoting his racial views. Joseph A. Fry's "Governor Johnston's Attempt to Unseat Senator Morgan, 1899–1900" (*Alabama Review*, July 1981) is helpful. *Memorial Addresses for John T. Morgan and Edmund W. Pettus* (Washington, DC, 1909) offers a wealth of detail about both of Selma's "Grand Old Men."

Jackson's *Story of Selma* also treats Selma's involvement in the 1901 Constitutional Convention in some detail. William Cook McMillan's *Constitutional Development in Alabama, 1798–1901: A Study in Politics, the Negro and Sectionalism* (Chapel Hill, NC, 1955) details the events leading up to the "disfranchisement" convention of 1901. Horace Mann Bond's *Negro Education in Alabama: A Study in Cotton and Steel* (Washington, DC, 1937) provides an African American perspective on the 1901 convention, along with a depiction of how "separate but equal" was implemented for Alabama schools in the early twentieth century. Sheldon Hackney's *Populism to Progressivism in Alabama* (Princeton, NJ, 1969) offers further insights into Black Belt politics during this period.

Official Proceedings of the Constitutional Convention of the State of Alabama, 1901 (Wetumpka, AL, 1940).

Chapter 6

Martin T. Olliff's *The Great War in the Heart of Dixie: Alabama during World War I* (Tuscaloosa, 2008) includes an essay on the response of Alabama's black residents to the war.

James Benson Sellers's *Prohibition Movement in Alabama 1702 to 1943* (Chapel Hill, NC, 1943) is still the classic study of that subject, as is Lee N. Allen's "The Women's Suffrage Movement in Alabama, 1910–1920" (*Alabama Review*, April 1958). Joanne Varner Hawks' "A Select Few: Alabama's Women Legislators" (*Alabama Review*, July 1985) and Marie Stokes Jemison's "Ladies Become Voters: Pattie Ruffner Jacobs and Women's Suffrage in Alabama" (*Southern Exposure*, Spring 1979) tell us about Harriet Hooker Wilkins.

Glenn Feldman's *Politics, Society and the Klan in Alabama, 1915–1949* (Tuscaloosa, 1999) does not think much of the conservatives' "soft" opposition to the Klan. The role of the Klan in state politics during the 1920s is traced in Virginia Van Der Veer Hamilton's *Hugo Black: The Alabama Years* (Baton Rouge, 1968). Glenn Feldman's "Race, Class, the Southern Conference, and the Beginning of the End of the New Deal Coalition" (included in *History & Hope in the Heart of Dixie*, ed. Gordon E. Harvey, Richard D. Starnes, and Glenn Feldman, Tuscaloosa, 2006) is revealing.

Chapter 7

Alabama during World War II is portrayed in Allen Cronenberg's *Forth to the Mighty Conflict* (Tuscaloosa, 1995). Carl Morgan's essay, "Craig Air Force Base: Its Effects on Selma, 1940–1977" (*Alabama Review*, April 1989) is worth consulting.

The conservative South's rebellion against the national Democratic Party is traced in Virginia Van Der Veer's *Lister Hill: Statesman from the South* (Chapel Hill, NC, 1974) as well as William D. Barnard's *Dixiecrats and Democrats* (Tuscaloosa, 1974). Harris Wofford's "Preliminary Report on the Status of the Negro in Dallas County, Alabama" (Yale Law School paper, 1953) provides a wealth of information about race relations in Selma and Dallas County in the early 1950s. Neil R. McMillen's *The Citizens' Council* (Champaign, IL, 1971) focuses on white resistance to integration.

Chapter 8

Cynthis Griggs Fleming, *In the Shadow of Selma* (Lanham, MD, 2004) portrays Wilcox County's travails.

Dan T. Carter's *The Politics of Rage* (New York, 1995) has the best account of the police riot in Marion that led to Jimmie Lee Jackson's death. Stephen L. Longenecker's *Selma's Peacemaker: Ralph Smeltzer and Civil Rights Mediation* (Philadelphia, 1997) offers invaluable details about the lead-up to King's arrival.

Sheriff James G. Clark Jr. gives his partisan account in *The Jim Clark Story: I Saw Selma Raped* (Birmingham, 1966) and Amelia Platts Boynton Robinson gives hers in *Bridge across Jordan* (Washington, DC, 1991). Sheyann Webb and Rachel West Nelson provide a child's-eye view of 1965 in their "as told to Frank Sekora," *Selma, Lord, Selma: Girlhood Memories of the Civil Rights Days* (Tuscaloosa, 1980).

Richie Jean Sherrod Jackson's *The House by the Side of the Road* (Tuscaloosa, 2010) provides a fresh look at Dr. King and other black leaders when they were "off duty."

Chapter 9

The "antipoverty wars" are treated in Susan Youngblood Ashmore's *Carry It On: The War on Poverty and the Civil Rights Movement in Alabama, 1964–1972* (Athens, GA, 2008). J. L. Chestnut and Julia Cass's *Black in Selma: The Uncommon Life of J. L. Chestnut, Jr.: Politics and Power in a Small Southern Town* (New York, 1990) displays more nuance than you would expect from a partisan account.

Rob Hereford's MA thesis for the University of Georgia, "A Study of Selma and Dallas County 1930–1970" (Athens, 1992) offers insights into the area's economic history

Concordia College Selma's struggles are depicted in Dr. Richard C. Dickinson's *Concordia College Selma: The Miracle on Green Street* (St. Louis, 2006).

Chapter 10

Thornton's *Dividing Lines* has the best coverage of the 1990 debacle, although the author's "Patching Up the Peace in Symbolic Selma" (*Commonweal* 1990) is worth a look. The Alabama Advisory Committee of the US Civil Rights Commission issued a report, *Crisis and Opportu-*

nity: Race Relations in Selma, in 1991. Gay Talese's *A Writer's Life* (New York, 2006) suggests that Selma has suffered from the prejudice of the national press. Peter Applebome's *Dixie Rising* (New York, 1996), Tom Dent's *Southern Journey: A Return to the Civil Rights Movement* (Morrow, NY, 1997), and Tony Horwitz's *Confederates in the Attic: Dispatches from the Unfinished Civil War* (New York, 1998) all devote a chapter to Selma since 1990.

Index

Page references in italics indicate an illustration.

ACKNOWLEDGMENTS

This history of Selma owes much to the encouragement and support I received both from scholars and from fellow Selmians.

Mike Fitzgerald, one of the leading authorities of Alabama during Reconstruction, generously read and commented on all ten chapters. His suggestions improved the book significantly, and it's not his fault that *Selma: A Bicentennial History* isn't better than it is. Chris McIlwain of Tuscaloosa has encouraged me enormously by sharing with me much of his research on the 1850s and 1860s in general and on the Saffold family in particular.

Anne Falkenberry Knight tracked down dozens of photographs for me and shared her memories of life in Selma. Janet Gresham took pictures of various sites for the book. A number of Selma families were kind enough to loan me pictures of their relatives; the Dinkins family was particularly helpful, graciously sharing pictures from their generations of service to Selma University.

Various friends took the time and trouble to read over the manuscript. Jamie Wallace added a wealth of details to my narrative of the 1970s and 1980s; Dick Morthland enlightened me about Selma's economic history; Harry Gamble, Grady Perryman, and James Ware all read over my account of the 1990 school crisis.

There are many others who deserve credit for helping me tell Selma's story, and I am grateful to them all.